THE NORU: BOOK III

FALL OF THE CHOSEN

Lola StVil

Copyright © 2015 Lola StVil
All rights reserved.

This book is dedicated to Elizabeth Rivera

When I think about you, I think about the beautiful Latina singing "rump shaker" at the top of her lungs in the hallway of our high school before Drama class; your gold curls bouncing playfully in the air. That is how I will remember you: playful, pretty and positive.

May you rest with Angels…

BOOK I

Santini
"THE GENTLEMAN" Moss

"It's better to do a dull thing with style than a dangerous thing without it."
— *Charles Bukowski*

CHAPTER ONE
CRY

For the record, no motherfucker can summon me to a meeting. I'm not some low-level demon with simple-ass powers. On the contrary, I'm high ranking and feared by many. And if they don't fear me, at the very least they hesitate before taking me on. Yet here I am, standing in the middle of his black marble and stone lair, moments after he calls on me.

My name is Santini Moss, but in the Demon world I am simply referred to as "The Gentleman." That's because unlike other demons, I don't resort to brute violence and hand-to-hand combat. I don't pulverize my opponents with bare fists and firepower. In fact, when I battle, I never even have so much as a wrinkle in my shirt. Which is a good thing because my clothes are, in a word, exquisite.

I look at my reflection in the waterfall display at the center of the lair. I'm six feet tall, buff, and have dark hair. I'm always in a suit and tie because wearing anything else would be uncivilized.

Every single one of my suits is tailored; my ties and pocket squares are silk. In addition, only top designers craft my shoes. Today I'm wearing a Tom Ford charcoal grey three-button suit with a metallic sliver paisley tie and pocket square. And lastly, I am wearing my signature shades from Dolce Gabbana. I am, to be honest, a handsome demon.

The only flaw I have is the six-inch scar on my right cheek. I got it when I was in battle with a demon that attacked one of my human maids,

Joanna. I don't like humans normally. They are genius with fashion but worthless otherwise. However, Joanna had been with me the longest. She minded her business and knew enough not to ask questions. Yet she was bold enough to demand her money when her pay was late.

I could have killed her, but she seemed willing to accept death. I liked that about her. Most humans are weak and fear everything. However, Joanna refused to give in to fear. She's also the best cleaning lady I've ever had. She's meticulous and never has a hair out of place. I made her the head of the cleaning staff. She manages my mansion with precision and skill.

We routinely have these chats that I happen to enjoy. We talk about wars that humanity has waged with each other throughout its existence and why they did or did not work. We were in a heated debate about the logistics of the Spanish Revolution when we came under attack.

I managed to kill every one of the demons, but not before one grabbed Joanna. In saving her, I was injured. A Swoosen blade caused the scar; any injury caused by that kind of blade won't ever heal.

I thought Joanna would run screaming as fast as she could out of the city. I thought she'd be driven insane by what she witnessed. Normally humans need to be killed after they are made aware of our existence. But the next day Joanna came to work on time and ready to clean, as if nothing happened. She's a tough old woman and I respect the hell out of that.

I look at my reflection yet again; even with the scar, I'm still handsome. But it's not just about my looks. I try and take care of myself. Get a workout in at least three to four times a week. That's hard to do in between killing humans, angels, and disrespectful demons. You see, I believe that presentation is important. Anyone can be a killer. But what I bring to the party is…style.

I look at my watch; he's been keeping me waiting in his frigid lair for half an hour now. Again, I am not normally summoned, but when he calls on you, you come. I think back to when I first met him.

The Demon world was in complete chaos because we had no leadership. The source of all evil was killed, so the Demon world waited for its next all-powerful leader. But while we waited, we did what was in our nature to do: fight. We formed different factions and went to war with each other.

I had managed to lead a team of over three dozen demons. We ran an impressive import and export business. We handled everything: human slaves (Pawns), Wednesday, Coy Paste, and other lethal drugs. We also supplied items to Hun's market, the market where beings go to find new and wonderful ways to inflict pain on their enemies. My business was booming. In fact, I was attending to a business matter the day I first met him. That day plays out before me as if it's happening now…

I pull up ahead of the motorcade in my chauffeur driven midnight colored Bentley (I'm wearing a dark blue Armani suit with matching tie and pocket square). We walk into the place where most demons in my business congregate: "STK" restaurant in Los Angeles.

The driver opens my car door. I step out and take in the scene: glamorous patrons dripping in diamonds, high-end handbags, and luxury cars. I love Los Angeles. Here all things evil sparkle. And everywhere you look there are Runners to make our lives easier.

Unlike Pawns, who still have their souls, Runners are humans who have traded theirs to evil in order to gain material things. We own most of the humans on Wall Street and ,well, just about every famous entertainer you can think of. That's why we demons love LA. It's a city full of humans to do our bidding. They will do anything from park our cars to murder. We own them.

We enter the trendy restaurant and find a pleasant civil atmosphere with humans, Runners, and demons. I signal for my guys to surround the room. I find the demon I came for: Morehouse.

He's a stout, big bellied prick with a full beard and long hair. He's engaged in a conversation with another demon, whom I've never seen before.

I head over to the table and pull up a chair alongside them.

"I really need to have a discussion with my friend Morehouse. I think you should leave," I instruct the stranger alongside me.

He exchanges a look with Morehouse and then wisely gets up and walks away from the table. I signal for the waiter to come over.

"Good evening, what would the gentlemen like from the bar?" the waiter asks.

"I'm in the mood for something sweet with a smoky finish. What would you recommend?" I ask as I survey the Coy Dark menu.

"We have an extensive Revere collection. Perhaps you'd care to try our newest acquisition: Malice."

"That would be perfect, thank you," I reply.

"And for you?" the waiter asks Morehouse.

Morehouse looks back at me like a human child who's been told he has to enter a haunted house alone.

"Morehouse, the Runner asked you a question, don't be rude," I suggest.

"Nothing…I…nothing," he manages to choke out.

The waiter walks away and leaves just the two of us alone to talk.

"You know what I hate, Morehouse?" I ask.

He shakes his head "no."

"I hate gossip. It's such a childish thing. Wouldn't you agree?"

"Yes," he whispers.

"Yet, listening to gossip is a part of my job. So I have no choice but to do it. But gossip isn't always reliable. For example, the word around town is that you have a cargo of Coy Paste you need shipped into Germany and you intend to use our competitors to do it. Is that true?" I ask nicely.

"Well, it's…I'm not trying to be a problem," he vows.

"I had to cancel an appointment with my tailor tonight to meet with you. That's a problem, Morehouse."

"I'm sorry," he says.

"We have always handled Germany. And we have yet to fail you. All we ask in return is a little loyalty," I remind him.

"Stern and his crew offered to charge me twenty percent less than you guys. Maybe if you can match it, I'll consider working with you again," he replies.

"See, now that upsets me." I sigh.

He shrugs his shoulders and looks back at me with a cocky expression. I take off my shades and look him in the eye. I signal to one of my guys, and they bring over a black box about three feet long and place it on the table.

"What's this?" Morehouse asks.

"Oh, this? It's a gift from some of my guys. They know I'm a collector," I reply as the waiter comes by and pours dark red liquid into my glass.

"What do you collect?" he asks.

"The bone that connects the wings to a demon's shoulder blades," I reply as I open the box. Morehouse looks at the bloody wing bone and then back at me.

"Before you ask, that once belonged to Stern," I inform him.

Morehouse jumps up and summons a fireball in the palm of his hand. My guys are on him before he can even blink. They pin him to the floor with his face in the carpet. Morehouse has a crew too. All of whom are now surrounded by what they know are far more powerful demons.

"I don't mind that you shopped around for a better deal, but we have history and we should have been notified that you were thinking of leaving us," I inform him.

"You would have killed us," he mumbles from the floor below.

"Well, yes, but it wouldn't have been so…bloody and garish. It would have been a nice, beautiful, peaceful death. But instead you showed no loyalty and we will take over your company and kill every one of your—"

"—Wait! Let's make a deal. Please, please," he begs.

I signal for the guys to pick him up and place him on the chair.

"I'm listening," I tell him.

"You can go back to our old deal," he offers.

"No, that won't work for me now," I reply.

"Okay, okay, we can have a new deal. I'll pay you twice what I did before."

"I don't know…" I admit.

"Wait, I can throw in all the Pawns I have," he pushes.

"Well, I do like a good slave…"

"So what do you say?" he asks desperately.

"No deal."

"WHY?" he shouts.

"Because you have no loyalty. I don't deal with demons I can't trust. Good-bye, Morehouse," I reply.

He starts to scream because he knows what's about to happen. His dark wings flap furiously against the air. He tries to get away, but my guys pin him to the chair, forcing him to endure what's to come.

I take my shades off and a black beam emanates from my eyes and makes direct contact with Morehouse. Immediately blood starts to seep out of every pore. Soon it runs from his eyes, nose, ears, and mouth. He dies in seconds, with a shocked look on his face.

The ability to make someone's body "cry" is a special one. Most demons and even angels can't do what I do.

I signal for my guys to eliminate every being in the restaurant. Instantly demons are being ripped apart, incinerated, and beaten mercilessly all around me. Normally I would only need to kill a few key demons in Morehouse's operation, but with our world in chaos, it's important that motherfuckers remember just how cruel you can be. That way they won't dare cross you.

I sit back and sip my Coy Dark across the table from my former business partner. I'm halfway done with my libation when I spot a figure sitting still in the corner, watching me.

The figure isn't the least bit afraid of the chaos that surrounds him. In fact, he seems bored by it. I look closer but can't really make out his face. Pissed off that my crew would allow a Runner or demon to remain unharmed, I shout out to them.

"WHY THE HELL IS THAT GUY STILL ALIVE? I SAID KILL EVERYONE!" I demand.

They run up to the stranger's table. He makes no move to flee or defend himself. Instead, he calmly scans over the faces of my demons. Then every single member of my crew gets down on one knee and bows their head before the stranger. It's not just his complete control over my crew that shocks me, it's how the room has changed.

The air fills with a dark energy, unlike anything I've ever felt before. He looks to be in his teens, but one look into his troubled dark eyes tells me he is no kid. The expression on his face isn't rage or malice. It's something far more sinister—control. His demeanor brings to mind a peaceful ocean surface—filled with deadly sharks below.

I've heard about Malakaro before. He's young but has managed to start making a name for himself. It isn't the fact that he has killed so many that makes him noteworthy, it's his strategy that sets him apart from the rest. He knows exactly who to kill, who to learn from, and who to manipulate.

He's on the short list of possible replacements as the source of all evil. I'm also said to be on that list, so I'm guessing he's here to battle me. I would never say it out loud, but being in the presence of the young evil instills fear within me.

Malakaro is the first of his kind, in that while he is no doubt evil incarnate, he isn't a demon at all. He's a Noru. That means he is the child of a guardian, a superpowered angel. Actually, Malakaro happens to be the firstborn of the most powerful guardian leader, Marcus Cane. His mother, Bianca, was Quo, meaning she was half human and half angel.

Marcus went on to have a family with the Angel of death. Together they have two kids. There's a newborn named Sam. The little fucker is said to be immortal. And then there's his ten-year-old sister, Pryor. That little bitch showed signs of enormous power from day one. Angels get everything. It's a real fucking shame.

Many demons have plotted ways to kill them. But that's just a death wish. Marcus and the rest of his team have all banded together and keep their kids under watchful eye. And even if that wasn't the case, going after the children of Death is a bad idea.

Since Malakaro doesn't have any demon blood in him, you might wonder how the hell he got to be so damn vicious. Well, the demons I've talked to cite the wicked ways of his mother, before her death and the stunning rejection he faced from his father.

Although Marcus did not know of Malakaro's existence, I'm guessing Malakaro took it as rejection nonetheless.

I study his face in search of a sign of goodness and there simply isn't any. I like that in the guy.

"I'm not going to bow," I assure him.

"If I wanted you to bow, you would be speaking from the ground," he informs me in a soft, chilling voice.

"Then what the hell do you want? Did you come here to try and kill me?" I ask.

"I've never tried to kill anyone before," he responds.

"If you're coming after my crew, I'll—"

"I have no need for your toys, Santini."

"Then what is it?"

"I came with an offer. You should work for me," he says simply.

"Yeah, I don't think that's gonna happen. I've got my crew," I reply.

He smiles. Then without warning every one of my demons reaches out for something sharp: blades, silverware, or jagged pieces of broken plates. They then stab themselves in the chest and proceed to slice their chests open. Everyone in the room is dead.

"I came to you because I admire your loyalty. Do you wish to join me?" he asks.

"If I say no, will you make sure I end up like them?" I ask, signaling to the mass grave on the floor.

"I do not want my second in command to follow me under duress. I can promise you that if you say no, I will not kill you today. However, I would kill you myself if that's what were needed to reach my goal. So should you someday need to die for me to reach my goal, yes, I would kill you."

"What exactly is your goal?" I ask.

"You have twenty-four hours to make up your mind," he says, ignoring my question.

He then rises slowly and walks past the corpses of my demons with complete indifference. I look back at him as he heads towards the exit.

"Wait!" I demand.

He stops walking and faces me.

"Yes," he replies.

"This goal of yours, would we have to kill a lot of angels?" I ask.

"Quite a few."

"And I'm guessing we're taking over the world, right?" I push.

"That comes after," he says.

"After what?" I ask.

"After my family reunion."

***

I would have been highly pissed off at Malakaro for killing my demons if I wasn't so busy being impressed. Nothing I heard about him did him justice. The level of sheer wickedness in him is to be commended. Yet I'm not sure joining him is what's best for me. At least not without finding out more about this angel turned evil. I decide to research Malakaro and find out what's behind the mystery.

Finding out about the vicious Noru proves to be very difficult. No one knows anything about him other than the fact that his mother was killed and his father never knew him. No one can tell me where Malakaro grew up, what his life was like, or how he ended up being so twisted.

When an important event occurs in the world of angels and demons, it's written about in journals called Muses. There are libraries all around the world that carry thousands of Muses. But the biggest collection of recorded events in our world can be found in the Library of Congress, in a secret room. I fly there and discover absolutely nothing that could help me learn more about Malakaro.

I put in calls to all my contacts and each time they come back with the same info as before. I am about to give up when a low level demon agrees to give me information in exchange for letting him live. He doesn't have details of Malakaro's life, but he does give me the address of a historian who might be able to help me.

"I've gone to libraries all over the world, and I found nothing," I yell at him.

"Yeah, but this guy is different. He's a Quo. His name is Henry…something. We trashed his bookstore one time just for fun. He was obsessed with Quo history. He might know what happened to Malakaro since his mother was Quo," he reasons.

I had spent hours trying to find the angel version of what happened but it never occurred to me to research Malakaro's Quo side. I take the info but kill the demon anyway (he wore brown socks with black shoes, so I did the world a favor).

The demon's info leads me to the small nothing town of Cherry Grove in Mississippi. There, I find a bookstore called Tea & Pages. It's well kept but devoid of patrons. It's a small space with large antiquated books from floor to ceiling. It holds two big plush purple velvet armchairs at the center of the room. In between armchairs is a small round coffee table.

As soon as I enter, a bell goes off and notifies Henry that he has a guest. He shouts out from the back and says he will be right out. I take another look around and then plop down on one of the armchairs. I put my feet up on the coffee table and wait for the old man to come out and shit his pants when he sees a demon in his store. I look at my watch; I have just enough time to hear what the old fart has to say. Then I can make up my mind one way or the other.

Not long after, Henry enters the room. He has silver hair, dark rimmed glasses, and a slight hump. In his hand is a tray with a teakettle and a teacup.

"Get your feet off my damn table, demon," he instructs.

"You dare speak to me in that insolent tone? Do you know who I am?" I challenge.

"Yeah, what of it?" he asks.

Is this old man serious?

"Do you want to die?" I ask.

"After my tea, yeah sure," he replies.

"Look, old man, I need some answers and I was told you have them." I explain the situation to him.

"So you think there might be detailed accounts of Malakaro's life written by his Quo mother?" he asks.

"Yes. I need you to go back there or wherever you keep the journals and look for it," I order.

"No need. I know my Muse collection backwards and forwards. I don't have any journals from Malakaro's mother."

"Don't lie to me, old man," I say, charging forward and grabbing him by his shirt collar.

"I told you, I don't have any details from Malakaro's mother," he says.

I look deeply in his eyes and I can tell he's being honest.

"Damn it!" I shout, letting the old fool go.

"I have something better; I have his father's secret journal. I came by it years ago from a collector who had mistakenly mixed it in with a box of Quo history books. I kept it thinking it might be worth something someday."

"Bullshit. Marcus Cane was an open book. He wrote down everything that happened on each mission. I've read all the journals and they don't mention Malakaro at all. Marcus didn't even know he had a son," I reply.

"That is where you're wrong, demon. Marcus Cane knew very well he had a son. In fact, Marcus and Malakaro met on three separate occasions."

CHAPTER TWO
NO QUESTION

Jason,

I hope this Muse finds its way to you one day. Knowing you like I do, I have no doubt that if you want to find this, you will. I'm not sure what I hope to gain by writing this other than to set the record straight. I want you to know two things: no matter what anyone tells you, you were wanted from the very start.

The second thing I need you to know is that walking away from you was in fact the hardest thing I've ever had to do in my entire life. I had my reasons and they were good ones, but that doesn't stop me from feeling like I failed you. Abandoning my own flesh and blood is absolutely the lowest point for me.

My wife, whom as you know is also Death, was working in the light when her colleague Fate contacted me. I found this surprising, since Fate is known for keeping secrets. He is the hardest member of the council to get information from. Mostly because everything he reveals will somehow change the future. It may be a small change or a major one, but Fate rarely takes that chance so we do not have any idea what tomorrow will look like.

Yet there he was at my doorstep. Once I opened the door and let him in, I could see that he had paused the world. Every single human was standing still in mid action. I told him that I would have met him somewhere else, but I had just put your sister, Pryor, down to Recharge, or to take a nap as the humans say.

Fate didn't look put out by having to come over. In fact, he looked like he was glad to be there. He asked to see Pryor and promised not to disturb her. I took him to her room and there he looked down at my three year old and her odd looking stuffed bear. The bear was wearing a pink tutu over a black ninja suit. Fate, not having the ability to foresee everything, looked at me, confused.

"She likes human toys. She likes the bear dressed as a ballerina, but she also wants the bear to know how to fight. So she asked us to make her a Ninja-Ballerina bear."

"Marcus, she is precious," he said.

"Thank you. Her mother and I are very proud of her," I replied.

"She's going to do amazing things one day," Fate told me.

"Right now, we're just working on getting her to stop scribbling on the walls and control her powers so that she doesn't take flight in a crowd of humans."

"She really is quite lovely," he said with a hint of regret in his voice.

That put me on edge. Fate doesn't just make house calls.

"What's wrong? What do you know? Is it about Pryor? Is she going to be okay? Is there a demon after her? Who is it? Who do I need to kill?" I demanded.

"Marcus, calm down."

"No, tell me what you know."

"Let's discuss this outside so we don't wake the Ninja Ballerina," he suggested.

We step out into the hall and immediately I started pacing, thinking of a hundred different things that could go wrong with Pryor.

"Marcus, I need you to remain calm, it's essential," he said.

"Tell me what's going on. Should I call Emmy?" I asked.

"Your wife and I talked she knows that you and I would have a word. She also knows that there are things she is better off not knowing. That's part of the job. Sometimes Fate and Time need to keep things from Death. That's what happens when Death is a working mom with a family," Fate reminded me.

"Okay, just tell me what's going on," I asked.

That's when he told me all about you. He told me that your mother, Bianca, left instructions for you to be placed with distant human relatives should something happen to her. He said your energy started growing and that's how they were able to find you—by tracking your energy. It was a complete shock to me that I had a son. Right away I demanded that he take me to you. And that's when the second shock of the night came my way.

"There's been a growing dark power on the outskirts of my visions of the future. With every passing day it has grown stronger. And today for the first time, I had a full flash of what's to come. This new evil is without measure. It won't just harm humans; it will send everyone and everything into a dark void where only ash and flames remain."

"We always knew that Lucy would be replaced by a new evil," I reminded him.

"But not like this. The new evil about to come our way isn't angry or wrathful. It's a methodical, deliberate seeker of blood and death."

"Do you need me to assemble the team? I can do that, but first I need to see to my son," I informed Fate.

"Marcus, the evil's name is Malakaro. He's your son."

***

After getting the news, I called my wife and she came to Earth immediately. We gave Pryor her bath, and then we called Tony, our long-time angel babysitter and friend. He watched Pry while we went to our favorite place to think things over, the Green mountains. My wife watched as I paced up and down restlessly.

"Marcus, talk to me," Emmy said.

"I…I don't know. I have no idea where to start," I confessed.

She took my hand in hers and forced me to stand still. She then placed her hands on either side of my face tenderly and said the oddest thing.

"How do you feel about baseball?" she asked.

"What?"

"For the wallpaper. I'm thinking that or maybe basketball. Or we could do angel related sports like Runner ball," she replied.

"Emmy, babe, you're losing me."

"When your son comes home to us, I want his room to be made up already," she replied with a smile.

"You want him to come stay with us?"

"Where else would he go? We're his family. He's a part of you, so he's part of me."

"I want that too, but Emmy, Fate said—"

"Ah, screw Fate. Don't tell him I said so, but he's not always right. You and I know that more than anyone else. It doesn't matter what anyone says. I know you and I know there's no way you would just stand back and let this kid grow up without you. Maybe he's gonna be evil because he isn't exposed to good. We can change that."

"Exactly! That's what I was thinking," I said.

"Malakaro is probably just a lost kid who doesn't feel wanted. We take him in and show him that he's not only wanted, he's loved. He stands a good chance of being good. How could he not? You're his father," she reasoned.

"So you're okay with this?" I asked.

"Bianca was awful and manipulative, but that doesn't mean her son will be the same way. This kid deserves to know his dad. And Pry will love having an older brother."

"He's probably going to be really angry that I wasn't there for him," I told her.

"Don't worry, you can make it up to him. This is the start of something wonderful. It won't be an easy adjustment but we can do this," she assured me.

"Yeah, I think so too. I mean, I really do," I replied.

She beamed back at me. She was even more beautiful then than the day I first met her. Not many women would be okay with raising another woman's child, but Emmy welcomed it.

"Marrying you was the wisest thing I've ever done. Thank you for this," I told her as I pulled her towards me and kissed her. She pulled away unexpectedly. She then smiled and took off in the air.

"Where are you going?" I shouted.

"Shopping! Our son is coming home. He's gonna need stuff!" she said happily.

***

Fate wasn't happy about our decision to take you in. He thought it would be a terrible mistake and that we would regret it. However, Emmy and I insisted that Fate allow us to bring you home. So Fate reluctantly arranged a meeting between you and me. Emmy stayed behind because she wanted to give us time to talk. She didn't want to get in the way of our first encounter.

Fate and I entered your human school and he paused everyone on site. We walked down the long hallway to your first grade class. It was the longest walk of my life. On one hand I was so excited to meet you, but on the other hand I was scared of what I would find.

I worried that my absence had already made you bitter and resentful of me. I worried that you hated me and that I would never be able to make it up to you. Fate told me that you were being raised by Quo who loved you very much, but I needed to see for myself that you were well cared for.

I also debated whether or not to tell you who I was when we first spoke. Should I tell you that I'm your father right away or wait? How would you take it? Would you agree to move in with us or want nothing to do with me? And what in the world would I say when you ask me about your mother? Bianca and I never got along, but I didn't want you to hate her, she was after all your mother. What could I say to make this whole thing better?

"Marcus, we're here. He's inside the classroom waiting for you," Fate said.

"Okay, he's been living with half angels, so he obviously knows about our world, right?" I asked.

"Yes, Malakaro knows the basics. His relatives saw to that," Fate replied.

"Good," I said as I looked through the small glass opening in the door.

I saw you standing there. You were a little over three feet tall and wore a black and blue school uniform. You had jet black hair like your mom and your wings flapped gently above you. You were perfect.

"That's my son," I said proudly as I looked at over at you.

"Before you go in, promise me this: talk to Malakaro first. See who he is now before you decide whether or not to take him in."

"Fate, there is nothing you can say that would make me turn my back on him."

"Just talk to him—before he knows who you are, have a conversation with him, Marcus. That's all I'm asking."

Highly irritated, I shook my head and focused on the little boy before me. I walked into the class to come take you home. I walked up to you and you turned to face me. You had these intense "saucer" wide eyesbursting with wonder and curiosity. It took everything I had not to pick you up and take you home right then and there.

"Hello, Malakaro," I called out to you softly.

"My name is Jason." You corrected me as you studied my face.

"I thought your name was—"

"No, call me Jason. It's my dad's name."

A lump forms in my throat when I hear the pride in your voice as you speak about sharing the same middle name as me, a father you have never met. I knew you would be part of my family and that I would spend all my life making up for my absence. We would care for you and love you.

"Hello, Jason, I'm Marcus."

"That's my dad's name," he said, intrigued.

"What do you know about your father?" I asked.

"He's like you; he has wings. And he can do anything," you said, clearly impressed.

"Really?"

"Yup, and he is strong and he can fight," you informed me.

"How do you know that?" I asked.

"Because he's my dad; my real dad. Not the Quo I live with."

"Mr. and Mrs. Cross treating you okay?" I asked.

"I don't like them," you replied.

Why? Did they do something to you?" I asked, on high alert.

"They make me wear a hat and gloves even when it's not that cold outside. They make me do my homework even when it's stupid and they sing with the radio in the car; they sound awful."

I burst out laughing. You smiled back at me. There is no denying it; you have your mom's stunning good looks and her charm. Yes, your mother could be charming when she needed to be.

"Your parents don't sound that bad," I assured you.

"But they are always telling me what to do."

"They are grown-ups, they know more than you," I remarked.

"But they're just Quo," you informed me.

"Quo are important, Jason. They matter. Just like humans matter," I replied as I got down to your level so we could be eye to eye.

"I want them to be good at it," you pleaded.

"You want them to be good at what?" I asked.

"Being my pets."

Your reply caused tightness in my chest. I didn't let that deter me. There was still time to teach you right from wrong.

"Why did you want to see me? Are you my new flight teacher? Are we going to have another flying lesson?"

"Not right now. So you like to fly, what else do you like to do?" I asked.

"I play with Roger. I ask him to sing and he does," you said, heading over to the bluebird in the cage in the corner of the room.

"He looks like a really cool bird. Hey, I heard you could do some pretty amazing things. Is that true? Can you show me what you can do?" I asked.

You shook your head "yes." You lifted your hands and you were able to lift the cage door without touching it. The bird quickly took to the air and circled the classroom. Once out, you had the bird fly around in exactly the pattern you commanded. There were times your concentration was off but still, you showed an impressive control. I excused myself and headed back to the hallway where Fate was waiting.

"I did what you said; I talked to him. And guess what? He's a kid. Just a kid with powers who wants to learn more about life. He's not some horrific monster. He's a child, my child, and you are out of your mind if you think I will let you keep me from my son!" I vowed.

"You have got to look at the bigger picture, Marcus."

"There is no bigger picture! He's my kid and I am going to take him home—today."

"He's never been able to set the bird free from the cage before. He's tried a hundred times before and today is the first time he's been able to successfully open that cage,"

Fate said.

"So what's your point?" I demanded.

"The point, First Guardian, is that his powers increased because he was near you. It's called Absorption and it's a rare ability. His natural powers are coming to the surface even without be trained to tap into them. He learned to fly on his own. He learned to focus his power enough to move objects, and when you came near him he tapped into your power and was able to control a living thing," Fate replied.

"Will he always be able to Absorb powers from other beings?" I asked.

"No, at one point he won't need to do that. He will have enough of his own."

"Okay, so for now he needs some help so he taps into powers of angels near him. There's nothing wrong with him wanting to learn to use his powers," I reasoned.

"Marcus, who do you think you are speaking to? I am Fate. I don't waste my time in family drama. I didn't come to you to tell you that one day your son would break curfew and get drunk off Coy. I came down here to tell you that the evil coming is ubiquitous and unrelenting; everything in the world will bow to it. Your son will be that evil."

"You don't know that for sure," I protested.

"Damn it, Marcus, listen to me!"

"No! You don't know what he will become. He could change his life. He could be good. I'm not going to give up on him. He's my son. How the hell can I walk away from him?"

"You have made some controversial decisions in the past but I understood them. I knew that they all came from your desire to protect the ones you love from danger. Walking away from this kid is the best way to do that."

"I can help him. I can teach him right from wrong. I just need some time with him. I will take him home and—"

"And what, Marcus? He has managed to connect to his powers even though he has limited contact with angels. Can you imagine how much power he will collect from you alone? Not to mention the fact that he will be living with your wife, who in case you forgot happens to be Death. He can tap into her powers too."

"What do you want from me?" I raged.

"We want your permission to bind his powers."

"What? No! He'll be defenseless. You know how much danger our children face."

"Marcus, Malakaro will not face danger; he is the danger."

"Don't call him that. He likes to be called Jason. That's his middle name. He likes that name," I replied, mostly to myself.

"I know you want to be there for him and that may have been possible if you were just any angel. But you're not. You're a Guardian. Many, including that boy in there, covet your powers."

"He doesn't even know who I am."

"No but he daydreams about meeting his all-powerful father. Most kids do. But unlike most kids, his father really is all-powerful. He can't have access to it. He can't be around you," Fate begged.

"He's a kid. He's confused and he feels rejected. That's why he's lashing out. I'll take care of him. He's my responsibility. I will raise him."

"Marcus—"

"No! I'm done talking about this. I'm going to get my son and bring him home. If you, Time, or anyone else tries to harm him, I'll rip your fucking souls out," I vowed.

"I'm working on patience, Guardian, but don't test me," Fate replied.

"You're wrong about Jason. He's a good kid. I did crazy things when I was a kid, but my dad stood by me. He didn't turn his back on me, and I'm sure as hell not gonna do that to Jason."

"Because he's just a kid, a misguided soul?" Fate asked.

"Yes," I replied urgently.

He signaled for me to look inside the classroom; I followed his stare and saw Jason standing by his teacher's desk, looking down on the bird. It wasn't moving. I rushed inside and asked him what happened.

"He saw the window and he wanted to fly away. So I put him back in the cage. I told him to sing but he wouldn't sing anymore because he was mad at me," Jason said.

"But now look, he's dead, Jason. Why did you do that?"

"I told you, he wouldn't sing for me. And if he won't sing for me, he shouldn't be allowed to sing ever again."

I stepped outside in the hallway and leaned on the wall for support. It was the certainty and coldness in his voice that caused a chill to run through me.

"I'm sorry, Marcus. Really, I am," Fate said.

"He's intelligent, he's focused and strong. Those are good qualities for angels," I whispered to myself.

"They are also characteristics essential in evil."

"No, I can't do it."

"Marcus!"

"No, okay? I can't abandon him. Please don't ask me to do that."

"You walked into that room and you saw it for yourself. The kid has a very black and white way of looking at things. That bird displeased him and he killed it. What happens when you take him in and you displease him? What happens when Pryor displeases him?"

Pryor...

"Marcus, do we have your permission to bind his powers or not?" Fate asked.

I looked into the room and saw you were now playing with the pet hamster on the other side of the room. I worried what would happen if the creature should disobey his master. I turned to Fate and spoke in a voice coated with regret.

"Yes, bind his powers, but not forever. We can revisit this issue in a few months."

"It doesn't work like that. If we bind his power it will be for five years."

"That's way too long," I declared.

"If he is going to learn right from wrong like you say, he'll need that time. We can revisit this issue in five years," Fate said.

"Okay, but I have to be there for him. I have to watch him and make sure he has what he needs."

"You can't do that. I told you, if you are anywhere near him he will use you and your power."

"And I told you, I can't just abandon him."

"We will see to his well-being. We will guard him. But the less he knows about you and who you are the better."

"You think he would seek to destroy his own father?" I asked in disbelief.

"I can almost guarantee it."

"Fine, what do you have in mind—and if your mixture causes him pain in any way you can forget it," I said.

"We're going to give him Dew; it's painless. All it does is suppresses his powers," Fate said as he headed towards the classroom. I turned away, unable to watch.

He's just a kid. He's my kid…

My chest tightened and the agony of abandoning my own flesh and blood spread through my veins. I saw a flash of his smile in my mind's eye and I was on the verge of calling the whole thing off but then I saw a flash of my little girl and the dead bird.

Fuck!

When Fate came out of the classroom I planned to bombard him with demands. I wanted to be kept informed of Jason's progress, his grades, his health, everything. But then I look in Fate's eyes and find something I have never seen on the face of a council member—fear.

"What is it?" I asked.

"Dew is the most potent power suppressor that there is and yet it didn't work on him."

"What does this mean?"

"It means there is no question about it: Malakaro will kill us all."

CHAPTER THREE
ANGEL'S DILEMMA

I reread the last line a few times. It isn't just what was said but the being that said it. According to Fate, Malakaro will be the undoing of angels. If this guy is as powerful as Fate thinks he is, I'm definitely up for joining him. I take a closer look at the journal. There are only two more entries. The old man starts to say something. I tell him to shut up and I continue to read.

Jason,

Over the years, while I couldn't physically keep an eye on you, I tracked your progress closely. You were given the best possible human and angel education. Anything you needed or wanted I made sure you had. When I gave something to my daughter, Pry, I made sure that I sent you something too. I wrote to you and expressed how proud I was of your progress and how intelligent you were turning out to be. Jason, not a day went by where I didn't think about you; not one.

The reports I was getting about you spoke in glowing terms of your intellect. They said you were brilliant and resourceful. They said you mastered vocabulary, reasoning, and logic. They were all taken aback by how mature you were for your age.

"Why can't I take him home now? It's been five years," I asked Fate.

"You think he's gotten better and that he no longer poses a threat but you'd be wrong, Marcus," Fate insisted.

"I've read his letters to me; I think he's becoming good."

"Yes, he's gotten good—at hiding just how bad he can be."

"This is crazy. He's a good kid. He was misguided; he killed a bird once. He made a mistake. But that was a long time ago. You've read the reports, my kid is remarkable," I argued.

"Yes, Marcus, he is very impressive. But you are failing to look at the bigger picture: he has no empathy."

"He just needs to be around angels that love him," I suggested strongly.

"Angels whose powers he can absorb to use for his own."

"I left him with you for five years. That's more than enough time," I protested.

"I would like you to take a look at this," Fate said.

He took out an orb the size of a grapefruit.

"This a called a Simulation Reply. It's a game the instructors give the children. They have programmed it so that the being looks like them. The student controls the figures inside the globe. They are given different scenarios and they decide how to handle it."

"What's in this scenario?" I asked.

"This is called 'Angel's Dilemma.'"

"What happens in this scenario?" I asked.

"There's a man, a human. He is separated from his family by shark-infested waters. He does not know how to swim, but he longs to get back to his loved ones. That longing has caused him to try and get across many times and many times he has failed. He is wounded and unable to try again. It is a 'no fly' zone, so angels cannot take to the air. And in the water along with the sharks are Soul Chasers. As you know they are orbs that tear apart the soul and are thus fatal to angels. The students were tasked to protect the man from danger."

"The point of the exercise being that sometimes we have no choice but to give our lives up for the greater good," I replied.

"Exactly. There is no way for the angel to cross the river and serve, but he can get the human safely across before dying."

"And how did Jason do?" I asked.

"He scored highest in the class."

"Really?"

"Yes. Some students lost points because they hesitated to jump into the water because of the Soul Chasers, which is typical for young angels. Other students spent too much time trying to figure a way around the Soul Chasers and the man bled to death. But Jason was quick and certain in his actions. He scored highest in the class."

"Why do you make that sound like a bad thing?" I asked.

"Watch what your son did."

I watched the simulation take place inside the globe. There was a mini version of a wounded man lying alongside a riverbank. Across from him were his three kids and his wife, who frantically called out for him. The man on the ground dragged himself back towards the water. It was clear he intended to try once again to get to his family. Jason looked down at the wounded man on the ground and without the slightest hesitation, he shot a Powerball at the man's wife and kids. All three died instantly.

Shocked, I looked over at Fate. He handed me the globe and told me the instructors had yet to ask Jason why he chose to kill the family instead of helping the man.

"We thought maybe you'd like to ask him yourself," Fate said.

I sighed deeply and opened the door to your classroom. You didn't quickly turn to look at me like you had the first time we met. Back then you were five, now you're ten and you weren't as quick with your emotions. In fact, it was awhile before you turned to face me.

"Hello, Marcus," you said, devoid of any emotion.

"Hi, Jason."

"I enjoyed the puzzles you sent me, thank you," you said.

"You're welcome. Can you turn to face me?" I asked.

You did as I asked. You had grown even more handsome than before. I hugged you and you returned my embrace—slowly. I chalked it up to your being young and embarrassed by emotion.

"How have you been?" I asked.

"Fine."

"Your instructors tell me that you are a pretty smart kid."

"Where are your powers? I can't feel them," you said.

"I took a suppressor. When I'm around you, you absorb my powers. It's not your fault, but you're too little; it's too much power for you."

"Is there really such a thing as too much power?" you wondered.

"Yes, Jason, there is."

"Okay," you replied, not fully convinced.

"I'm told you've been reading angel history. I know you have questions about certain things." I started carefully.

"Yes, I do. I suspect you're my father, is that true?"

"Yes, I am. Your mother and I…we were together for a brief time…it was all very unexpected."

"From what I gather, she had me to use me as some sort of tool to gain power."

"Yes, I suspect that was her intention—but that doesn't mean something is wrong with you or that you're not wanted. You are. I want you in my life. You're my son and I love you."

"But you have another child, right?"

"Yes, her name is Pryor. She's seven."

"Is she away at school like I am?" you asked.

"No, she lives with me."

"Can I live with you too?"

"Do you want to?"

"Yes, can I? Please?"

"I want that, Jason, but first can you tell me about the Simulation Reply game," I asked.

"I scored better than anyone else in the class," you said proudly.

"Yes you did, because you made the quickest decision. And I'm proud of you, but son, you didn't meet the goal of the game. The goal was to save the man, not hurt his family," I pointed out gently.

"The goal was to save the man from danger and that's what I did," you said with certainty.

"How did killing the family keep the man safe from the danger? The danger was the sharks in the water," I reminded you.

"No, the danger was the man's desire to be with his family. That's what made him want to cross the shark-infested water, so I eliminated the family. That took away his desire to cross and kept him safe."

"But, Jason, now his family is gone and he's unhappy."

"The goal was not to make the man happy; the goal was to keep him safe."

I sighed heavily and raked my hand through my hair. You smiled back at me.

"So, am I going home with you?"

***

I couldn't take you home then. It hurt me so bad to walk away from you once more. The next time we met another five years had gone by. And again I kept up on your progress and again you failed to grasp certain basic angel concepts.

I consulted one of my best friends, Rage. He is the only demon I know who turned good. I don't know what I wanted him to say, but I somehow hoped he'd have a solution to my problem. Instead the only thing he told me was that sometimes beings are born bad.

As hard as it was to do, I had to put the issue of you and me to the back of my mind and focus on my new son, Sam. He's two years old now and has been ill for weeks now. He's weak, unable to fly, and constantly needing to Recharge. We took him to a Healer and she told us someone had sent him a virus. I didn't want to believe you could do something that terrible but when the Healer said it was a virus that could only be made by blood relatives, I knew it was you.

The virus wasn't enough to kill Sam, but over time it would drain him of his powers completely. That would leave him defenseless and at the mercy of demons everywhere. After the Healer fixed Sam, I went over to the school to see you and ask if you knew anything about this. Even before I asked, I had my answer. You were smug and calm as we spoke.

"Why would you do that to him?" I asked.

"I didn't do anything."

"DO NOT LIE TO ME!" I shouted.

"Why not? You lie to me on a regular basis. I dare say it's the cornerstone of our relationship."

"Jason, I know you're mad at me but—"

"Malakaro."

"What?"

"My name is Malakaro. And really, Marcus, we need to stop meeting like this."

"You could have gotten Sam killed," I replied.

"If I wanted him dead I would have sent a different poison."

"Why would you want to hurt Sam at all? He's never done anything to you."

"He took something away from me."

"What?"

"You. You were mine. Then he took your attention away. Someone needed to be held accountable."

"You poisoned my son."

"I didn't kill him."

"That's not the point. If we didn't heal him in time he would have lost his powers. Do you know how cruel that is?"

"Yes. I remember when you tried it on me."

"Is that what this is? Revenge? Jason, we just wanted to make sure your powers didn't get out of hand. But what you did to Sam was wrong. It was immoral. Do you get that?"

"According to one of your precious humans, Friedrich Nietzsche, 'It is a prejudice to think that morality is more favorable to the development of reason than immorality.'"

"He was wrong. Being moral is far more favorable," I corrected you.

"Have you been moral, Marcus?"

"I have failed at times."

"Yes, you have. You never took me in. I wanted you to welcome me as you had my sister. But you never did because I never fit into what a Noru is supposed to be. I was kept away from you because I wasn't weak minded; I didn't pray at the altar of feeble humans. But I knew that I mattered to you for the simple fact that I was your only son. Then you went and had another male child. Taking away the only connection I had."

"You hate me for having another son?"

"I was the only one with that title—Marcus Jason Cane's son. I put up with being a family secret because it was the only way I could have a relationship with you; you, the all-powerful First Guardian."

"Jason, listen to me. Having Sam doesn't make me love you any less."

"So despite my cruel actions, you will take me home with you?"

I looked away from you, not sure how to reply.

"I didn't think so," you said quietly.

"You weren't ready to come home; you posed a threat," I pleaded with you.

You looked over at me and smiled slowly.

"Oh, Father, I haven't even begun to threaten you…"

***

The next and last entry isn't by Marcus, it's written in a softer handwriting. You can tell a woman wrote it. I look at the old man and he signals for me to keep reading. That's when I find myself reading a passage from a member of the council—Death.

Malakaro,

When my husband came back from his meeting with you, I couldn't find him. I had searched all the usual places, I asked the other Guardians and no one had seen him. I knew that meant he went to the one place he goes to when he's at his lowest—his human mother's grave. She died some years before from a drug overdose. Sure enough I found him leaning on the tree standing by her headstone, looking up as if there would be answers written in the sky.

"Hi," I said softly.

He looked up at me and there was no other way to describe the look in his eyes other than to say he was broken. I have never seen him in that much agony in all the time I have known him. It's like something got ahold of his soul and was twisting it; slowly killing him.

"Marcus, honey, what is it?"

"The poison, Jason sent it to Sam."

He told me about the conversation the two of you had. I tried to control my temper but already I was causing the sky to darken and thunder had started exploding.

"You're certain he did it?" I asked.

"Yes. There's always so much darkness in him. I tried to find something, some spark, some hint of light, but…"

He was too overcome to move on. I pushed back my rage as a mother and tried hard to focus on being his wife. I held him as tightly as I could while he unraveled.

"I can't help him, Emmy."

"I know."

"He tried to take my son's life…I can't just let him…what did I do to make him so evil? What did I say? How did I break him?"

"This isn't your fault. Some beings are born that way and there's nothing anyone can do."

"I'm an angel. I'm the First Guardian. Why can't I save my own son from evil?"

He moaned and slid to the ground, heartbroken and defeated. I sat beside him and took his hand, but it wasn't enough. It'll never really be enough. Marcus has always wanted to save the ones he loves more so than the average angel. He lost his life as a human trying to save his mother from herself. He doesn't know how to give up on the ones he loves.

"I would do anything to get him to turn good. Anything at all, but I can't put the kids at risk. I can't let him hurt my family."

"You have done everything you could do. But it's time to walk away," I said sadly.

He gasped as if he was physically in pain and bowed his head.

"He hates me. He hates our family and he would do anything to hurt us. I can't reach him. I try and I try but…I lost him. I lost my son."

"No, Marcus, you have a son. His name is Sam. He's three years old. He's bright, sweet, and has made you his whole world. You also have a daughter who at only twelve years old already shows signs of being a powerful leader. But more importantly she has kindness, mercy, and compassion."

"She got that from you," he said in a quiet whisper.

"She got it from us. They both did. You are an exceptional father. Maybe one day he'll find his way back to good, back to you. But for now, let it go. Let him go. If not, we stand to lose everything we worked for."

"I know I have to cut ties with Jason, I just…I don't know how," he admitted.

I reached out and handed him a green pill called Blank. Once you take it, you forget whoever is weighing so heavily on your soul.

"If I take this I won't remember anything at all about Jason," he said.

"Honey, his name is Malakaro. And I don't know if he really will be a threat to the world tomorrow. All I know is that he's a threat to our family today. And his only connection is with you. We need to sever that connection," I replied.

"Yeah, I know…"

"You don't have to decide to take the pill now. If you need time to think it over—"

"No, there's nothing to think over. He tried to hurt Sam. That can never happen again. And as long as I know about him, I'll inquire and try to find a way to help him. He'll use that to get at you and the kids. I have to take the pill—now," he said.

It was an extra potent dose, and in a few hours he forgot every detail having to do with you. Fate and Time told me that you were not a subject that would disappear so easily but I didn't care. I was just glad that Marcus found some peace. He's back to his old self. He doesn't even recall making the journal entries he's made here. I thought about throwing this Muse away but I didn't because it was important to Marcus.

I am going to confess something to you. I lied to my husband when I told him that maybe you could turn good in the future. You and I both know that's bullshit. You are just as evil, broken, and twisted as your mother was. In the start I was open to taking you in because everyone deserves a chance, but you have shown that you are exactly what Fate said you'd be—wicked and devoid of compassion.

I am surprised however, because while you may have taken on your mother's evil streak, apparently you don't have her intelligence. Going after my kid was a bad move because now you've pissed me off. So take this last entry as a warning:

You want to come after Marcus or me, that's fine. But you go after my kids and I will peel the flesh from your bones with my teeth. Try me.

Xo

Death

***

After that day in the bookstore, I have been faithfully following Malakaro. I am more than happy with my decision. Sure it sucked to kill Joanna. I mean, I really liked her. But my boss pointed out that my feelings for her could be seen as a weakness. He hated weakness. So, not long after I joined him, I sent a demon to capture and kill Joanna, my only human friend.

Hey, focus on the now , Santini, and stop flashing back to the past.

After scolding myself, I look at my reflection in the waterfall once again. Yes, I'm still as striking as I was when I first met Malakaro all those years ago. And of course everything is working out perfectly.

We are on our way to collecting all five vials of Rye. A Rye is a mixture consisting of unimaginable evil powers. This crazy angel scientist guy named Pinter created it. We need to locate all five Rye and mix them together.

We will then divide the mixture into two parts. My boss will drink the first part. There's only one being that can ingest the second part of the mixture. He or she is called the Alago. We don't know who that is yet, but when we do, my boss will force that bastard to drink. Then together the two of them will become the perfect evil.

"Santini, enough with your reflection. Vanity is a human failing. Let us not share in it," Malakaro says as he comes down the steps, followed by his black panther, Makayla.

"Sure, Boss, sorry," I reply.

The panther growls at me. I daydream about skinning that damn thing, but she's my master's favorite pet.

"I know we have one Rye vial already. Do you have a lead on where we can find the second one?" I ask.

"Not yet. But I didn't summon you here for the vials. I bring you news. An hour ago, my helpless little sister was captured by The Center." Malakaro says matter-of-factly.

"The Center? I've heard things about that place...I thought it was a myth—a place where angels torture other angles," I reply.

"I assure you it is no myth."

"What are they doing with Pryor?"

"Killing her…"

BOOK II

AADEN "SILVER" CASE

"Always go too far, because that's where you'll find the truth"
— *Albert Camus*

CHAPTER FOUR
CRASH

I walk up the steps of my dad's house and head to my room. There, I find a girl in my bed; naked. She lies on her side, props her head up with the palm of her hand, and greets me with a smile.

Okay…

"Hello, Silver" she says seductively.

"Hi," I reply calmly.

"I heard you were coming back here to get a few things. I thought I'd wait for you," she informs me.

"I see."

"You don't mind, do you?" she asks.

"No, but maybe you should put some clothes on," I suggest.

"Why?"

"Well for one thing, you look cold," I reply, signaling towards her protruding nipples.

"I'm naked by choice. If I wanted to put my clothes on I would have done so."

"Fair enough."

"Is this making you uncomfortable?" she asks.

"No, but I think maybe a blanket couldn't hurt," I reply.

"Why do you want me to cover up? Don't like what you see?"

"I do. You're beautiful; you always have been."

"So, why are you still standing across the room? Come, join me," she purrs.

Crap.

"I'll come over, but I need you to put something on."

"Okay," she says simply.

She reaches over to the side of the bed and picks up an article of clothing from the pile of clothes she had discarded at the base of the bed. It's a blue silk scarf. She places it around her neck and of course it does nothing to conceal her body.

"There. Happy?" she asks.

I can tell she's been drinking—heavily.

"This is a very bad idea," I warn her.

"Actually, I think it's the smartest idea I've ever had. You know what tonight is?"

"It's certainly not sobriety night," I reply.

"It's 'Fuck it!' night. That means tonight we say 'fuck it' to everything that's been bothering us. And just have fun."

"What's been bothering you, Key?"

"Nope, we won't talk about that stuff."

"Okay, but why don't you put your clothes on so we can talk," I suggest.

She laughs and starts walking towards me.

"Talk? Is that what you do with a naked girl, Silver?"

"You don't want to do this, trust me," I warn again.

"Oh, but I do. I really do."

"Why?" I ask as I shake my head, baffled.

"You're Silver, the first and only half demon, half angel. Every girl fantasizes about being with you. It's been said your touch is rough and commanding but gentle when it needs to be. So c'mon; show me."

"You know I can't do anything with you," I remind her.

"Don't worry. I brought a bottle of Trickk. So even though Ruin has your Rah, you and I will still be able to screw."

"And what about Bex?"

"You think he cares what I do?"

"Yes, Key, I think he does."

"Then you're as delusional as I was."

"We were all on a high from rescuing my dad from the Forest of Remains. You and Bex were fine. That was just a few hours ago. What happened?"

"You know what happened."

"No, Key, I don't," I reply as I walk past her and drape her with the sheet from my bed.

"We laughed tonight, Bex and me. We laughed. I can't even remember what we laughed about but we did. We celebrated making it out of the forest by going to our favorite spot—the tulip field in Holland. Have you ever been there?"

"No, I haven't."

"It's painfully beautiful. There are endless perfect rows of red, blue, and yellow tulips. It's the most beautiful place on earth. Truly," she says as tears quickly fill her eyes.

"Key, did Bex break up with you?"

"We were exhausted, so we lay there in each other's arms and Recharged in the field. His cell phone rang and I picked it up. It was one of the Healers in training from the Clinic. She was checking up on Bex. I said that he was fine and that I would look after him. And she said, 'Oh, you must be the girl he was calling out for while he was under. Wow, he's really into you—Pryor.'"

I can feel a sharp pain travel across my chest. I try to quiet the frenzy of rage that is growing inside me but I fail. Every inch of me is tense and on high alert. Pryor isn't mine. Well, not officially. But still it angers me to no end to know that Bex is thinking about her.

"That doesn't mean anything, Key," I lie.

She laughs this sad dark laugh and shakes her head.

"Do you know what it's like to watch someone you love just walk away from you little by little? I close my eyes and test myself. Do I remember what his laugh sounds like? What his touch feels like? I have to remember precisely all the places he's touched me. Because it's just a matter of time before…"

"I know for a fact that Bex would never hurt you."

"STOP LYING TO ME!"

"You and Bex just need some time."

"No, what we need is for Pryor to be gone. I hate her. I hate her. I wish she died in that cave," she blurts out. She is so shocked by her statement she places her hand in front of her mouth. Her eyes widen in shock.

"I didn't mean—I just—I gotta go," she says as she heads for the window.

"Key, wait!" I call out.

She doesn't even slow down. I send a group text to the team and then take off after Keyohmi. She's flying erratically and with no regard for the humans down below. I call after her but she makes no attempt to slow down. She zips through the air at dangerous speeds and nearly collides into a skyscraper.

"Damn it, Key, slow down!" I demand.

My warning does no good at all. If anything she is more reckless than before. Then without slowing down, she careens towards the ground. I call out for her to wait for me, but once again she dismisses me. She lands so hard on the ground she dents the surface of the street.

I land right behind her. We're standing in a seedy alley somewhere in Ibiza, surrounded by nightclubs. Before I can stop her, she runs into one of them. I take off after her once again. Inside the club there is a sea of angels, demons, and humans. They dance and jump around wildly to the absurdly loud pulsating music.

It's hard to track Key because the lighting is designed so that the club goers are in silhouette. The only chance to really see anything comes when the strobe light hits the crowd. But then all I can see are half dressed club goers with bight makeup bouncing up and down as they grind on each other.

I finally spot her in the middle of the zoo that is the dance floor. I cut through the dancers and head for her. She sees me and goes even further into the crowd. In her rush to avoid me, the sheet falls off her and hits the floor. The club goes nuts. Everyone cheers and hollers at the top of their lungs. They pump their fists, flap their wings, jump in the air, and paw at Key.

Key isn't bothered by the attention; she loves it. She dances with anyone and everyone around. The crowd is in such a frenzy the very foundation of the nightclub starts to sway.

Fights regularly break out in these kinds of places. I can only imagine what would happen if the demons that surround us realize Key is a Noru. The chance to take one of us out would be far too tempting. The only thing saving Key right now is the poor lighting.

"We need to get out of here!" I shout.

"Hey, I know her!" someone yells from the crowd.

"She's Noru!" someone else adds.

It happens all at once: We are under siege by demons from all sides. They tackle us as the humans scatter. The angels in the crowd go back to "duty" mode and fight back. In dire need of a distraction, I hurl a fireball at the disco ball and it explodes and rains shattered reflective glass.

I use the distraction to get to Key. But a demon near her takes aim and sends a blade straight for her. I leap forward and block his weapon by using a nearby demon's corpse as a shield. I fire back at the demon. It lands in the center of his chest. He dies quickly. I then reach out for Key to guide her to safety. I don't see the fireball heading towards me until it's too late. Thankfully, a Powerball hits my attacker in the arm, causing his fireball to go astray.

I look over and find that it's Bex who has just saved our lives. He looks over at Key, who looks back at him as if she couldn't care less about the drama surrounding us. Bex knows as well as I do, this is no time for a heart-to-heart. He swallows hard, takes his jacket off, and drapes it over his girl.

"Get her to safety. I'll take care of the demons," he says.

I grab Key and head towards the back room and close the door. I take the drunken Noru and sit her down in a chair in the corner. She keeps whispering that she's fine over and over again.

"Stay here, I'm gonna go back out there and help Bex," I tell her.

"No! Stay with me Silver. Pry is gonna be so pissed," she says as she laughs. Her laughter quickly turns to hysteria. I quickly walk up to her and take her hands.

"Key, everything is going to be fine. But I need to go and help Bex," I tell her.

When she doesn't reply, I call out to her. That's when I see it: Her eyes are completely flooded with a silver liquid. She is overdosing on something. I've seen it with club girls before.

"Shit! Key, what did you take?" I scream.

She is no longer conscious. Her body goes limp and she starts to slide off the chair. Bex comes in and tells me he has everything under control in the front. That's when he sees her on the floor.

"What happened?" he demands.

"She must have taken something," I reply.

"Key, Key!" Bex says, shaking her.

She doesn't answer. Bex rushes out of the room and scours the building looking for a Healer first aid kit. Most clubs have them for this very reason. Meanwhile I send out a quick text.

"I found these two, but I don't know what they do," Bex says frantically.

"We can't give it to her if we don't know what it does. It might make it worse!" I suggest.

"Well, we can't just sit here and watch her die, Silver!" he yells.

"We could take her to the Healers at the clinic," Bex says.

"Or you could just look on the inside of her lower lip," someone offers.

We turn to find Ruin standing on her Port, looking bored.

"Thank Omnis, you're here. You have to help her," Bex begs.

"Ah, not really," she replies.

"Diana!" I call out.

"It may have escaped your notice, but I'm not your pocket genie slash Healer, okay?"

"Ruin, please help her," Bex says frantically.

Diana looks over at me and then at Key's body.

"Look on the inside of her lip. If it's blue then she took 'upper' mixtures. You can use the vial on the right to cure her. If she took 'downers' to calm her, the inside of her lip will be green. In that case use the other vial," she says.

Bex places his shaking finger on Key's mouth. He gently pulls back her lower lip and studies it.

"The inside of her lip is not blue or green; it's purple. Purple spots," Bex says.

"Shit!" Ruin says, leaping off the Port and hurrying over to Key. She searches desperately for something in the small pouch she always carries with her.

"Ruin, what's going on? Tell me!" Bex begs.

"Your girlfriend didn't take an upper or a downer. She took both at the same time," Diana explains quickly.

"She's Paused," I whisper with quiet dread.

"What the hell does that mean? Talk to me," he shouts.

"When you take mixtures to both calm and excite you, there is this crazy high you can get from it. It's a high that fills you up with euphoria and makes you feel as if you are taking in the power of a thousand Para angels," I inform him.

"The trouble is when angels do it too much it causes a bacteria to build up in the bloodstream. That then throws the angel's body out of balance. So the body can no longer guard against an overflow of euphoria," Diana adds as she takes three vials from her pouch and starts to mix them.

"That's crazy, you're saying she's dying because she's happy?" Bex asks.

"Euphoria is just as powerful as a Powerball. Imagine your system is equipped to handle a pint's worth but now it's having to deal with a gallon. The overflow is seeping into her system and shutting it down."

"In other words, Para, your girlfriend is overdosing on synthetic happiness. I'm guessing she did that because her life is crap; only now the fake happiness is killing her. I can go into more detail or you can shut the hell up and let me save her."

Bex agrees to Diana doing whatever she feels she must do. She takes out a thin, scalpel-like knife and presses it just below Key's ear. Blood starts to seep out of Key's body and onto the floor. Only it's not silver colored like it should be. Instead it's a horrid bruise color.

"We have to get the overflow out before I can introduce the treatment into her system. It will kill off the bacteria and restore her body's natural balance," Diana says.

"We can't just let her bleed out!" Bex protests.

"I will stop the bleeding when we start to see silver colored blood, that means the infection is all out."

"What happens if her blood doesn't turn silver or if it's so infected, by the time we get to the healthy blood color, she's already bled out?" Bex says, more frantic now than I've ever seen him.

Diana and I exchange a quick worried glance but neither of us replies. I go over to him and force my voice to stay steady.

"Bex, Diana is brilliant. I trust her completely."

"Okay," he says softly.

There is no doubt about it. The Para angel is in hell right now. For the next two minutes, we watch as a member of our team bleeds on the floor. Just when Bex is about to seriously lose it, we see a stream of silver colored blood trickle out from Key's neck.

Diana acts quickly. She applies the thick greyish mixture she created and we watch as the incision on the side of Key's neck starts to seal itself.

"If it worked, in a few moments the color should start to return to her face. She'll open her eyes," Diana tells us.

Bex is on his knees and has sandwiched Key's hand between his. All three of us look on, silently praying to Omnis that Key opens her eyes.

We wait.

We wait.

We wait.

Key stirs just slightly. Bex gasps, weak with relief. Diana and I exchange a look once again. It was a close call. Bex doesn't know exactly how close because the fact is most angels don't survive being "Paused." When Bex speaks to Key, he struggles to stop the shaking in his voice but we can hear it clearly—the future king of Paras is at the mercy of a girl. I know exactly how that feels...

"You're okay, I promise. You're okay," he tells her.

"What the hell happened here?" someone asks from the doorway.

"East, I called you and the whole team like an hour ago. Where were you?" I ask.

"I was in the middle of something. I came as soon as I could—Key, are you naked under that jacket?"

"It's a long story," I reply.

"Yeah, I've got time," East offers.

Bex flashes East a warning glance and zips Key's jacket all the way up to the collar.

"Seriously, Key, are you okay?" East replies.

"Yeah, she's gonna be fine, thanks to Diana," I add.

"Wow, you're handy to have around. I'll have to remember that," East quips suggestively.

"Yeah, like you could handle me," she whispers, loud enough for him to hear.

"Where's Pry? Did you leave her out front with the demons?" I ask.

"All of the demons have taken off, Silver. The front is clear."

"Knowing her, she probably chased them." I sigh, shaking my head.

"I'll take a look around the neighborhood," East says.

"And find out where Swoop is. I called her too. She's supposed to be here," Bex says.

"It's my fault. She was trying to save me," a quivering voice adds.

We turn our focus to the two beings that have just entered the room: Randy and Swoop.

Randy has a gash on his right temple and his lower jaw is bruised. Swoop looks out at us and she isn't her usual off-the-wall-with-energy self. Something is seriously freaking her out. Key notices it too and asks Bex to help her up.

"Swoop, what is it? What's wrong?" Key asks her twin in a weak voice.

Swoop looks around the room but stops when she makes eye contact with me. I've known Swoop since she was born and I have never seen her look this afraid and this worried—for me. Dread starts to work its way along my body. Everyone in the room grows eerily silent. Whatever she's about to say, it's going to be bad; really bad.

"East, go get Pry, tell her something's up and we need her back here," I order.

East turns to leave, but Swoop calls out after him.

"No, don't go outside. Pry's not outside," Swoop says.

"Where is she?" East asks.

"They took her," Randy says as his eyes fill with tears.

"Who took her?" Bex asks.

"The Center."

CHAPTER FIVE
HOLLANDER

As soon as the words come out of Randy's mouth, a blanket of rage comes over me like nothing I have ever felt before. It's a perfect storm of loathing, vengeance, and desperation. My wrath is fueled by its desire for one thing: death. I know there will be death—there must be death. Yes, today many will die…

It only takes seconds for me to set fire to the entire street. The chaos that ensues means nothing to me. The team pleads with me but again that means nothing. I take to the air with such speed the windows in the surrounding buildings shatter as I fly by them.

I don't stop to examine the damage in my wake. I fly furiously until I get where I need to go: Shanghai, China.

I look down at the city of skyscrapers and focus my attention on the tallest one: Shanghai Towers. The mega tower is over two thousand feet tall and has over one hundred and twenty stories. It is currently Para headquarters.

The team has followed me to China, but that doesn't stop me from raining Powerballs down on the Para's sacred landmark. The blasts from my palms are so strong the foundation of the building starts to shake. At once Paras take to the air to investigate.

I attack them with no regard for their lives whatsoever.

They try to surround me, but my powers are far more lethal than theirs and so they end up mostly trying to shield themselves. Meanwhile the team insists on calling out to me, but their voices are barely audible in the rage and frenzy of my mind. There are Powerballs hurling in every direction but that doesn't stop me from getting to my goal: the top level of the tower. There is where I will find him—Ross Hollander.

Hollander is the one in charge of the Paras while Bex's mother is stuck in the light. Although Bex is the next Kon, meaning the next king, until he is ready to take his position, Ross Hollander serves as the interim Kon. And if he doesn't give me what I want, he will be the first on a long list of angels to die today.

At top speed, I smash through the large bay window of the penthouse floor. The Paras are right behind me with a hail of Powerballs and Soul Chasers. The Soul Chasers are orbs designed to suck the soul from me. But little do they know, I don't even think I have a soul at this moment; not anymore.

The pandemonium around me only fuels my rage. I land and the building sways beneath my feet. The black marble floor reveals my reflection back to me. I don't recognize myself. My wings have lost most of the greyness they once harbored. They are now as black as my eyes. I look down the long hallway and see the Para angel I came for. He has hair the color of snow and bright blue eyes. He stands guarded by a sea of Paras.

His guards take flight and attempt to tackle me. I don't attack them, it would take too much time. Instead I use my powers to dismantle the building and cause further destruction. In the pandemonium I am able to get close to Hollander.

There are only three Paras now in my way. I quickly remove them as obstacles by breaking various bones in their bodies on contact. They are skilled, but so am I. And I have something they do not: an unrelenting desire for vengeance. When I make my way to Hollander, his eyes widen in utter shock as he takes in the scene.

Hollander goes to attack me, but I'm quicker. In one swift motion, I pick him up and fling him down to the ground, facing the floor. Before he can even think to get away, I stomp on the area between his wings and his shoulder blades with my boot.

He is unable to move. I grab ahold of his wings and start to pull on them. Hollander begins to scream. The team enters the building and calls out for me to show mercy as they race over to me.

"Silver, no! Please stop!" Swoop begs as they come towards me.

I take out a flat coin-like object from my pocket. It's called a Kork. It creates an instant sheer barrier. It only lasts a few minutes, but that's all I need. I hurl the Kork towards the team and the army of Paras headed my way.

Immediately, a blue neon swirl emanates from the Kork. It forms a blue tented barrier and divides the room in two. On one side is the team, the Paras, and Diana. On the other side is me and a soon-tobe-dead Para if he doesn't comply.

"WHERE IS SHE?" I demand.

"Who?" Holland shouts.

I yank harder at his wings as the team bangs on the barrier, begging me to stop. Hollander cries out again, and again, I pull mercilessly at the base of his wings.

"I don't know what you're talking about" he insists.

"YOU'RE THE INTERIM KON; NOTHING THAT HAPPENS WITH THE PARAS CAN HAPPEN WITHOUT YOUR CONSENT. YOU AGREED TO LET THEM TAKE HER. NOW WHERE IS SHE?"

"I don't know what you're—ahhhhh." He groans as I slowly yank his wings from his shoulders.

"I'M GOING TO ASK YOU ONE MORE TIME AND THEN I'M GOING TO RIP YOUR FUCKING WINGS OFF. WHERE IS PRYOR???"

"I told you, I don't know!" he lies.

"I'M DONE TALKING; NOW YOU DIE," I vow as I pull his wings halfway off.

His bloodcurdling screams fill the halls and coat the entire tower. The team implores me to spare him but there is no reasoning with the rage that engulfs me. I don't give a shit about anything or anyone but her. And if he is not helping me, he's in my way and must be dealt with.

"He's not lying!" Randy shouts at the top of his lungs.

I turn to him in my wrath-filled haze and wait for an explanation.

"How the hell do you know?" I ask, refusing to even loosen my hold on the Para bastard.

"Look at him, if he knew anything he would have told you; listen to his voice, there's genuine shock that Pry has been taken," Randy reasons.

"Bullshit! He's hiding something," I push.

"What if it's not the Paras that run the Center? What if it's just a select few? What if it's a hidden society among the Paras? If so, there are ways we could lure them into the light. Just like the group of super villains in the DC Comic book series," Randy says.

"This isn't a comic, Randy!" I scold.

"No, think about it. There has never been any media about The Center. Why is that? They want to remain secret. That includes their identity. Whoever runs The Center is doing so covertly," Randy pleads.

"And I'm telling you, I don't give a shit about what he says, he knows something! He's gonna tell me now or die," I promise as I go to pull out the rest of Hollander's wings.

"She'll never get over it!" Diana shouts at me.

"What the hell are you talking about?" I bark.

"Pryor; when you get her back and she finds out what you did in order to save her...she'll never look at you the same way," Diana replies.

"She's right, Silver. You do this and it changes everything," Bex adds.

Then in the haze of my hatred, Pryor's face flashes in my head. She looks at me with pleading eyes. Those damn perfect purple haunting eyes...

"Are you sure about knowing ways to get to The Center?" I ask Randy.

"I have a few ideas—ones that don't involve murder. Ways that Pryor would approve of."

I look down at Hollander. I release him from my hold but before he can gather himself, I get down to the ground and make him a promise.

"When I get her back, if there's so much as a scratch on her, I'll peel the flesh from your body and eat your fucking soul..."

***

Just as I stand up, the Kork fades and the barrier disappears. Suddenly a slew of Paras come my way. I'm still livid and have no issue taking them all on. But Swoop leaps into the air, latches on to me, and does a series of summersaults that send us both tumbling out the window. I straighten up mid-fall and gain my balance, but she urges me not to go back to the tower.

"Please, Silver, don't," Swoop says again.

"The Omari are coming, we need to go, now!" East warns.

We look out in the distance and the trained Para assassins have indeed taken to the sky. They are nearly impossible to outfly and they never lose sight of their target. If they start after us, they won't stop.

Everyone else on the team echoes Swoop's suggestion. So we take off. Unfortunately the Omari are on our tail and determined to catch us. Suddenly, Bex turns back and raises his hand in front of the army of Paras headed for us.

"What's he doing?" Randy asks East, who is helping him maintain his balance on the Port.

"Bex is the next Kon. So even though Hollander is in charge, when the future king tells the Omari to stand still they have no choice," East replies. We look back and sure enough the Omari stand motionless in the air awaiting Bex's command.

"You guys go. I'll take care of this," Bex says to us.

The team exchange uneasy looks but we decide to do as Bex says. We all take off and head back to the house in New York City. As soon as we get home, Key runs upstairs to change and Randy bombards me with questions.

"Okay, first, do you have any recollection whatsoever about where you were when you were at The Center?"

"Even if I could recall, it wouldn't matter. It's located on a Whirlwind," I inform him.

"I have no idea what that is," Randy admits.

"A Whirlwind is a location that isn't fixed. It changes every hour. The Center is in the middle of a Whirlwind. That means one hour it's in Boston and the next it's in Rome," Swoop adds.

"So there's no way to pinpoint its location?" he asks.

"You can if you know the origins. That's what I was trying to get out of Hollander," I reply.

"Why would they take Pryor? She hasn't done anything," Swoop reasons.

"It's my fault. They wanted me to stay away from her but I couldn't," I admit.

Ruin glances at me with a mix of hurt and sadness. I know she has feelings for me, but I can't lie about how much Pryor means to me; not anymore. And even if I could, Ruin sees right through me. She always has.

"But why should The Center even care that two teenagers hook up?" Randy asks.

"They didn't bother to explain. They just said to stay away or there would be consequences."

"You never asked why?" East says.

"You don't know what it was like there—let's just stay focused on Pryor," I order.

"Okay, well we need to start at the beginning. We need to know what The Center is and what its function is," Swoop says.

"I'll tell you what their function is: torture. Plain and simple," I reply.

"No, I think Randy's right. We need to know more," East tells us.

"Since it's on this Whirlwind thing, we may not be able to find it, but we can do the next best thing: find out who is behind it. Just give me some time to gather the materials I need," Randy adds.

"We don't have time, Randy. She's been gone for hours!" I yell.

"Yeah, and the reason she is gone is because she sacrificed herself so I would not get hurt. So let me help her the best way I can. Let me do what nerds do best—research."

"Randy, we can't just—"

"Silver," East warns.

I reluctantly agree to give Randy a few hours to do some research and figure out who could be involved in The Center. He heads to the kitchen with his laptop. Diana volunteers to clue Randy in on everything she knows about The Center, which unfortunately isn't much.

"Swoop and East, can you two help Randy?" I ask.

"I will, I just have an errand to run first," East says.

"Seriously, there's something you need to do that's more important than finding your friend? Your leader?" I ask, baffled.

"There's nothing more important, Silver, you know how I feel about Pryor. But I need to do this. I'll be back in a half hour. If something comes up I'm just a Port ride away," he says.

It's only then that I realize he's waiting for my okay on the matter. The fact of the matter is with Pryor not around I am the new leader. A role I really don't relish.

"Fine, but you get half an hour, no more," I reply.

He thanks me and hustles out of the house quickly.

"What is he up to?" Swoop asks.

"Something he doesn't want us to know about; something I'm pretty sure is against the rules," I remark.

"Says the guy who nearly ripped a Para's wings off," Swoop teases me. I look back at her and my anger has subsided (at least for the time being). And now I am left with only my fear that she's hurt—or worse.

"Silver, it's going to be fine," Swoop says as she embraces me.

"She's been with them for hours. The things that they've had time to do…" I reply, mostly to myself.

"We'll get her back. I'll go help Randy and we will come up with something, believe me," Swoop replies.

As Swoop rushes off, her twin sister comes down the steps, now fully clothed. She sees me head for the door and calls out after me.

"Silver, where are you going?"

"I can't do this, okay? I can't just stand here knowing that she's…I feel like I should…I have to do something, anything. She needs me."

"Yeah, Pryor does need you. She needs you to stay calm. She needs to know that you have control over everything, including your emotions," Key scolds.

"Okay, okay, you're right," I reply.

"Now, we will figure this out as a team, okay?" she says.

"Yeah, okay. We will find her," I say to myself.

It doesn't matter what I say out loud, the frenzy and panic in my chest won't subside. And now that the wrath has died down slightly, it leaves more room for longing. And longing for Pryor leads to—yes, there it is. Pain.

I gasp and place my hand over my chest. It feels like someone has taken a knife to it and is cutting it open. I reach into my pocket and pop a blue pill I take to control the pain. I don't take it often because it can be habit-forming. But right now, I really need to keep this pain under control.

"Are you okay?" Key asks.

"Yeah, yeah, I'm fine. What about Bex? Any word from him?"

"No, but I don't expect to hear anything. If he has an update, he might contact East or Swoop."

"He's pissed at you?"

"He won't look me in the eye," she says sadly.

"There's been a lot going on," I offer.

"I was so stupid. How could I hurt him like that?"

"Look, I'm no expert, but he has some things to explain too. So when this is over, you two need to figure things out," I suggest.

"You're right and we will. Bex and I will get past this. I really want to."

"I know," I reply softly.

"Then can you help me?" she asks.

"Help you how?"

"We are already in so much drama, if Bex finds out that I came to you and tried to...you know...can we just keep what happened in your bedroom between us?" Key asks.

"YOU SLEPT WITH HER?" someone shouts.

We look towards the kitchen and find Diana standing in the doorway, livid.

Fuck!!!!

"Diana, it's not like that," I explain.

"You lying asshole!" she accuses.

"What?" I reply, clueless.

"You had me believing that you changed for the redhead. That you were some kind of an angel. The whole time you've been giving it away to every Noru, Para, and Quo. Tell me, Silver, exactly how many girls are you currently fucking?"

"It's not like that, Ruin. You don't understand," Key says.

"The hell I don't; Silver acts all 'good' and convinces everyone that you're different but it's all it is: an act. He will sleep with any and everything. So exactly how many bottles of Trickk did you two go through? How many times did he have you convulsing in fits of ecstasy? Hey, did he do that thing with his tongue?"

"Diana, enough!" I caution her.

"Ruin, it's none of your business what did and did not happen between me and Silver!" Key rages.

"I've lost everything in the name of helping Silver, so it is my business," she protests.

"You have no idea what we're talking about. In fact, why are you even here?" Key demands.

"Oh, so now that I'm done saving your life all of a sudden I'm not needed? Just like a junky, ungrateful."

"I am not a junky! I had too much to drink one time," Key says.

"Oh, please save it for someone who doesn't know what a Tic looks like. You're living off of Coy, drugs, and delusions. The fact of the matter is nothing you do will change what's happening with the redhead and your boyfriend."

"You have no idea what you're talking about and you really need to shut up now," Key says, growing hysterical.

"How can you be Noru and so damn weak? Don't you get it? Silver and Pryor are going to be together. There's nothing you can do about it. You will lose Bex just like I lost Silver. The fact is no one ever wins at love. And believe me, sweetheart, sleeping with Silver is the same as a human putting a gun to their head. It will only bring pain."

"For the last time, I did not sleep with Silver!" Key protests.

"Then what the hell were you doing in his bed? Tell me, I'd really like to know," Diana demands.

"Yeah, me too," a voice says from the front door entryway.

I don't have to turn towards the door to know who has entered the house—judging from the look on Key's face it could only be one angel—Bex.

CHAPTER SIX
OUT OF OUR HANDS

By now both Swoop and Randy are back in the living room. They watch as Bex looks at Key with a mix of fury and hurt. Yet when he speaks his voice is not raised, rather it's steady and calm.

"Did you sleep with Silver?" he asks.

Keyohmi looks back at him with regret and profound sadness. She's about to say something but when she opens her mouth nothing comes out.

"Bex, you and Key need to talk about this alone," I advise.

"Why? It seems like everyone in this room already knows what's going on; everyone but me. So, catch me up, Key," he says.

"We are not doing this now; am I clear?" I demand.

"Fine," Bex retorts.

"What happened with the Para?" Randy asks.

"What happened is that Silver tried to execute a high ranking Para in front of everyone," Bex replies hotly.

"I needed answers," I remind him.

"Yeah, well now we have to be even more careful because if the Paras know that Pryor is gone, they will try and rescue her themselves and take this mission out of our hands," Bex says.

"The Paras are the reason that the Center even exists," I remind him.

"We don't know that. And when we decided to send you off to The Center, we didn't know—"

"We?" I ask.

"I was asked to weigh in and I voted to send you to The Center."

I don't remember tackling Bex. It happened quicker than even I could process.

"DO YOU KNOW WHAT THEY DID TO ME IN THERE?" I scream.

"I didn't know," he vows.

"And now they have her. They have her and it's all because of you!"

"We didn't know, Silver," he insists.

We argue between blows and the team tries in vain to separate us. Finally, Swoop stands between us.

"Swoop, move!" I warn her.

"No, you two need to stop. We don't have time for this," she reminds me.

"You and I...we are done. You got that? We just work together. We are not friends and I promise you if something happens to her...Bex, I will kill you," I vow in a deadly tone.

"Nothing is going to happen to Pryor. Now can we be grown-ups, please?" Key says.

"This from the girl who can't stay out of other people's beds?" Diana says.

"Diana, enough!" I bark.

"Why is it so hard for you to just shut the fuck up?" Key asks.

"Don't be pissed off at her for what you did," Bex protests.

"I didn't do anything," Key replies.

"Then how the hell did you end up sleeping with a half demon?" Bex adds.

"I had a little too much to drink and I went to see Silver at his dad's house—but nothing happened, I promise," she pleads.

"So you didn't end up in his bed tonight?" Bex asks.

Key opens her mouth but no words come out. She bites hard on her lower lip in an effort to keep from bursting into tears.

"Key, it's not a hard question. Were you in Silver's bed?"

"Yes," she whispers.

He nods slowly and starts to make his way upstairs. She calls out after him.

"I talked to the Healers at the Clinic. They told me when you were unconscious you called for Pryor—not me. Pryor."

"So you end up in another guy's bed because I may or may not have mumbled something in a half-conscious state; a state that your suspicion put me in. Key, I asked you if everything was okay between us and you said yes."

"I was trying to keep us together," she reasons.

"You lied to me, you try to poison me, and now you're screwing my teammate? That's not keeping us together."

"Bex, you don't understand."

"Yeah, I do, and I'm sorry if I called out another girl's name. I didn't do it to hurt you. I don't even recall doing it. But the question isn't why I called on Pryor. The question is with everything that's happened with us, why would I call on you?"

Key doesn't have a reply. Instead she just stands there looking wounded and in pain.

"This conversation ends; now," I inform them.

Everyone looks back at me but they remain silent. Her sister takes her hand as the couple exchange a glare between each other.

"What happened with the Paras? Are they sending the Omari after Silver?" Randy asks.

"No, I took care of it. I made an arrangement with them," Bex says.

"What kind of arrangement?" I ask.

"I can't get into it. Let's just say it's handled," Bex insists.

"How much do they know about Pryor's disappearance?" Swoop asks.

"They don't know she's gone," Bex replies.

"What, why not?" Key says.

"Because if they did, they would launch a rescue mission—right after they put us under lock and key. The fact is no other team will work as hard as we will to get her back. We let everyone know she's gone and suddenly the mission is out of our hands."

"Bex is right. Besides, we don't know who we can trust," I tell them.

"But didn't Silver already announce that Pryor was gone?" Swoop says.

"I convinced them you were drunk and talking crazy. I made it so that everything you did tonight was due to a bad reaction to drinking and drugs. I told them that I would see to you getting some help," Bex says.

"And just like that, they let it go?" Randy asks.

"Well…yeah, sort of," Bex says.

We all exchange a look of concern.

"Bex, what aren't you telling us?" Swoop says.

"I told you everything," he replies.

"I agree with Swoop. I know I just started learning angel history but you guys don't do well with angels trying to kill each other. There are usually consequences from the stuff I've read," Randy remarks.

"Like I said, we made a deal."

"What deal did you make, Bex?" I demand.

"It doesn't affect any one of us personally and we need to get back to looking for Pry," Bex says.

I would like to push the issue but he's right. So, I order everyone to get back to work. That is, everyone but Diana. I tell her to meet me upstairs. Meanwhile, the team gets back to work. As Diana and I head upstairs, we catch a glimpse of Key reaching for Bex's hand as they enter the kitchen. He pulls away…

***

"What the hell is your problem?" I shout the moment we are in my room alone.

"You're putting this on me?" she replies.

"Why do you have to act like this?"

"You're out there nailing everything that moves and I'm the one to blame?"

"Damn it, Diana, don't do this."

"Do what?"

"Make me regret contacting you."

"The way you're acting, you already regret everything, including the day we met."

"That's not true."

"Liar! You hate the guy you were back when it was just us. But that guy—that demon—was important to me. He mattered to me and you just want to act like he never existed and that's bullshit."

"We can't do this. We can't keep having the same discussion over and over again. You wanted me to be a full-blown demon and I can't do that. I can't turn my back on the Angel world."

"An hour ago you marched into headquarters and damn near ripped that angel's wings off. It felt good. You're just too afraid to admit it because then you would have to face the truth—you are a demon. More so than any other demon I have ever encountered."

"I did what I had to do," I reply as I turn away from her.

"You did what was natural."

"I am never gonna be the guy that you want me to be. Do you get that?"

"Did you sleep with her?"

"Diana, you and I are not together!"

"Then why do you keep calling me?"

"I needed you to help Key."

"Silver, there are hundreds of Healers you could have called but instead you called me"

"So?"

"Wow, you really aren't going to say it, are you?" she pushes.

"Say what?"

"You miss who we were before this stupid team came between us. You miss doing whatever you wanted and being accountable to no one. You miss us."

"Diana...you have to start dealing with the fact that you and I are not involved."

"You're accusing me of not dealing? Silver, you can't even say Pryor's name. You're the one who is refusing to deal with things."

"I'm done with this conversation," I reply, shaking my head as I head towards the exit.

"You're treating me like I'm some delusional lovesick human. The only one delusional in this room is you. You refuse to face facts: you might never find the location of the Center."

"Get out."

"You might never get to her in time."

"GET OUT!"

"Everyone here knows the truth except you: Pryor's probably already dead."

I grab her by the throat and slam her up against the wall with such brutal strength she gasps. The sheer fury coursing through me makes my hands shake. She looks back at me with delight.

"There he is—my Silver. The demon I love."

My father ingrained in me that hitting a girl was a sign of a weak angel. I've hit female demons before but it was always in self-defense. But outright attacking Diana leaves me feeling disgusted with myself. Yes she provoked me, but it's still a crap move on my part.

"I'm sorry," I reply as I let her go and step away from her.

"Don't be. It's the first honest moment you've had in months."

"Calling you was a really bad idea on my part. I thought we could be…I was wrong to call you. It won't happen again."

"So you want me to go away?"

"I want your help, but you can't give it without causing pain to everyone around you. And I can't have that. So yeah, you have to go."

"You are so ungrateful." She swears.

"I know you saved Key's life and—"

"I'm not talking about her. I'm talking about you. I tried to save you from yourself. I took your Rah so that you could not do anything with her."

"That's not the reason you took my Rah."

"The hell it isn't. I tried to keep you away from her because I knew what it would do to you if she were taken to The Center. Yet you did everything to undo all my work. Now you're standing here scolding me like a damn child when you're the one who has no self-control."

"You took my Rah to punish me. Don't try and pass it off as some altruistic move," I counter.

"Okay, maybe I did. Maybe I'm a selfish bitch who wants what she wants. But you were told to stay away from Pryor and you didn't. You let your feelings for her take over. You wanted her and nothing else mattered, not even her safety. Tell me, what does that make you?"

Her words attack my soul with the ferocity of a Soul Chaser. I gasp softly as she utters the thought I had been running away from since this all started.

"Silver, you want me gone, fine. I will go. Just remember this: you can blame it on Bex, you can murder every Para there is, or even set the world on fire, but the fact still remains: Pryor is gone because of you."

***

Diana goes downstairs and leaves the door open, allowing me a perfect view of Pryor's room across the hall. Against my better judgment, I enter and close the door behind me. Right away I'm greeted by her scent: lilies and summer rain.

I walk over to the framed pictures on her dresser. Many of them are pictures of her parents and her little brother. I pick one up and study it. Everyone smiles back at me from the frame.

I remember the day they took that picture. It was the day she successfully flew around the world on her own. It meant she mastered flight, a proud day for most angels. But Pry was mad because she thought she should have flown faster. She had the second best time in our class but that wasn't enough. Finally our instructor agreed to let her try again, unofficially. She did better than any one of us would have guessed. She was beaming.

There are other pictures on her dresser, most of which I recall: pictures of her and the team. All our training sessions, trips around the world, and outings were well documented.

Next to the photos I spot a small orb. It's a Reply. I activate it with my touch and it reenacts Pryor laughing and sticking her tongue out playfully. She's the most beautiful thing Omnis has ever created. Hearing her laughter triggers a surge of longing unlike anything I have ever felt. I put the Reply down and that's when I spot—under her bed—the box.

We had jokingly called the box "Mini Omnis." We called it that because the box was always out of our reach. We tried a dozen times but could never find it. When we asked Pry what was in her secret box all she would say was that it's the place she puts things she can't live without.

For years we speculated about what she was keeping in there. Bex thought she was keeping some secret mixture that would do her chores for her. The twins joked that Pryor was keeping a demon there to practice her powers on. East often said she was keeping some crazy mixture that caused her hair to be the shade of red it was.

Whatever she was keeping in the box, it was very important to her. She hid it under her bed and covered it with a Triplex. A Triplex is an invisible coating that makes it impossible to see an object even if it's right in front of you unless you know it's there.

She must have forgotten to place the coating back on.

I pull out the white wooden box from under the bed. It has different complex patterns carved on the side of it. I'm not sure what treasures she's hiding in there but for some reason I feel as if knowing the answer will bring me closer to her. I sit on the edge of her bed and open it. There's only one thing in there—a hammer.

Not too long ago she came to me upset and ready to give up on the thought of us being together. She said she was trying to knock down the wall I had put up and she needed something to give her hope. I sent the hammer to her. And here it is, in the place she puts the things that matter most.

"Damn…" I whisper softly to myself.

That's when it happens. The weight of her absence forces my head down and despair washes over me. The thought that she is in pain renders me weak and shakes me to my very core. But what takes me over the edge is that what Diana said was right—it's my fault. I'm the reason she's been taken—or worse.

Please, Omnis, don't take her from me…

"We have a problem," Key says.

I look up and find her standing in the doorway.

"Oh, I'm sorry. I didn't mean to—are you okay?" she asks.

I clear my throat and gather myself. I then place the box back under the bed.

"Are you sure you're okay?" she asks, studying my troubled face.

"Yeah, I'm good. What's up—did Randy find something?"

"Um…no, not yet. But we were monitoring social media to make sure news of Pryor's disappearance was still under wraps and there was breaking news on twitter about Bex."

"What news?" I ask.

"We now know what he had to do in order to ensure the Omari didn't come after you. They are forcing him to give up something," she replies sadly.

"What?"

"Us—Bex is leaving the team."

CHAPTER SEVEN
SUSU

It's ten minutes later and everyone gathers in the kitchen except East, who still has not replied to the texts I've sent him. We confront Bex about leaving the team but he is resolved to do just that.

"They can't force you to leave the team," Swoop protests.

"She's right. We have to fight this, Bex," Randy says.

"It's my fault, they can't take it out on you," I tell him.

"The Paras feel that my loyalties have been shifting. They want me with them, and as the next Kon, that's where I belong," Bex argues.

"So you actually want to leave us?" Swoop asks.

"No, but I think that they may have a point. I'm not behaving like an angel who will be king someday. I stood by and let Silver torture one of my own. What kind of king does that?" Bex pleads.

"You couldn't have stopped me, Bex. I blocked your path. There was no way you could have gotten to me to prevent me from hurting Hollander," I remind him.

"The truth is, I would have let you hurt him. Him and a hundred other Paras if it meant we would find her," Bex replies.

"I'll talk to them. I'll tell them you tried to stop me but that you had no choice."

"Silver, it doesn't matter to the Paras. All they know is that I stood by and watched you inflict pain on my own kind," Bex says.

"If they want to send the Omari after me then let them. You can't give up your place on this team," I tell him.

"If the Omari come after you, they will kill you. They won't capture you and take you away. If you're caught by them, you're done. We have our differences, but I'm not gonna let that happen," Bex says.

"When are you leaving us?" Swoop asks.

"I told them I needed a few days. They were reluctant but finally agreed in the end. That means as usual we are short on time, so we better get back to work because as of now we have nothing to go on," Bex reminds us.

"Actually, I think I may have something," Randy says, guiding us into the kitchen to view what's on the screen of his laptop.

"Whoever runs The Center must hate Noru. So I've been focusing on beings that have voiced concern about you guys existing. While there aren't many, the few are very vocal about it," Randy explains.

"How did you compile this list?" Bex asks.

"I've taken names from every angry tweet, Facebook post, blog entry, and news feed. If they have bitched about it, they are on this list," Randy replies.

"There's over two hundred angels on here. How will we narrow it down?" I ask.

"I've already done that. Everyone on this list still actively hates you guys for being so powerful and expresses their dismay. Everyone except this angel," Randy says, pointing to the profile of an older, slender Para angel with dark rimmed glasses and silver-white hair.

"Who is that?" I ask.

"His name is Colton Bishop. Take a look at this," Randy tells us.

He shows us Bishop's webpage. His entire site is dedicated to the reason why Norus should not only be banned from the Angel world but should be destroyed altogether. This angel genuinely hates us.

"What does the site prove? Other than that he's a raving lunatic?" Swoop asks.

"Once he created this site, he posted on it regularly. He took great pains to make sure it was current and filled with anti-Noru propaganda. Then all of a sudden he took the site down. He erased all traces of himself online and in the media. I had to do all kinds of Hacker-Ninja things to find what little info I did."

"Maybe he changed his mind about us," Key offers.

"Not this guy. He has a whole manifesto here about the dangers of Noru. There are only two reasons why he would stop shouting that the Norus should be destroyed. He's dead or he has found a better way to get his point across," Randy reasons.

"It's not a strong lead, Randy. But it's all we have. Good job," I tell him.

"I know a few places I could check out, places that cater to embittered, paranoid angels who think everyone is out to get them," Bex offers.

"Great. In the meantime, the twins can go to Hun's Market and see if there's a Seller there who might know something. Sellers are notoriously nosy. They deal in gossip just as much as they do forbidden objects."

"It's worth a shot." The twins agree in unison.

"When this is all over, we will deal with this crazy thing about you leaving the team. That's just not gonna happen," I say to Bex.

"I didn't know you cared," Bex teases.

"Luckily I don't have to like you to have you on the team," I reply.

"Well then, Ruin should fit right in," Swoop says.

"Where is she?" Randy asks.

"She's gone," I reply.

"She's a real pain but she's a fantastic Healer; we could use her," Key replies.

"I know she's gifted, but she also brings issues with her. Anyway, she's long gone by now," I tell him.

"She's probably lurking somewhere nearby," Randy replies.

"Why would she hang around after I told her to go away?" I ask.

"Because she has nowhere to go. She doesn't have a good handle on the whole 'not being evil' thing, but for a demon, she sure has saved a lot of angels," Randy says.

"Randy has a point and besides, if she's not with us, she's going to turn to the only other being she has a connection with—Malakaro. Wouldn't you rather her be here than with him?"

"You're right. I'll go get her and bring her back," I reply.

"No one is going anywhere until I get some answers," the demon at the front door demands.

I turn and find my father, Rage, standing in the doorway.

***

"Who has her?" my father asks as soon as we are alone.

"Who has who?" I reply.

"Don't screw around with me, Aaden. I know something is wrong."

"There's nothing wrong. I went on a stupid, drunken bender," I lie.

"That's crap and you know it."

"You don't think it's possible that I just lost control?" I ask.

"No, not like this. Look, I made the mistake of believing what others were saying about you once and I won't make it again. I know you, Aaden. You know better than to get into drugs."

"Dad, everything's fine," I assure him.

"The hell it is. The only being in the world that can affect you this much is Pryor. If she were somehow in danger, I have no doubt that you would take on the entire Angel world. Now what's going on?"

"It's nothing we can't handle."

"Damn it, Aaden, I will not ask you again!" he says in no uncertain terms.

I have no choice but to update him on the past few hours; right away he is livid and ready to take action.

"You have no idea where she is?" he asks, on high alert.

"No, The Center is in a Whirlwind. So there is no permanent location," I reply.

"Okay, I'll take care of this. I'll take out as many angels or demons as I need to, but don't worry, I'll get her back," he says, in a frenzy.

He goes charging for the door. I quickly stand in his way. He looks at me, puzzled.

"Dad, you have to let me do this on my own."

"Pryor's my best friend's daughter. Everyone on the Guardian team vowed to look after the Noru. I am the only team member here, I have to find her."

"You want to help, that's great. We're not going to turn down help from anyone. But I have to take the lead on this. Pryor isn't here, that makes me the First Noru as of now. This is my team and I have to lead them."

"I won't sit back and let them take the only child Marcus and Emmy have left. You need to step aside and let me take care of this," he rages.

"If Mom was alive and someone took her, would you step aside?" I challenge.

He looks like he's going to argue but then thinks better of it. He manages to calm himself down as he studies me.

"It's not your fault they took her," he says after a moment of silence.

"It is. They told me to stay away from her and…"

"I don't care who they are, they don't get to decide who you end up with. Screw them and their bullshit rules. You love her?" he asks.

"Yeah, I do." I met my father's serious stare.

"Does she love you?"

"She has never said it but…I think so."

"Then go get her," he pushes.

"And you'll stand down?"

"You're the First Noru right now, so if that's what you want, then yes."

"We could use your help," I offer, knowing he would lose it if he were completely cut from the mission.

"Anything you need," he replies. I tell him about Randy's theory about a secret society.

"That would explain why I haven't been able to find anything on The Center. The bastards are operating underground."

"It's very likely. Have you ever heard of a Para named Bishop?" I ask.

"Colton Bishop?"

"Yes."

"Sure, he's a loudmouth Para-conspiracy nut. He wouldn't shut up about the 'dangers' of mixing angels with other beings. When you and the other Noru were born he went into overdrive. He ranted for weeks about how it never should have happened. But I haven't seen or heard about him in years. You think he has something to do with The Center?"

"Randy thinks it's a good bet. Could you dig around and see where he is?" I ask.

"I'll get on it," he promises.

"Also reach out to any contacts you can in the Demon world. Also ask Sellers, Pawns, anyone and everyone. We need to find this Bishop guy. He's our only clue right now."

"Okay, I'll take care of it."

"Thanks."

"How's the team holding up?" he asks.

"They're trying to deal but it's hard on them. The twins are just getting over not having their parents around and now their leader is missing. Easton is worried like crazy because he keeps trying to look calm and collected. Randy is trying to focus his research so that the reality of the situation doesn't hit him."

"And Bex?"

"Things with the Para and I are…complicated," I admit.

"Whatever your issues, put it aside and focus on Pryor. She's all that matters."

"Believe me, I know," I reply.

"There's something else," he guesses as he looks into my unsettled face.

"Diana's here. She helped us out earlier and I wanted her to stay but she's so…"

"Diana," he says, nodding with understanding.

"Exactly."

"Whatever you do, keep Pryor's disappearance a secret. If the Angel world finds out, so will her parents. And they won't survive even the possibility of losing another child."

I rake though my hair with both hands. My father studies me once again. It's as if he can see the tension traveling throughout my body.

"Aaden, talk to talk me."

"What if I don't find her?" I whisper.

"Bullshit, you got this. I know you do," he assures me.

He then does something that's always embarrassed the hell out of me: he embraces me and tells me he loves me. I fought hearing that when I was a kid but that never stopped him from saying it. But today, I don't fight him back. Today it feels good to hear. Today, I say it back.

After he looks me over, he makes me promise to contact him should we need any help. Then he heads for the door and I call out to him.

"Dad?"

"Yeah?"

"When Mom died…how did you do it?"

"Do what?" he wonders.

"Live without her. Pryor's only been gone for a few hours and I can't…"

"Aaden Grey, you are not allowed to have those thoughts. Pryor will be fine. Her father is First Guardian, he taught her to be strong. And her mother is the most stubborn woman you will ever meet. I'm telling you that girl just refused to die. And Pryor is the very same way. She will make it through this. It's your job to make sure you do the same."

***

The team flies off to hunt down more details while Randy works furiously on his laptop. Diana reluctantly heads back towards the house. In no mood for a second round of fighting, I head out before she gets to the door.

East is not answering his phone. I don't want to worry the others but I don't like not knowing what's going on with him. I use the GPS tracker Pryor had us all install on our phones. Thankfully he did not turn it off.

I find East at the shelter on West 28th Street. It turns out I don't even need the GPS to tell me where he is because he's shouting so loudly he can be heard out in the street. Worried, I rush inside the shelter and find him in the middle of a crowd of humans, trying to stop a fight.

East stands in front of a small-framed girl with curly hair and caramel skin. He blocks her from taking a swing at a giant overweight guy with long stringy hair. The crowd holds the guy back but the person who really needs to be held back is the girl. Although the guy towers over her, she is determined to get at him. I recognize her; it's Marisol.

Easton met her a few months back and saved her from an abusive boyfriend. In doing so he exposed us. Then she transferred to our school and Pryor had him Mind wipe her. I knew he was involved with some girl since he was disappearing all the time, but I didn't know who it was.

"You touch that boy again and I'll make sure you're locked up!" Marisol vows as she lunges full force at the mammoth-like man.

Easton is the only thing standing between her and a violent end. The man yells back and vows to kill her if she ever so much as speaks to him again.

"You come near her and it will be the last thing you do in this world," East promises the man.

"This bitch attacked me for no reason," the man says.

"You deserve it, you coward! Does beating the hell out of your kid every night make you feel like a man?"

"Go screw yourself, little girl," he counters wrathfully.

"You touch that kid again and I'll cut your damn balls off!" she shouts.

I like her.

I don't intervene because East can take care of himself, especially in a crowd of humans. He doesn't need my help. Although at some point it may take the two of us to hold Marisol back.

Fearing that so long as the large man is in her presence, she'll never calm down, East guides her kicking and screaming out of the crowd and takes her to the back of the building. I follow, hoping to get his attention.

"What do you think you're doing? That guy could have killed you!" East scolds.

"Hey, I'm not the problem. He's the one getting drunk and taking his pathetic life out on his son," she argues.

"I'm not defending him, but you need to get yourself under control."

"I'm not going to sit back and let that ape hurt anyone," she protests.

"Okay, start from the beginning," East says.

"James comes into the shelter every day with one injury after another. He gives me these weak excuses like falling down on his bike, but it's a lie."

"Are you sure?"

"Yes, I'm sure. When his father comes in to get him, he's so scared he nearly wets himself," she explains.

"You could have called the cops," he replies.

"No, because then they would move him to another foster care family and they might be worse than this guy."

"So your solution is to confront his foster father and threaten a man three times your size?"

"I wanted him to know that I'm watching him. And if he ever hits his son again he's gonna have me to deal with."

"Oh, and what will you do?"

"Kick his ass," she replies confidently.

"Okay, I get you wanting to go all 'Kill Bill,' and by the way, that's sexy as hell, but you could have been hurt," he warns.

"My ex-boyfriend ripped me apart daily and that was my fault. I gave him permission to destroy me because I never spoke up. I'm not gonna do that anymore, East. I can't. The day I walked out on my ex, I vowed that I would never remain silent while someone was suffering. I will help put an end to it. That's who I am now. Please don't ask me to be anyone else," she says passionately.

"Sunny, I don't want to change you. But thinking you can tackle that guy all on your own is crazy," East replies.

"Well, then strap on the straightjacket and bring on the meds," she says stubbornly.

"This isn't funny. You punched that guy and he could file charges. You'd go to jail. That's okay with you?"

"Depends. Would I get conjugal visits?" she asks with all sincerity. East smiles despite himself.

"Yes, I would come and 'do' you in jail; that's just the kind of classy guy I am," he says.

"Who said the conjugal visits were with you? We just started seeing each other. I have lots of options," she teases.

He smiles and gently pulls her towards him. She looks into his face and beams up at him as she wraps her arms around him. He brushes a stray hair away from her face and tucks it behind her ear.

"What is with you and getting in harm's way?" he asks.

"James' dad is a bully; I hate bullies."

"You can't stop all the bullies in the world," he cautions her.

"Who says? I have a cape and everything."

"Marisol, please take this seriously." He groans.

"I had to take a stand. Or to quote a famed South African civil rights leader, Desmond Tutu, 'If you are neutral in situations of injustice, you have chosen the side of the oppressor.'"

"Why couldn't I fall for a simple girl, one who likes to shop and hashtag everything?" he asks himself out loud.

She laughs at his dramatic sigh. Then he looks into her eyes. At first I thought he was taken with her, but judging by the way he's looking back at her, it's more than that. East is in love.

"I'm sorry I made you worry. And I'm sorry I'm not more 'Uber glam,' but you're stuck with me. Is that okay?" she asks sincerely.

"Yeah, that's okay," he replies as he pulls her in and kisses her tenderly.

As their kiss grows, my comfort level decreases. I have no choice but to let them know I'm there before things get any more heated. I clear my throat.

"Silver!" East says, caught off guard.

"I'm sorry to interrupt, but we need you back at the house," I reply awkwardly.

"Is there news?" he asks anxiously.

"Is this about your angel friend?" she asks.

I glare at Easton. Marisol should not have any idea about angels, period. He didn't wipe her mind.

"Oh, I know. It's a secret. Sorry," she replies.

"Don't worry about it," I reply, smiling politely.

"Um…Marisol, this is Silver. Silver, this is Marisol. She's my girlfriend," he says proudly.

We shake hands and she asks if she can help in any way. East tells her we have everything handled and apologizes for having to leave. I turn away as he gives her a quick kiss good-bye. We start walking down the block in silence for a few moments. East is the first to speak.

"I'm sorry," he says.

"For leaving a mission to go talk to your girl or for not wiping her mind like you said you did?"

"Both."

"East, c'mon, what are you doing? You know Marisol can't know about us. When we get Pry back, she's gonna kill you for not doing what she told you to do. And on top of everything else, you're distracted from your mission. And we can't afford that," I remind him.

"I had made plans with her before all of this and I just wanted to cancel in person. When I got here she was in the middle of cursing out this guy and…knowing that Pry is in trouble made me want to make sure others in my life are safe. I just wanted to check in on her. Time got away from me."

"Okay, fine, but why didn't you wipe her mind?"

"Knowing there were angels on Earth gave her hope. I just couldn't bring myself to take that away," he confesses.

"At first I thought you were just hooking up with some chick and having fun, but I can see now it's more than that," I admit.

"Yes, it is. It's so much more. We started talking again and it's like we never stopped. I love her."

"But here's the problem. You just spent the past like half hour telling her to stay safe. Then you go and tell her the biggest secret in the world, the same secret that could place her in danger. Demons find out she's important to you and she becomes a target. You say you love her and that's great. But how much is your love going to cost her?"

He doesn't reply. However I can tell my words are weighing on him. He lowers his head as we walk in search of an alley to take off from.

"She seemed nice," I offer.

"She is. She's crazy but nice."

"She really would have tackled that guy, huh?"

"She would have fought him to her death. That's what scares me," he admits.

"I know what you mean. Pryor's the leader and the strongest of us, but every time we're in battle, I just…"

"You want to tell her to sit it out?" he guesses.

"Yeah. Not gonna happen though."

"Nope. Never," he agrees with a smile.

I update him on what Randy found as we head down the nearest alley. Just as we are about to take off, East gets a text. He reads it twice in disbelief.

"What is it?" I ask.

"It's Swoop; she says The Center sent us a message—"

Before he can get the rest of the words out, both of us take to the air. Once we land, we rush inside the house, where the rest of the team is already gathered.

"They sent us a Replay," Key says.

She holds the large orb in her hand and it activates. But there is no visual image inside the orb. Instead the message from the orb is auditory. It replays Pryor's terrified screams.

"No. No. No," Randy begs as his eyes fill with tears.

"Wait, there's a slight buzzing in the background. Do you hear it?" Swoop asks.

"Yeah, I hear it," I reply.

"What's the buzzing sound? What does it mean?" Key says.

I don't reply. I can't form the words.

"Silver, what does the buzzing mean?" Bex demands.

"It's the sound of one of the tools they used on me. It's called a Susu. I'd recognize it anywhere," I reply in horror.

"What do they use it for?" Randy asks.

"It's what they use to…"

The rage coursing through me makes it hard to keep talking. A fireball springs inside my palm and I fear in a few seconds the house we stand in will be nothing but ash. Sensing this, Swoop places her hand on my shoulder and speaks calmly.

"Silver, don't lose it. We need you. Just please talk to us. What does the buzzing sound mean? What are they doing to Pryor?"

"Cutting her open."

CHAPTER EIGHT
MRS. COLTON BISHOP

The team immediately comes at me with a thousand questions. They want to know what happened to me at The Center. They beg to know what Pryor has been going through since she's been there and what they are likely doing to her now.

I remain silent, which causes them to reach an even higher level of panic and frustration. The team's questions fill the room and together with the sound of Pryor's agony, form a perfect crescendo of torture in my ear. I throw the orb into the wall so hard it shatters and takes a large chunk of the wall along with it. The room falls silent. No more Pryor screaming. No more questions.

Without saying a word, I step over the rubble and head out to the backyard. I know I need to calm my rage and be a leader, but right now, I can barely think straight. The ire that grips me demands that I kill and destroy everything in sight. Not giving into that urge takes all I have. I lean back against the wall and look out at New York City. I hear someone enter the backyard. I turn and find him coming towards me.

"Bex, not now," I warn him.

"On my way back to the house, it took me three tries to get airborne," he says.

"Why?"

"No focus," he says, shaking his head in disbelief.

I don't say anything back.

"I have been flying since before I could talk and all of a sudden, I had no idea how to take off. The twins haven't Recharged and Randy hasn't taken his eyes off the computer screen in hours, not once," he says in a quiet tone.

"Why are you telling me this?"

"Because you are not the only one who is missing her. You're not the only one in agony knowing that she's being hurt."

"You're saying you know how I feel but the truth is you don't. You have no idea what they are doing to her; I do."

"Yes, and knowing what she's going through right at this moment can cripple you or motivate you. Make a decision and do it quickly."

***

It's a few minutes later and I have gathered the team. They look back at me; I've never seen them this edgy and anxious before. The twins fold their arms across their chests as if to brace themselves from what's to come. Randy is no longer crying, but sadness creeps behind his eyes. Bex taps his foot impatiently and Diana studies my every move.

"Okay look, I'm not Pryor. I can't do that 'nice and gentle' thing she does. All I can do is be honest and tell you what I know," I say to them.

"Fine, tell us what they are doing to Pryor," Key says.

"I will, when and if the time comes. But right now we need to stay focused," I reply.

"Why are you keeping this from us?" Randy asks.

"Because if you knew what was being done to her you'd do something reckless and get yourself killed or you'd curl up in a corner and beg East to wipe your mind."

My saying that just causes Randy to freak out more. Right away I regret my choice of words. I'm just not great at this leadership thing.

"Randy, we're going to get her back. And when we do, I'll be the first to tell her how helpful you were. So please keep helping and don't fall apart on me," I plead.

"Okay, I'm fine," he lies.

I know he's still terrified; his shaky voice betrays him. However, the fact that he's trying to look composed is good enough for me.

"I need you guys to trust me. Knowing what they are doing to your leader is their way of distracting us from finding them. We can't get pulled into that. We must stay focused at all cost. Is that understood?" I ask. Slowly they all nod in agreement.

"Great, now where are we on finding Bishop?" I ask.

"Every being I encountered had no idea where he could be," Swoop says.

"No one has heard from Bishop in years," Bex says.

"Yes! We got a location," Randy says, looking on his phone.

"You found Bishop?" Bex asks.

"No, but I found the next best thing: his wife."

"Bishop was married?" I ask.

"Yes, and for some reason he didn't just give his Rah away like angels normally do. He also got married and had a human ceremony," Randy replies.

"Why would he do that?" Swoop asks.

"I don't know. All I know is that we have a record of his marriage license. And if you give me a few seconds I can tell you who his wife is…" Randy says as he scans the screen of his phone for answers.

"What if she's in hiding like Bishop?" Swoop worries.

"It doesn't matter, we'll find her. Even if we have to threaten every demon, Seller, and Pawn there is," Bex says.

"We won't have to search for Bishop's wife; we already know where she is," Randy says, taken aback by what he sees on the screen.

"Where is she?" I ask.

"She's at school; Bishop is married to The Face."

***

We head over to the school moments later to see The Face. Her real name is Mrs. Greenblatt. Her job was to protect and look after us. It never occurred to any of us that she would be involved in The Center. Although I don't know why I'm shocked. The amount of double-dealing and bullshit in the Angel world is endless.

Still, I find the news upsetting. It's not that I like the Face. In fact we frequently argued. She was always a pain in the ass. She'd nag me to death about things I couldn't care less about like not skipping class, not using foul language, and following the rules. It's like I said, she was a real pain.

Yet there was something in her I respected. She never let my temper get in the way of lectures on being a better student. And even though I'd never say it out loud, I admired that she stood up to me and insisted we try to go on with our human education. Yes, most of the time, I wanted to staple her mouth shut, but I thought of her as a good being. I guess I was wrong.

We enter the hallways of the Livingston Academy and right away all heads turn towards us. The guys turn to face the twins and drool over their beauty. The girls put on their bright smiles and either walk towards us or gawk from a distance. A few girls smile at Randy. We're surprised by this new development but no one is as surprised as Randy. He's outright baffled.

"Are they looking at me?" he whispers to Swoop.

"That's right, stud," she teases.

"Last week I would have killed for that," Randy says to himself.

"And this week?" Key asks.

"I couldn't care less," Randy replies.

I understand why Randy feels the way he does. Not so long ago he was just a scrawny kid who longed to get in good with the popular crowd and maybe score with a chick behind the bleachers. Then out of nowhere he finds out that he's the Blue Rose heir.

The Blue Rose heir is the only being that can help Malakaro achieve his goal of evil domination by drinking the second half of a mixture. There are five vials he needs in order to make this mixture; he already has his hands on one.

Should Malakaro find out that Randy is the Blue Rose heir, he will come after him. The only one who can stop this is Pryor. And according to the angels, the only way she can stop Malakaro at that point is to kill Randy.

Many would be fearful of Pryor knowing that she is tasked to kill them, but not Randy. Instead he's here helping us find her. I keep meaning to check in with him and see how he's handling the fact that he's the heir but something always gets in the way.

Like being betrayed by the one that's supposed to be protecting us.

The more I think about it the more upset I get. Judging by the determined strides of the team, I'm not the only one who's pissed off by The Face. In fact, the first one to go bursting through the door isn't me; it's East.

"Where the hell are you keeping her?" he demands.

"Will you excuse us please, Ms. Gordon?" she says to the startled student sitting across from her.

The girl gets up from her chair and heads towards the door, yet she doesn't go through it. Instead, she finds herself staring longingly at Bex.

"You should go. Now," Key warns the student.

She smiles bashfully at Bex and hurries out of the office.

"How nice of you all to grace us with your presence," The Face says calmly.

"Look, lady, I'm in no mood to play around. Where is she?" I demand.

"Who?" she asks.

"You lie to me one more time, lady, and I'll bash your damn skull in," I promise her.

"Where is Ms. Cane? She needs to know that a member of her team is being insulting and downright offensive," she counters.

"Stop acting like you don't know she's been taken," Swoop snaps.

But judging by the shock on her face, Pryor's disappearance is news to her. The shock turns into concern and worry. And for the life of me, I can't see a hint of duplicity in her expression.

"You had no idea, did you?" I ask.

"Certainly not. That child is my responsibility," she says.

"Don't act innocent. You are married to the guy who took her," Key accuses.

"I have not seen my husband in years. Our union was…unwise," she says.

"Um, yeah, you think?" Randy says.

"Alright, everyone just calm down. We aren't getting anywhere like this," Diana says.

We all turn to look at her, in shock.

"What, because I'm a demon I can't be the voice of reason?" she declares.

"I can't believe I'm going to say this, but Ruin has a point," Bex says.

"The demon is calling for peace, the future king of Paras is agreeing with a demon, and Randy is the new hot kid on the block. Yup, it's the end of days," East quips.

"Start at the beginning, Mr. Case, so that I might catch up," The Fact instructs.

We tell her the events of the past few hours and leave out the parts having to do with our personal lives. She listens closely and doesn't say anything until we are done speaking.

"Now you know everything. It's your turn to talk," I order.

"Colton was a very good angel. He was sweet, intelligent, and caring. That's why I married him. We didn't have to have a human marriage, but since I'm half human he insisted we get married the human way to honor that part of me. That was the kind of guy he was," she says, lost in thought.

"What happened to him?" Swoop asks.

"He was always fearful of what could happen if one angel had too much power. Then he learned of the Noru. Six super-powerful angels who could take on Paras and win. It made him very nervous."

"Why? We never did anything to him," Key says.

"It's not what you did, it's what you had the potential to do," she replies.

"He began to research the possible outcome if the Norus took over the Angel world," she tells us.

"Take over? I'm sorry to tell you this, but your husband was a paranoid, suspicious conspiracy nut," Bex says.

"He had doubts about the Norus' intentions. He worried about what a team of super powered angels would someday be after," she says.

"You know what we're after, Mrs. Greenblatt? Happiness. That's it. That's all we want. But every time it comes within reach, it gets pulled away," Key says.

"Keyohmi—"

"I am not done," Key snaps at The Face.

Okay…

"We don't want to conquer the world or be the most powerful. We just want…we want security. We just want to know that the ones who say they love us today will still love us tomorrow."

"Key—" I argue.

"Still not done," she rages.

The room grows still. We wait for Key, who is apparently at her breaking point.

"You said that you would take care of us. You promised that you would be there for us. You can't just turn around and…you are betraying us by aligning yourself with someone else!" she says, looking over at Bex.

It's so clear to us by her tone and her rage that Key is really not addressing The Face. Her wrath is aimed at her boyfriend. Bex glares back at her. He's about to reply but then stops himself at the last moment.

"Okay, so when this is all over, I vote we chip in and send Key and Bex to couples' counseling, who's in?" East asks.

"I am," Swoop says.

"I could put in a few bucks," Diana says.

"Mrs. Greenblatt, go on," Randy says.

"Colton's concern grew with the appearance of Malakaro. He began to obsess about finding a way to fix the Noru 'problem.' So he came up with The Center."

"Do you know where The Center is?" Bex asks.

"No, but knowing Colton, it'll be hard to find. Again, he was a very smart angel."

"He has it on a Whirlwind," Randy says.

"I'm sorry, I have no idea where it could be. When he brought up the idea of The Center that's all it was, an idea. It was to be a place to study and learn about Noru powers," she tells us.

"And the only way to do that was to torture us?" I reply bitterly.

"That wasn't the original point of The Center. It was a learning institution. There was no torture or anything cruel," she says.

"I don't know what it was supposed to be but I can tell you what it is: It is a place where they cut you open and make you want to die. A place where they find your deepest fears and use them to suck your soul from your body," I bark.

"No, that's not what it is."

"THEN WHY DID I TRY TO KILL MYSELF?"

"Silver," Swoops gasps as I show The Face the scar where I ripped the base of my wings at my shoulder blades. The Face studies it, genuinely shocked by the nearly twelve-inch scar.

"Lady, there are things I could tell you about your husband that would make your skin crawl," I warn her.

"He started out just wanting to preserve the Angel world," she says.

"That may be where he started but that's not what's going on now," East says.

"Why did you leave him?" Swoop asks.

"We drifted apart. It happens. But we never got a divorce and he never asked for his Rah back. I guess neither of us wanted the end of our relationship to be…official."

"Does anyone?" Bex replies softly.

"Let's say your husband really did want to study us. How did he go from that to torturing us?" Swoop asks.

"Malakaro," she says slowly.

"What about him?" Randy asks.

"If The Center is what you say it is, then it must have happened when Malakaro emerged," The Face informs us.

"What happened? What is the real point of The Center?" Bex asks.

"Yeah, why didn't they just come after us and kill us?" Swoop adds.

"They didn't want to kill angels. He wanted to ensure their survival," The Face pleads.

"Yes, he wanted to protect the angels from some big bad teenagers. Got it," East says, shaking his head.

"The Center sent you a Replay with Pryor screaming?" The Face asks me.

"Yeah, about an hour ago," I reply.

"How did that make you feel?" she asks.

"Seriously?" Randy says.

"All the things The Center did to you, what emotion generally emerged?" The Face pushes.

"You know, the normal emotions that come from being tortured: joy, hope, and yes, love," I reply bitterly.

"Be serious. What did you feel during the times they were torturing you?" she insists.

"I was…afraid and anxious. But in the end, more than anything I was—"

"Angry," she says.

"Yeah, does that mean something to you?" I ask.

"They said yes," she says to herself.

"You want to clue us in?" I reply.

"A long time ago, Colton met with key members of the Para world. He wanted them to sanction the making of a forbidden device. I guess they agreed to it."

"What device?" Bex demands.

"A Deed," she replies.

Fuuuuuuuuuuuuuck!

The news makes everyone in the room lower their head in despair. Randy looks on, confused.

"Hello, human here. Need more info. What's a Deed and exactly how much will our lives suck because of it?" he asks.

"A Deed is a very fancy, old looking box with a lot of complicated patterns. It doesn't do anything major—except you know, wipe things off the face of the Earth," East says.

"I don't understand," Randy admits.

"It's what you humans would call a bomb. Except a timer does not trigger it; it's triggered by events," Bex says.

"For example, someone could make a Deed and program it to go off on a person's wedding day or program it to go off when the being reaches an unprecedented level of emotion," Key says.

"Like anger," I conclude.

"Yes. I think The Center has been trying to push you to reach a level of anger that would activate the Deed."

"That's why they sent you the Replay of Pryor screaming; they want you to lose it," Bex replies.

"What will actually take place should the Deed be activated?" Randy asks.

"The Noru die," Swoop says.

"Mrs. Greenblatt, how far would he go in order to activate the Deed?" Bex asks.

"The angel I know would never take a life. But I don't think he's the same angel anymore," she admits.

"That's crazy. Why doesn't he just take you guys on?" Randy asks.

"He'd lose. And it's not just about stopping the Noru. It's about making sure everyone knows how wrong it is for powerful angels to mix with other beings," Diana says venomously.

"As I said before, I don't know where The Center is. But I vowed to Pryor's mother that I would look after her and all of you. If there's any way I can help, I will," she offers.

"Are you sure you don't know where The Center is?" Bex says.

"I don't think you need to find The Center. A Deed won't work in a Whirlwind. It's too much movement. Colton would have had to leave it in one place. I think you should focus on finding the Deed. The Deed must be in constant communication with its maker; it's signaling to them," she suggests.

"So we find the Deed, and that will lead us to The Center," East says.

"Yes, I believe so," The Face says.

"Any idea where the Deed is?" I ask.

"There's only one angel who Colton would trust to make him a Deed. Our son Noble."

"You have a son?" Key asks.

"Yes. He's...complicated. But he's brilliant like his father. He might know the location of the Deed."

"When we find the Deed, can't we just destroy it and be done?" Randy asks.

"No, only the being that commissioned the Deed can destroy it," she corrects.

"Got it," East says as we head for the door.

"Fresh bread," The Face says to herself out loud.

"What?" Swoop says.

"Oh, sorry. I was just remembering something. He loved the scent of fresh baked bread. We honeymooned in the South of France and he couldn't get enough," she replies, sounding more like a smitten girl than the strict disciplinarian we had come to know.

That's when it became apparent: she's still in love with Colton.

"Lady, are we clear about what's going to happen?" I ask her.

"You're going to rescue Pryor," she replies.

"Yes; then I'm going to kill your husband."

CHAPTER NINE
TRUTH & CONSEQUENCES

By the time we leave The Face's office, school is over and most of the student body is gone, leaving the hallways and classrooms empty. We make contact with Noble, but he refuses to give any info over the phone. He does however agree to meet us. The team heads for the exit of the school but I stop them. They turn to face me, not sure what's going on.

"Bex and Key, you two need to figure something out before we go any further," I inform them.

"We don't have time for that. We need to go see Noble, right now," Bex counters.

"He said he'd meet us in an hour. He's not far from here; we have time. And the fact is you two can't separate your relationship from this mission. So find a classroom, a hallway, or whatever is close and figure this out," I reply.

"We have to put Pryor first. We can wait," Key says.

"I'm no expert, but judging by your outburst, either you're going to kill Bex or you're going to implode from pretending like you don't want to kill him," Diana says.

"The demon isn't wrong. You guys need to get your issues out in the open. We never have time on missions. But today we have a few minutes. Use it," Swoop advises.

"I'm torn. On one hand I think you two should talk. On the other hand I'd like to start a pool going to see how long before Key really loses it and sprays Bex's blood all over the lockers," East quips.

"Well, I'm not torn. You two are getting in the way, so figure it out," Randy adds.

"I don't want to do this in front of everyone," Key objects.

"Really? Because five seconds ago you were more than willing to put our business out there," Bex reminds her.

"I'm sorry if I can't be as contained as you about our relationship falling apart. I never learned how to be coldhearted like you."

"Are you really blaming me for you ending up in Silver's bed?" Bex says, shocked.

"Nothing happened between us," she urges.

"Yeah, I'm sure he just held you; that's exactly what Silver's known for. His gentle touch," Bex retorts.

"I'm going to let that go because controlling my temper is the only way to keep everyone alive, but Bex, don't push me," I warn him.

"We are breaking apart and it has nothing to do with Silver," she shouts.

"We're breaking apart because you keep pulling at us. You have done nothing but find ways to come between us. The big problem with 'Bex and Key' is Key!" her boyfriend accuses.

"YOU TWO GET IN THE DAMN CLASSROOM NOW!" I demand unequivocally.

The two of them reluctantly enter the classroom across the hall from us and close the door behind them. The walls of the school are thin, we should be able to hear them, but there is no sound coming from the classroom. I'm guessing Bex and Key are just staring at each other.

How does Pry deal with this every day?

"Not everyone can be as well matched as me and Marisol," East says as we stand in the hallway awaiting the couple.

"You're dating Marisol?" Swoop asks.

East tells them how much he cares about her and admits that he has yet to wipe her memory. The team warns him that she could be in danger because she knows about our world. He just keeps promising that he will look after her.

I want to point out that protecting the ones we love isn't always something we can do, but I figure that's a battle for another day. Anyway, after we get Pryor back, she's going to make East wipe her mind whether or not he wants to.

Just when I think I'm going to have to go inside the classroom and force them to talk, we hear Key's voice floating into the hallway.

"I didn't sleep with Silver. I need you to believe me," she says.

"Okay," he replies simply.

"But you're still pissed off, right?" she asks.

"What is the answer you're hoping for?"

"I don't know," she admits.

"What has gotten into you? Why are you acting like this?" he wonders.

"I feel like I'm trying to stop an avalanche from coming down on our heads and burying us. And you're not helping, Bex. All you're doing is denying that we're in trouble but we are. We are in serious trouble."

"So the way to help is to do as many drugs as you can and end up in another guy's bed?"

"I said I was sorry for that."

"And just like that everything is okay?" he challenges.

"I know that I messed up. And again, I'm sorry. I didn't mean to end up with Silver that night."

"I really can't do this right now," he says.

"Silver said—"

"I don't give a damn what he said. I will talk to my girlfriend when I'm damn good and ready," he shouts.

"Don't walk away from me. Honestly, just grow a pair of wings and tell me that you are still mad at me."

"Okay, you want to do this, then fine, let's do it. You know why I'm so angry at you?"

"Yes, you think I slept with—"

"No, that's not the reason I'm pissed off. That's not the reason I can barely look at you."

"Then what is it?" she asks.

"YOU ALMOST DIED!!!"

"What?" she says, completely taken aback.

"You lay on the floor dying. Your body went limp, and life was just draining out of you. I thought you were gone. I thought I would have to spend the rest of my life without you and it fucking hurt, Keyohmi. It hurt."

"Bear, I'm sorry."

"No, you're not. I think it's exactly what you wanted. You wanted to hurt me. You wanted to scare the shit out of me so that I could remember how much I love you. The only problem is I didn't need help remembering. That is until now. Right now, at this moment, I am having a hard time remembering why I love you."

"You want to break up?" she asks in a small voice filled with pain.

"I didn't say that."

"No, but it's what you want, isn't it?"

"Oh for Omnis' sake, Key, what do you want from me?"

"THE TRUTH!!!"

"About what?"

"Stop it, Bex! Please just stop acting like it's all in my head. I can't take it anymore. I know I'm acting crazy. I know I am a complete mess, but please don't do this to me. Don't pretend it's all in my head."

"Key, I—"

"Say it!"

"I'm not gonna—"

"DAMN YOU, BEX, SAY IT!"

"Key, this is—"

"SAY IT!!!"

"YES, I HAVE FEELINGS FOR PRYOR!"

Out in the hallway we listen as Key bursts into tears. Then she does something odd—she thanks Bex for being honest with her. He doesn't reply. Then suddenly we hear him calling out for her to stop. The team and I run into the classroom and find the window wide open.

"Where's my sister?" Swoop asks.

"She took off," Bex replies.

"Damn it! Swoop, go get her before she gets herself in any more trouble," I order.

Swoop takes off into the air.

"I'll go too," Bex says.

"No, we have a better chance of things going smoothly if Swoop goes by herself."

Swoop glares at Bex and takes off after her sister.

***

"So, how deep are these feeling you have for Pry?" East asks moments later as we head down the hallway. Bex shoots him a warning glance but East was never one to take hints.

"Seriously, how deep are they? Is it like a passing fling?" he asks.

"East, shut up," Bex replies.

"Oh come on, how deep? Did you write her name on notebook paper with a colorful marker?" he pushes. Diana starts to smile and even Randy can't help but join in.

"East, leave him alone," I reply.

"Oh no…you have gone way past the crush phase, haven't you? Admit it, Bex, you're ready to give her your Netflix password," East concludes.

Now, Diana and Randy are laughing outright. The more they try to stop the worse it gets. And the stern look on Bex's face only adds fuel to the fire.

"I think you guys should have a human wedding," East adds.

"I have the perfect dress for the occasion; it's black," Diana says.

"That way when Key kills Bex, you can go from the wedding straight to the funeral that will surely follow."

"Exactly," she replies happily.

"I'm gonna miss you, buddy. But seriously, when Key kills you for breaking her heart, what song would you like played at your funeral? Do you want to go spiritual old school or maybe something a little edgier like Pink Floyd?"

"No, I think something more like 'Stairway To Heaven'—Led Zeppelin," Diana replies.

"Guys, let's get serious; everyone knows the best funeral song, especially for a dead angel, is 'Angel' —Sarah McLachlan."

"I don't know, that's a little on the nose," Diana replies.

"How about—" Bex pins East against the wall by his neck before he can finish his sentence.

"Okay, okay, I can see now that you're not ready for open mockery. Noted," East gasps.

"When the mission is over I give you permission to take his head off, but for now let him go," I reply.

Bex releases East but takes a moment to glare at him. East gives Bex a charming smile and fixes his clothes. Randy and Diana start to hum various funeral songs under their breath.

East's cell rings. He looks at the number on the screen and instantly his relaxed demeanor changes. The conversation is brief. There's only a series of "Yes" and "Okay, whatever," but judging from the tone of his voice, something is wrong.

"What is it?" Randy asks.

"It's just…forget it," East replies.

The team and I exchange an uneasy glance. It's rare for East to take anything seriously, let alone get upset. There's usually only one thing that can get to him like that.

"What's going on with your family?" I ask.

"My dad forces us to take these stupid camping trips in the mountains once a year. It always takes forever to set up the tent, it invariably rains, and we end up trying to eat beans from a can. We always forget the can opener and have to use our powers and more often than not the cans explode," he replies.

"So you're upset because he's gonna force you to go again this year?" Diana asks.

"Um…no. I'm lucky, this year they went without me," he says quietly.

"That's a good thing, right?" Bex says.

"Yeah, yeah. Definitely. I mean, I didn't want go anyway, so…"

"Why did they leave without you?" I ask.

"My dad heard about what happened at Para headquarters and he thought the family should get away and avoid whatever fallout there may be," East says.

"Why would that make them take off without you?" Randy asks.

"East, I'm sorry. I didn't mean to make things hard for your family," I reply.

"It's not you. My dad is always looking for a reason to take off without me. I was once late from a training session by five minutes and he just drove away. The thing is, I saw him drive away as I was running up to the car. I swear to Omnis he saw me. He saw me and still kept driving," East says, lost in thought.

"I missed something. Why is your father such a dick?" Diana asks.

"The thing is he's not. He's the nicest guy to everyone but me," East says with an ironic smile.

"Why?" Randy asks.

"I have no idea. It's like I did something horrible to him and I can't remember. But whatever I did must have been really bad because…I just keep paying for it," East says sadly.

This isn't the first time we've heard about East's father, Frank, being cruel, yet it still gets to East. This time is no different. We hear the hurt in his voice. We're not sure what to say. Normally East is the one who can find humor in these heavy moments. When he's down and hurting, we're at a loss as to how to help.

"Fine, you big baby, we'll take you camping. But no beans and you have to promise we can kill things along the way," Diana offers.

"I could see myself roughing it. Okay, when this is all over, we'll go camping. We can be out in the great wide open. Live by our wits and nothing else. I'll bring my portable DVD player. We'll watch *Star Wars*," Randy adds gleefully.

"How is bringing your DVD player 'roughing it?'" East asks with a smile.

"It doesn't play Blu-Ray," Randy informs him.

"Wow, you're a brave man," I reply, shaking my head.

"Okay, we'll watch *Star Wars*, but just to be clear, Hans didn't shoot first," Diana says.

Randy's so insulted by her comment, his jaw drops. The look on Randy's face helps bring East back to his old self. Just then, my phone vibrates; I pull it out and read the text on the screen. I announce the news as I take to the sky.

"We gotta go; Swoop's in trouble!"

***

A few minutes later we fly into the dark Chicago skyline. Right away we are greeted by a slew of Powerballs and flames. The Kasters have taken over the area. Kasters are superpowered demons that have been chosen by Malakaro to hunt us. There used to be six of them, but Pryor killed one and Diana left them. So now they are down to four.

But losing two members doesn't stop them from wreaking havoc. They are spread out in the sky, poised to attack. There are very few humans around but the ones there flee in panic.

East uses his electric lasso around the Kaster named Twist. It wraps around the demon and starts draining him of his powers. Another Kaster, Wrath, creates a vortex in the sky and tries to pull East inside it. Unable to hold on, East is forced to release Twist and focus on not getting pulled into the vortex. Unfortunately, there is nothing he can grab hold of.

Bex, an expert in flight strategy, is able to maneuver around the vortex without getting pulled in and save East seconds before the hole swallows him. While they were able to avoid certain death, they can't stop the force of the closing vortex from knocking them both out of the sky.

The second they hit the ground, a Kaster named Manic seeks them out. Manic is always a pain in the ass to fight because he's a Partial. That means he's half animal and twice as hard to defeat. He takes the form of a winged beast with poisonous fangs. One bite from him and death isn't too far off.

I send a Powerball right at Manic and it lands on his hind legs. He howls and roars loudly. My strike gives East and Bex time to regroup, but they are no match for what's about to happen.

"Kill is getting ready to fire, stop him!" I order Diana.

Diana looks down from her Port and sees Kill, the leader of the Kasters, about to take out both Bex and East. She looks back at me and she's uncertain. At first I think maybe she doesn't want to attack her old teammates, but then I realize what the problem is: Randy.

In our hurry to get here we took Randy with us.

"Throw him to me!" I shout.

Before he can object, Diana pushes Randy off her Port. Randy screams as he plummets out of the sky. I catch him just in time, place him on a rooftop, and put a Holder around him. Randy bangs against the bubble-like prison, insisting that he be allowed to help. I pay him no attention and head back to the battle.

Diana dives down and attacks Kill by opening her mouth and inhaling his life force. This gives Bex and East a chance to escape the Kasters. I turn in search of Key and Swoop, but I can't find them in the air.

"Where are they?" I shout to East.

"Swoop's over here!" he yells as he heads towards a row of trucks.

I fly down to get to them but I'm tackled by Kill, who has managed to break free of Diana's powers. She now lies on the floor. I shout out to her and she assures me she's okay.

"So nice to see two demons connecting," Kill says venomously.

"I'm in no mood for you. So if you promise to go away I might let you live," I offer.

"I think I'll stay for the rest of this party. I already paid the fee to enter," Kill replies and he takes out his blade.

"You haven't begun to pay," I vow.

I hurl fireballs at him in rapid succession. He manages to dodge all of them as he tackles me to the ground. He cuts though the air with his blade until he makes contact with my skin. He slices into my forearm and laughs.

I groan as the blood comes rushing out of me and seeps down to the cement.

I send a Powerball to the base of the nearest skyscraper and watch as it topples over on us. The falling glass and metal causes Kill to lose his balance and drop his blade. I summon a massive orb of power, far bigger than what's safe.

I know it's a risk to summon up such a powerful weapon in a city filled with humans, but I need to get Swoop and Key. I yell to the team to take cover and then I send the Powerball right into Kill's face. The city of Chicago shakes violently.

Kill manages to move out of the way but not before the Powerball makes contact with his left arm and leg. The blast shreds his limbs off. Pieces of Kill are sprawled out into the night air.

Manic, in the form of a beast, runs to his leader's defense. Diana grabs the blade and stabs Manic in the back with it. The animal howls repeatedly. Seeing that Bex and the others have overpowered his team, Kill calls for them to retreat. Meanwhile his arm and leg have already started to regenerate.

"We're not done here; believe me," he says as he takes off into the sky.

I order Bex to secure the humans and get Randy out of the Holder. I take off my shirt and use it to stop the bleeding as I run towards the twins.

"Is Swoop okay?" I ask, looking down at her bruised body.

"Yeah, but she needs something to mend the wound on her side," East says.

I look closer and there's a silver colored pool of blood forming on Swoop's right side. Her eyes are barely open and she moans in pain.

"Swoop, don't worry. Everything's going to be okay. I promise," I reply, hoping my voice doesn't betray the worry I feel.

Diana begins to tend to Swoop. I look around, fearing Key may be hurt in the debris.

"Where's Key?" Bex asks as he comes running with Randy a few steps behind him.

"I was following her…got attacked from behind…I called but she never came," Swoop says in a weak voice.

"What do you mean, she never came? Swoop, where is Key?" I ask.

East signals for us to turn and look behind us. We do as he instructs and find a small-framed girl running towards us laughing uncontrollably. It's Key. Her clothes and hair are disheveled. She's jittery and unable to stand still. There is no doubt about it; Key is high.

"They have the best colors in that alley. So pretty," she says, sounding like a child.

She doesn't notice her wounded sister on the floor until Bex points it out. That seems to snap her out of her drug-induced haze. She falls to her knees before her sister and begs for Swoop's forgiveness.

"I didn't hear…I wasn't…I don't know what happened," Key says.

"What happened is that you came here to get high and your sister tried to stop you. Now she's injured because you were too stoned to hear her crying out for you! It's like you don't give a damn about consequences anymore," Bex shouts.

"Swoop, I'm so sorry. Don't be mad. I love you," Key pleads.

"Key, she could have been killed," East says.

"I know, alright! I know. I messed up, okay?" she shouts.

"NO, KEY, IT'S NOT OKAY!" I yell.

"I'm sorry."

"BEING SORRY DOESN'T MEAN SHIT TO YOUR INJURED SISTER OR TO PRYOR, WHO'S SOMEWHERE FIGHTING FOR HER LIFE. SCREW YOU AND YOUR APOLOGIES; YOU'RE OFF THE TEAM!"

CHAPTER TEN
WE KNOW YOU

I send East to Mind wipe the humans that witnessed the battle. In the meantime, Diana tries to help Swoop while Key looks on anxiously. I make a call to Noble and push back our meeting. The fact that we are once again delayed pisses me off far more than I can ever articulate. But we can't go without ensuring that Swoop is okay, especially now that we are down one member.

I thought Key's boyfriend would have something to say about my decision to take Key off the team, but the one who requests to talk to me isn't Bex; it's Randy. He asks that we take a walk while Swoop is being tended to.

"Alright, Randy, what is it?" I ask.

"This walk we're talking isn't for me, Silver; it's for you," he replies.

"I don't get it."

"Leaders need sounding boards. Someone they can talk to about the decisions they've made. I was that person for Pryor. So I'm offering my services to you for a small fee," he jokes.

"Randy, thanks but I'm fine," I tell him.

"Pryor says that at the start of every conversation we have. She tells me just how fine she is. Then she blows something up."

"I get what you're saying, but really I'm good."

"You're bleeding," he says.

I look down and realize that in addition to my arm, I have a six-inch piece of metal embedded inside my palm.

"I didn't even notice that," I admit as I pull it out.

"That happens when you're 'Incredible Hulk' mad," Randy points out.

"I know what can happen if I lose my temper. I'm trying to deal with it."

"Yes, and I want to help. Talk to me."

"Is that how it works? You ask Pry to spill her guts and she does?"

"Yeah, but it's okay if you need to warm up first. We can talk about the weather."

"What is there to say? I didn't want to throw Key off the team, but I have no choice. She's a liability. But she's also an amazing fighter and I don't know if leaving her behind is a good idea," I admit.

"For what it's worth I think you did the right thing," he says.

"Really?"

"If Key does anything to endanger the mission and we don't get to Pry in time, she would hate herself forever. Keeping her off the team, at least for now, is the best decision for everyone. Silver, you did the right thing."

"So why do I feel like crap?"

"Hero side effects."

"Is it this hard for Pryor?" I ask.

"Yeah, because you guys weren't just a team, you're a family. That means feelings are involved."

"I guess."

"Silver, I know you said that you didn't want to tell us what is actually happening to her but can I ask you one thing?"

"What's that?"

"Do they have blankets at The Center?"

"What?"

"When someone at school would pick on me or mess with me, I would push her away. But she would always insist on sitting next to me. She'd say I looked like I needed a hug and I'd tell her that hugs were for kids. But then she'd wrap her arms around me and say "This isn't a hug. It's just that you look cold and I want to keep you warm.' Tell me whereever she is there's something there to keep her warm," he asks.

He turns his face away so I won't see him get choked up.

"Randy, look at me," I order.

He reluctantly turns to face me; his eyes fill with tears.

"We will save Pryor. Do you hear me?"

"Yeah."

"And when we get her back you can wrap her up in the biggest blanket you can find. Okay?"

"Okay. Sorry, didn't mean to…they never lose it in comic books. I guess that's why I'm the sidekick," he says.

"That's crap. You're the reason we have a lead. Just because you can't fly doesn't mean you're not important to us. In fact, you're essential."

"Thank you. So what do we do now?" he wonders.

"As soon as Diana is done treating Swoop, we're gonna go drop off Key. I don't want her wandering around and getting herself hurt. So, we're gonna take her to someone we trust. Someone who will make sure she's taken care of."

"Who?"

"Pryor's grandfather; Julian."

***

We travel to Boston where the very original First Guardian leader lives. Julian is perhaps the most famous Guardian. He broke Omnis' rule and helped a girl named Femi get into the light. That mistake cost him everything. Julian is known for being both ruthless in his determination and fiercely protective of his family.

Stories about the lengths he went to in order to stop Pryor's mom and dad from uniting are legendary in our world. And in the end, he finally relented and welcomed Pryor's father but it was a long road.

"So Julian is an angel, right?" Randy asks as we walk up to the two-story red brick house.

"He was human, then he died and became a Guardian. Then he messed up really badly and well…it's a long story. But as of right now he has no powers. Although he knows all the players in the Angel world and is widely respected or feared depending on who you talk to," East says.

"And we can trust him?" Randy asks.

"So long as it's about keeping his family safe, then yes," I reply.

"I haven't seen Uncle Julian in forever," Swoop says, still sounding weak.

Diana was able to mend her wounds but warned us it would be a few hours before Swoop was back to her full strength. Key hasn't spoken much since I told her she was out of the team. I'm sure she hates me right now and feels like I'm overreacting. Bex has been pretty silent on the matter. I'm not sure if that's good or bad. All I know is that we need to find the Deed and we can't do that while we're busy watching out for Key.

We knock on the red door and a few moments later a beautiful human opens it. She has skin the color of coffee beans, long braids that frame her face perfectly, and a brilliant smile. She looks to be in her late fifties although it's hard to know for sure.

"Aaden!" she says, smiling even bigger as she embraces me.

"Hello Femi," I reply.

She greets everyone on the team and is happy to meet Randy, the best friend Pryor has told her so much about. Femi has no idea that we're angels. And although she was at the center of the biggest story in the Angel world, she has no memory of it at all. Looking at her now, I think it was for the best.

"Where's Pryor?" she asks.

"She has a school project so she couldn't make it. We were nearby so we thought we'd stop and say hi," East replies.

"That's great. Come in!" she says, opening the door wide.

We enter the nicely decorated home and are surrounded by framed pictures of Pryor and her family. The dark hardwood floor and soft lighting make the house feel like home.

"Julian, the kids are here!" she shouts towards the rooms upstairs.

"So Pryor used to spend a lot of time here when she was little?" Randy asks.

"Yeah, she lost control of her powers and ended up flying into the living room. That freaked Femi out. Julian had to get someone to wipe her mind," I reply in a whisper.

"Julian will be right down. You all have great timing. I just made a nice pot of beef stew and I also have fresh buttered biscuits and lemonade. Everyone have a seat," she says as she gathers the plates.

"Thanks, but we're not hungry," I reply.

Randy flashes me a quick look of panic. I always forget he needs to eat. East eats too but he's only half human and doesn't need to eat as often as a human does.

"Actually, Randy would love a plate," I reply.

"Certainly. You know, I have never seen any of you eat," she says.

We smile back at her, not sure what to say.

As she serves Randy a bowl of stew, Julian comes down the stairs. He looks to be a little older than his wife. He's put on a few pounds but is still in pretty good shape for his age. Just one look at us and he is already on high alert.

"Femi, honey, weren't you going shopping?" he asks.

"I was but I can't now. We have guests."

"Please don't change your plans for us," Bex says.

"Go, honey, you deserve to shop a little. I'll take care of the kids. Hurry, the stores are closing," he encourages.

"Well…there is a sale at Nordstrom…" she replies.

"Missing a chance to shop is a major crime," Swoop says.

"Okay, but I'll be back soon," she says as she takes her coat and heads out to the garage.

"Where's my granddaughter? What's a full demon doing in my house? And what drug is Keyohmi on?" Julian says, changing his tone the moment his wife is out of sight.

"How do you know I'm on—"

"Key, I'm the original First Guardian. I know what a stoned angel looks like."

"Oh. Well if you want to tell how awful I am, you're too late. I let everyone down and now I'm off the team," she says softly.

"I see. And where is my Pryor?" he asks.

We explain things to him. Then he curses the Angel world.

"First my Emmy is stuck in the light and now Pryor's gone. This Malakaro bastard is really starting to tick me off."

"Here, here," East says.

"And the demon?" he asks.

"This is Ruin. She enjoys walks on the beach, long sips of Coy Dark, and saving the occasional angel's life," East says.

He looks at Diana suspiciously. He's about to say something. Fearing the words that are likely to come from his brazen lips, I interrupt him.

"We need you to look after Key."

"Yup, I need to be babysat," she says sardonically.

"It's what's best for you," Bex whispers.

"If you care about what was best for me you wouldn't have feelings for someone else," she counters.

"Can you keep an eye on her?" Randy says as he swallows his food.

He must have been starving because he clears his bowl in minutes.

"Who's the hungry human?" Julian asks.

"He's Pryor's best friend. Can you watch Key?" I ask again.

"Yes, I can look after her, but is it wise to go without her? From what you've told me, The Center is full of evil. You really want to leave one of your own behind?" he says.

"We don't have a choice," I respond.

"Your parents are good angels. You twins are the most important thing to them. Why would you do such a stupid thing like this?" he asks Key.

"She's been under a lot of pressure," Swoop says, taking her sister's hand.

"That's what being Noru means—pressure. Suck it up, kid," Julian says.

"You don't understand," Key replies.

"The hell I don't. I chased my wife for a million lifetimes. I know more about love than all of you combined. And you know what I learned after finally getting what I want from Omnis?"

"What?" she asks in a sad voice.

"Everything that bastard put me though was necessary. How else would I know to appreciate it?"

"I don't want to be like this, okay? But when I try to pull myself together…I know Bex is just an angel like any other angel but…" Key stops and lowers her head to the floor.

"Babe, I told you that I'm not leaving you," he insists.

"But you have feelings for Pryor," she reminds him.

How Bex feels about Pryor is something I bury deep inside and I refuse to think about or process. Yes, I always knew how he felt, but now it's out in the open and I hate it. Yet focusing on it right now would be foolish. And so would trying to focus on the other question that's been nagging at me. The question I'm afraid to ask out loud.

Does Pryor have feelings for Bex?

"It doesn't matter. The point is I let everyone down. And you guys need to go on this mission without me like Silver said. I didn't think it was possible to fail on every level. I can't even do my job. Swoop could have died today and it would have been my fault," Key says.

"It's okay, Key," Swoop says.

"It's not okay. I'm sorry, guys. I'll stay here with Julian. You can take my wings away to ensure I do," Key says.

She then turns around so I have access to her Deck, the spot behind her head where the leader can touch to strip a team member of their wings.

"She sounds really sincere. I think she regrets her actions. Are you sure we can't take her?" Swoop asks.

"Look, I want to, but we don't know when she's going to go off the rails again and want more drugs. When this is over, Key, I promise we will get you the help you need but for right now, there's no way we can take you. I mean it's not like they have a pill that makes addiction disappear in a matter of minutes," I tell them.

"No, not in minutes, but there's something that can be done in hours," Julian says.

"You mean a Soak?" Diana says.

"Yes," Julian replies.

"What is that?" I ask.

"Yes! A Soak. I don't know why I didn't think of it myself," Key says, getting excited.

"What is it?" Randy asks.

"It's a black vial that's used to clean the soul. It clears all the fear, doubt, and uncertainty normally attached to your soul. It makes it easier for you to resist drugs because you feel complete within yourself," Key says.

"Why isn't this more widely known?" I ask.

"It's fairly new among Healers," she says.

"I heard of it from the inventor herself. She's pretty proud of it. You can give it to Key and in a few hours that will get rid of her addiction," Julian says.

"It won't get rid of it, but it will give me the extra strength I need to resist it," she pleads.

"Has it been tested? I don't want you to take anything that could harm you," Bex says.

"It's perfectly fine. I want to try it. Silver, what do you think?" she says, filled with hope.

"Julian, can you and Key excuse us?" Diana says.

"What? Why?" Key asks.

"It'll just be for five minutes," Diana says.

"No, I'm not gonna leave; I deserve to hear whatever you're about to say," Key counters.

"I saved your life. All I'm asking is that you give me five minutes alone with your team. Then when you come back you can continue to glare at me. I promise," Diana insists.

Julian takes Key upstairs and leaves the rest of us in the room. We turn our attention to Diana, who looks worried.

"We have a problem," she says.

"Yay, another one!" East says sarcastically.

"What do you mean?" I ask.

"Once you drink the vial of Soak, it takes you to your darkest fear. I mean it literally takes you there. It makes you disappear into your fear. Then it forces you to face whatever it is that frightens you."

"So Key will be pulled into a scenario where her and Bex aren't together?" Swoop asks.

"If that's her biggest fear, but I don't think it is. That's why we have a problem," Diana says.

"Whatever the fear is, she can get past it. I have faith in her," Bex says.

"That's great, but it will also reveal things she didn't know she was afraid of."

"Wait, you mean…?"

"Yes, East, Soak will undo your work. It will give her back her memory—all of it," Diana tells him.

That's when I finally understand why Diana is worried about Key taking the vial.

"Wait, East never did any work on Key. Key's never had her mind wiped," Bex responds.

"That's not exactly true…" East says carefully.

"What are you talking about?" Bex demands.

Crap, why now?

"Okay, Bex, we need to tell you something but you have to stay calm and know that we did what we did because it was the best way to keep Key from getting locked away," I warn.

"What happened? What memory did you take from her?" he demands of East.

"Over a year ago, you two had an argument. I'm guessing it was about Pryor but I'm not sure. Anyway, Key was upset and she went out to a bar and took some pills. It caused her to temporarily lose her powers as a side effect. She was leaving the bar and five humans attacked and raped her. By the time she came to, she had her powers back. And when she realized what was done to her, she killed all five of the humans," I reply.

I have never seen Bex look so tormented before. When he speaks his voice trembles from anger and profound sorrow.

"Raped?" he says, unable to wrap his head around the news.

"I know it's hard to hear. When Silver told me, I totally lost it," Swoop admits, placing a hand on his shoulder.

"Bex, I'm sorry. We would have told you but it was best no one knew. I only told Swoop because I needed her to make sure Key didn't start drinking again," I tell him.

"This is my fault," Bex says.

"No, the people to blame are dead," East reminds him.

"How is this not my fault? That girl out there, my girl, faced the worst thing that could possibly happen to anyone because of me. I don't even remember the fight but I'm sure I said something about Pryor. Something that made Key mad and…"

"Bex, it's okay," East says.

"And today, I told her I couldn't remember why I loved her. I said that to her. And meanwhile she's going through this?" Bex says to himself.

"You guys argued. Bex, we all say things when we argue," I assure him.

"What do I do? How do I help her? How do I…"

"She doesn't know. I wiped her mind," East reminds him.

"Wait, she killed five humans…you took the blame, Silver?" Bex asks.

"I told her to go and that I would take care of it," I say.

"You went to The Center for Key. I thought you really killed those humans…I didn't know…" Bex says, utterly bewildered.

"Look, it's nothing, okay? It's what families do: protect each other," I reply.

"So we aren't gonna let Key take the Soak, right?" Swoop says.

"I think she should take it," Diana says.

"What, you said taking it was a problem," Bex says.

"Taking the Soak without knowing she'd been raped is a problem. But if you tell her what happened to her, she'll know what she's in store for when the Soak takes her back to that night," she replies.

"No, I'm not gonna tell her," Bex says.

"Why not?" Diana pushes.

"Because it would crush her," Bex snaps.

"You guys never learn," she says, shaking her head.

"Excuse me?" Bex says, baffled and insulted.

"How many times has Key asked you if you have feelings for the redhead? And how many times have you lied to her?"

"This is different," Bex replies.

"No, it's not. Stop keeping this from the ones you say you love. It doesn't work. And you know why, because we know you. We women, who stand by you guys both in bed and in battle, we know you. We know what words to say to hurt you. What to say that will haunt you. And when you are wounded and your spirit broken, we know what to say to heal you. So when you look in our face and lie to us, it makes us girls want to stab you in the face."

"Okay…" East whispers.

"You don't understand. I was trying—"

"Para, you lied! You looked into the face of the girl you claim to love and you lied to her. You could have come clean and had a grown-up conversation, but instead you did what felt comfortable for you: you lied. And now you are doing the same thing again in this situation," Diana accuses.

"It was the worst night of her life. Why would I bring that moment back to her?" Bex says.

"He's right. I wiped her mind. If she doesn't take the Soak, she'll never know she was raped," Easton replies.

"Just because you wiped her mind doesn't mean you wiped her subconscious. Somewhere inside, that girl knows she's been violated. I mean, look at her behavior. The first thing she does is find a guy to sleep with when she's high."

"Maybe it's a coincidence," Randy says.

"No, it's not. I know because I—I know other girls that have been assaulted. They either get really shy and withdrawn or they go to the far end of the spectrum and use sex to try and get their power back."

"Diana?" I call out softly once her voice starts to tremble.

"What?" she snaps.

"Are you okay?" I ask.

"Yeah, fine," she lies.

"If fixing her subconscious is the key then we are out of luck. I don't know how to do that," East tells Diana.

"Nor should you. Seriously, five humans climbed on top of that girl and inserted themselves inside her. They walked away with a piece of her and maybe it's time she gets it back. Tell Key the truth," Diana says emphatically.

"You just don't get it," Bex says.

"Yeah, I do. You're protecting Key's innocence. Yet a few hours ago she was in Silver's bed. I hate to break it to you, but the treasure you're guarding has already been stolen."

CHAPTER ELEVEN
THE GIRL IN THE ALLEY

I expect Bex to get extremely upset with Diana and challenge her at every turn. Looking around the room, I am not the only one. We all know what's about to happen. It will be an all-out argument, yet another thing we don't really have time for. However, when Bex opens his mouth his tone isn't confrontational at all; it's remorseful.

"You're right," he says softly.

"Look, I'm not trying to be a bitch but—wait, did you just agree with me?" Diana asks, stunned.

"Yeah, I did," Bex replies.

"Anyone else feel a chill?" East asks jokingly.

"Bex, are you saying you want to tell Key, because I'm not okay with that. She may be your girlfriend but she's my twin and I'm not gonna let you hurt her even more so than you have already," Swoop declares.

"Swoop, it's the only way she can get better," Bex pleads.

"Do you know what this could do to her?" Swoop replies.

"It can't be any worse than what she's been doing to herself," Bex insists.

"Wrong, telling her could send her over the edge."

"Swoop, we need to do this. If the Soak can help her fight her addiction, then I don't see how we have a choice," Diana replies.

"First of all, there is no 'we.' Secondly, the only reason we are allowing you to tag along is because you saved Key. And while that's one thing in your favor, it's the only thing. So stay out of this," Swoop informs her.

"I am only trying to help but do whatever you want," Diana says, shrugging her shoulders.

"Key is my sister and I have a say-so in whether or not we tell her something that will devastate her," Swoop counters.

"What other choice do we have?" Bex asks.

"I'll take care of her. I'll make sure she doesn't take any more pills," she replies.

"You'll watch her for the rest of your life?" East asks.

"If I have to, yes," she says stubbornly.

"Bird," I call out to her.

Swoop turns to face me. I haven't called her "Bird" in years. I used to call her that back when she was learning to fly. Her wings were weak and fragile. She was learning basic flight patterns but she insisted on trying to outfly every bird in the sky. She marveled at their speed and once asked her parents if Omnis would ever let her fly as fast as the birds. They reassured her that she would someday be even faster.

"Silver, Key's not like family to me, she is family. How can I let Bex tell her something that will crush her?" she asks.

"Bird, she can't go on this way. She either faces the truth or it will wreck her whole life. The next time she gets high and loses her powers, there may not be anyone around to cover for her. You want to protect her, then arm her with the truth. We should have done this when it first happened," I explain.

"Maybe Ruin and Bex are right. Maybe knowing just how bad things got with her drug use will help her fight her urges," Randy says.

"In the end, Bird, you are her sister and if you don't want us to tell her we won't. But just so you know, she may turn to harder drugs. She could someday be a full-on Tic," I add.

"What's a Tic?" Randy asks.

"It's an angel drug addict that is so far gone, their wings and soul start to…" Swoop is too emotional at the thought to finish her statement.

"Bird, what do you want to do?" I ask.

"Okay, Bex can tell her," she replies in a small voice.

We call for Julian and Key to come downstairs and join us.

The two of them enter the living room. Key looks suspicious and worried. She then looks at our faces and it confirms that something bad is coming her way.

"Okay, so what's going on?" Key asks.

"We want you to take the Soak," Swoop says as she takes her sister's hand.

"That's great!" she replies.

"But before you do, there's something you need to know," Bex says.

"What is it?" Key says.

"Let's go into the other room," Bex suggests.

He walks over to her and lovingly places his arm around her. She looks into his face and sees the pain reflected in his eyes. She grows fearful and looks back at him anxiously. The two of them head for the dining room.

The doorway that separates that room from ours is made of glass. Once they enter and close the door, we don't hear them but we can see everything. Bex has his back turned to us, but we have a clear view of Key.

Bex begins to gesture as he recounts the worst night of Key's life to her. With every passing moment Key grows more and more apprehensive. Swoop takes my hand and squeezes it tightly.

From what I can gather, Bex is at the end of the story. He tells her exactly what happened to her in the alley. She shakes her head "no" and violently pounds against his chest. The more he tries to calm her down the more she rages against him. She strikes blow after blow as if fighting him off will rescind the horrible news.

Swoop, unable to take in the sight of her older sister's agony, buries her head in my chest. East gently strokes her back and Randy places his hand on East's shoulder. Julian looks on, concerned. As much as we want to intervene, all of us know that this is overdue.

Bex holds on to Key and no matter how much she tries to fight him, he refuses to let her go. Finally exhausted, her rage subsides and gives way to heartbreak. She sobs repeatedly as she crumbles to the ground.

Bex, unfazed by her attempts to push him away, kneels down to the ground and takes her in his embrace. This time she doesn't push him away. She clings to him as if her life depends on it. I fear, that in many ways, it does.

***

Some time passes, more time than we have to spare, but there is no way to rush what Key is facing. I know Pry wouldn't want me to go in there and force Key to come to terms with such a horrific event. So we stay where we are until Key is ready to face us.

When she emerges from the dining room, Bex is right behind her. He takes her hand protectively as she stands before us. Swoop leaps out and holds her tightly; she apologizes to her sister for allowing Bex to tell her the truth.

"No, I needed to know." She replies in a weak voice that barely escapes her throat.

"I took your memory and I'm sorry. I didn't think…we just wanted to help," East tells her.

"I know," she replies.

She turns to face me. It's hard to read her expression. All I know is that for the first time since I've known her, Key seems…small. It's as if she's been reduced to a mere shadow of who she once was.

"You went to The Center because of me. I don't know how to…what do I do to thank you?" she asks.

"There's a good chance I would have killed the humans myself," I admit.

"Why didn't you tell them it was me?" she asks.

"We don't betray the ones we love," I remind her.

"I will make it up to you. I don't know how but I will," she vows.

"Don't worry about Silver, he enjoyed the downtime while locked away. Taking the rap for you gave him a chance to work on his knitting patterns," East replies.

"He's right, there's a scarf in your future," I reply, smiling.

She embraces me. I feel her body tremble slightly against me. She's scared. I embrace her and whisper in her ear that everything will be okay. When she pulls away and looks at me, I can see she's not sure if anything will ever be okay again.

"Okay, I'm ready for the Soak, what do I have to do?" Key asks.

"I don't know everything but I can guess something really messed up has happened to you. Is that right?" Julian asks.

"Yes," she replies simply.

"I didn't know you had endured a trauma. I thought it was just regular heartbreak. This changes things," Julian adds.

"How so?" East asks.

"We need to be sure that the Soak is the right treatment for you," he replies.

"It's the fastest way to get me better. I need to rejoin my team," she says.

"I get that, but remember you aren't just an angel. You're a Noru. That means you are stronger than other angels but so are your inner demons," Julian warns.

"You think she could lock herself in?" Diana asks.

"It's very possible. In that case taking a Soak would do more harm than good. In fact, it could be the worst thing for her."

"Wait, I don't get it," Randy says.

"This time you are not alone, Randy. I have no idea what's happening," East replies.

"A Soak is often referred to as 'The room with no doors,'" Julian explains.

"Why?" Randy asks.

"Going inside a memory is dangerous. You can get stuck there. Key being Noru I know she can face whatever normal demons haunt her subconscious. But as I said before, since she's about to face major trauma, those inner demons might not be so easily slain."

"What exactly does she have to do once she's taken the Soak?" Bex asks.

"Her body will stay but her mind will go back to that night. Once there, she has to literally stop running from the memory and let it play out. But her subconscious will try and fight it."

"He's right. The event you are facing is utterly terrifying and your mind will do anything to run away. Ironically, the more you try to escape, the less likely you will be to make it out in time," Diana says.

"The Soak has a timer?" I ask.

"She has three minutes to confront what is crippling her or she won't be able to come back. She'll be locked in that night forever. It's called Enderma. It's the Angel world's version of a coma," Julian says.

"Then forget it. She's not doing it," Bex says.

"I agree," Swoop replies protectively.

"Then we won't do it," I reason.

"Wait, I want to do this," Key protests.

"You could get stuck. You would be locked into your nightmare," I remind her.

"Is there any other way for me to beat my addiction?" she asks Diana.

"Yes, there are lots of other vials you could take," she replies.

"You see, we don't have to do this," Bex says, relieved.

"But the other vials will take longer to work, right?" Key persists.

"Soak can help you get better in a few hours. But other mixtures take longer," Julian adds.

"How much longer?" I ask.

"Three to six weeks."

"No! We can't wait that long. Pry needs us. If we do the Soak then I can get better quickly and get back on the team. Silver, I want to do this, please."

"Pryor wouldn't want you to risk getting stuck," I reply.

"I have placed this team in danger numerous times. We would already be on our way to save Pry if it wasn't for me. Don't you get it? I need to do this," she pleads.

"Okay," I reply reluctantly.

"Silver, you can't agree to this. Did you hear what Julian said? She could get stuck there," Bex shouts.

I signal for him to step away from the team so we can talk.

"This is a bad idea," Bex says as soon as we're out of earshot.

"It's not my favorite option but look at her, Bex."

He looks across the room at his girlfriend. She has her arms folded against her chest and her head is down.

"She's feeling powerless and I think taking the Soak will give her a chance to get some of that power back. I don't think she wants to do this; I think she needs to," I inform him.

"So, what have you guys decided?" Julian asks.

"Key will take the Soak," Bex says with great trepidation.

As we start setting up to administer the Soak, I have only one thought.

If Key isn't strong enough to face what happened in the alley, we will lose her forever…

***

Julian brings out a glass basin and places it on the table at the center of the room. Diana helps him add various mixtures and pours them into the bowl.

"Hold out your hand," Diana says to Key.

Nervously, Key does as requested. Diana uses a blade from her pouch and cuts into Key's palm. She winces slightly as the silver blood drips from her hand and down into the pool of mixtures. Julian plucks a feather from her wings and drops it into the bowl as well. The mixture turns from light grey to black, then it begins to swirl around on its own.

"As it starts to build up speed, the Soak will seek out the angel whose blood and feathers were placed in the bowl. It will reach out for you. Do not fight it. Let it enter you. Once it does, you will lose consciousness and be taken to the night of your worst fear. We will watch it play out in the basin," Diana says.

"We'll be able to see what's going on in her head?" Bex asks.

"Exactly," Julian replies.

"What do I do once I get there?" Key asks.

"Endure," Diana replies.

"You need to face whatever the fear is. Your instincts are going to be to run, but that would be a mistake. Stay, face it, and you'll be back here before you know it," Julian says.

"Like we said before, you only have three minutes. So the faster you confront the humans who did it, the better," Diana reminds her.

"Will everything look exactly as it did that night?" I ask.

"No, it will look like whatever Key interprets it to be. We don't know what it'll look like until she's inside the moment," Diana explains.

"When I face my fear, then I'll immediately be pulled out of the Soak?" Key asks.

"Yes," Julian says.

"How will she know how much time she has left?" Swoop wonders anxiously.

"We told her she has three minutes, her subconscious is aware of that. It may reflect in the time limitation in many different ways. There may be the sound of a clock ticking or a watch somewhere in the alley. Whatever it is, pay attention to it. Once your time is up, if you have not faced your fear, you will be left in the alley—permanently," Diana cautions again.

"Okay, I got it," Key says bravely.

Bex takes her face in his hands and kisses her gently.

"I know we have a lot to work out but I love you. I love you so much," he says.

"I know," she replies softly.

Suddenly Swoop bursts into tears and covers her mouth with her hand. Key reaches out for her twin, the two embrace, and Key promises she will return.

"What if you don't? What if you stay in that awful moment forever?" Swoop sobs.

"Hermes is about to unveil its new lineup of crocodile handbags, you know I'm not missing that," she teases her twin.

"We have one more mixture to add, then the Soak will enter you," Julian says.

The contents of the bowl move in a circular pattern and furiously pick up speed. The black mixture is now a miniature twister. It brings with it a gust of wind that threatens to throw us to the floor and shakes the foundation of the house. We are all forced to hold on to whatever is near us.

"The Soak is fully formed. We need to add the final ingredient now." Julian shouts above the roar of the growing tornado.

Key braces herself and signals that she's ready. Julian drops a red liquid into the growing twister. Right before our eyes, the twister leaps out of the bowl and inserts itself into Key's eyes, nose, and mouth. The Soak picks her up off the ground, spins her in the air, and slams her faceup onto the floor.

"Key!" Bex shouts in a complete panic.

"She's okay, she's inside the Soak, look," Diana says.

We look inside the basin on the table and watch an image start to form on the surface of the remaining mixture. The worse moment of Key's life plays out before us.

Key is back in the alley of the bar where I found her that night. Above her, dark rolling clouds invade an angry crimson sky. A black bird with red eyes descends from the sky and perches itself along the roof of the building. Soon it's joined by another and then another. The three birds look down at her.

The sky opens its gaping mouth and spits at Key in the form of an icy rain. It pours down on her with brute force. She gathers her jacket in an attempt to stay warm. Then she hears an ominous chanting coming from all directions. She looks around frantically but can't find its origin.

Without warning one of the birds cries out and red blood seeps from its eyes. It falls to the ground, dead. Key looks over to where the bird fell and finds the animal's blood has formed the shape of an hourglass. Key's mind has given her three birds, one for each minute. She's down to two birds, meaning she has two minutes to confront her fear.

Suddenly, shadowy figures spring up from the cold wet concrete and surround her. Key's eyes widen with terror as the shadows get closer. She tries to take to the air only to find that her wings are gone. But the shadows go past her and head for a small tunnel a few yards away. Fearful that the second bird could die at any moment, Key bravely follows the shadows into the tunnel.

In the distance, she watches as the shadows come to life in the form of ravenous beasts with decaying flesh, fiery eyes, and fangs. They gather and converge on their prey.

She hears sobbing coming from the center of the vicious circle. She recognizes the voice; it's hers.

Key dares to look even closer. She sees the "past" version of herself looking back at her from the floor. In the entryway of the dark tunnel, rain water rushes in and carries the corpse of the second bird with it. Key now has only one minute left to confront her fear.

She rushes to defend her "past" self from the creatures. In the midst of the battle, her former self manages to grab hold of Key and whisper something in her ear. We don't hear what Key's "past" says to her. Whatever it was, it shocked and disturbed Key. So much so that she curls up into a ball and sobs.

In the entryway of the tunnel, the third bird makes its way towards her, its feathers falling with every step and its movements unsteady. Key sees the last bird. She knows she now has less than a minute before the bird dies. Less than a minute until she is locked in her nightmare forever. The problem is, Key no longer cares...

CHAPTER TWELVE
KILL HER!

The panic in the living room is unlike anything I've seen before. Bex and Swoop are beside themselves, demanding that Diana and Julian wake Key up.

"We can't wake her. She has to confront her fear or stay there, you know that," Julian replies.

"Fine, if she can't come out, I'll go in and get her," Bex vows.

"You can't enter. It's not your subconscious, Bex; it's hers," Diana reminds him.

"Well we need to do something, she's just sitting there too traumatized to move," East says.

"How much time does she have left?" I ask.

"The last bird is falling apart. It's shedding and its eyes are glazing over," Randy says.

"I need an actual number," I demand.

"She has thirty seconds left," Julian says.

"Key and I are from the same bloodline. Maybe if I drink the Soak, I can enter her memory," Swoop says.

"It doesn't work like that. You drink that Soak and we have no idea what it will do to you," Diana counters.

"I don't care. I'm willing to take that chance," Swoop replies.

"I'm not. Bird, you can't drink the Soak. Key wouldn't want you to," I remind her.

"I don't care. I can't lose her," Swoop says as she heads for the basin.

"Wait, we can't get her out but can we talk to her? Can she hear us?" Randy asks.

"It's worth a try. Swoop, talk to her," I tell her, desperate for her to get away from the basin.

Swoop runs over to Key and kneels beside her. We all kneel down and beg Key to get up.

"She's still curled up in a ball, but she's shaking her head 'no' inside the Soak. That means she can hear you," Julian says as he looks into the basin.

"It won't matter if she can hear us if nothing we say changes her mind," Swoop replies desperately.

"Key, baby, please get up," Bex pleads.

"Key, you can do this. Get up!" East begs.

"Damn it, Key, get up!" I demand.

"Twenty seconds," Julian calls out.

"She was doing fine. I don't understand what happened," Randy says.

"Her past self said something that completely destroyed her. But I couldn't make out what it was," I reply.

"Fifteen seconds."

Shit!

"Key, we need you, please get up!" I beg.

"Seven seconds."

"Please, please come back," Bex says as he rests his head on her chest.

"Damn it, Key, please get up!" Swoop cries.

"Does anyone know what the past said to her?" Swoop says hysterically.

"I don't know. What's the one thing a rape victim fears the most?" East asks.

"Six seconds." Julian announces urgently.

"Move!" Diana shouts, suddenly jumping into action.

She makes us move away from Key. She then kneels down beside her. The rest of us rush to the basin to see what's happening; the black bird falls on its back. Its eyes are closed and its wings show only slight movement. The bird is going to die.

"Key, listen to me. I know what she told you. And she lied to you," Diana tells Key.

"Five seconds," Julian says.

"She said you deserved to be raped because you're high, but she was wrong, no one deserves it," Diana cries.

"Four seconds."

"She's the reason you're locked in there. She's the fear. You have to destroy her!" Diana shouts.

"Three seconds."

"YOU DIDN'T DESERVE TO BE RAPED AND NEITHER DID I. YOU WILL GET THROUGH IT. YOU WILL GET THROUGH IT. BUT FIRST YOU HAVE TO KILL HER. KILL HER!" Diana screams.

Just as the black bird takes its last breath, Key picks up a sharp stick that's beside her, leaps to her feet, and plunges it into the center of her "past" self. Everything goes dark. The bird is dead.

Racked with worry, we turn to Key's body lying on the living room floor. We don't know if she got out in time. We watch her with bated breath to see if she has come back. There is no movement. Key is perfectly still. No one says a word. We just look at her and silently beg Omnis not to take her from us.

I look over at Bex and the sheer heartbreak in his eyes is more than one should have to bear. Swoop's eyes are swimming in tears.

Please no...

Suddenly Key bolts upright and gasps for air. She latches on to Diana and sobs in her arms.

"It's okay. It's okay," Diana whispers.

"She said it was my fault. She said..." Key cries.

"It's over. The past is gone," Diana replies, gently stroking Key's hair.

"It hurts," Key confides.

"I know. But it's not forever, promise," Diana replies.

And for the next few moments we watch a demon guide an angel out of hell...

***

We place Key in the guest bedroom and Diana gives her a mixture to help her Recharge. Julian promises that he will look after her and that the hard part is over. Key should be back to full strength in a few hours. I tell her that as long as she is able to resist her habit, she can rejoin the team.

"You guys need to get going," Key says in a light whisper.

"I know, but we just want to make sure you are really okay," Swoop says, taking her hand.

"I am, but Pry is not. So just leave me here and I will join you guys soon."

"Key is right. We need to go, now," I reply.

"I can stay with you while the team goes to talk to Noble. Then I can join them in the search for the Deed," Bex says to his girlfriend.

"I know you want to be here with me, but it really would help me rest knowing that the whole team is helping to find Pryor. Go," Key tells him.

"I think she's right. We need to get back to the mission, like right now," East adds.

"You look weak," Bex says to her.

"Yes, and I will look better when I rest. I will rest when you get the hell out," she teases him.

"Fine, I'm going," he says, giving her a kiss.

"Maybe I should stay," Swoop offers.

"No! Go. All of you," Key insists.

"Okay, get some rest," Swoop says as she kisses her twin on the forehead.

My cell phone vibrates and I pick up the call. I have a quick conversation with my dad and recount it to the team.

"No one knows where Bishop is, but according to the demons my dad has talked to, Bishop never works alone," I tell them.

"So he could have a partner?" East asks.

"Word on the street is he has an apprentice," I reply.

"Does Uncle Rage know who the apprentice is?" Swoop asks.

"No, but he's headed to meet a contact of his and he'll let us know as soon as he gets any info. In the meantime, we need to be in the air headed for Noble," I order.

Bex turns to Key, whose eyes are nearly shut. The mixture is working. Soon she will be knocked out. The look of concern on Bex's face is undeniable.

"Julian will text you updates on Key every half hour," I promise him.

"My wife will gladly fuss over her. She loves taking care of people. Don't worry about it," Julian says.

He nods and agrees to come with us, as does Swoop. As they say their last good-byes, Julian takes me aside.

"You know why I'm not worried that my granddaughter is missing?" he asks.

"Actually no, I don't," I admit.

"Because I know your father. He's a wrathful fucker. And your mother may have been an angel but I have seen her in battle; she was ruthless when she needed to be. So I'm not worried because I know you inherited all these traits from them. I'm not worried because I know you will do whatever it takes to get my grandchild back. Am I wrong?" he asks.

"No, you're not wrong. I will find Pryor. No matter what," I promise him.

"Good. And if someone needs to die to make that happen, angel or demon, do not hesitate. Do you hear me?"

"Absolutely."

As Julian walks away, in my mind's eye, I picture the powerful Guardian he used to be. I picture him fiercely defending the angel and human worlds from evil. I wonder if he misses it. I wonder if he ever longs to have his wings back…

Relieved that things are squared away with Key, I text Noble and let him know we are ten minutes away. Then, I look outside the window and I see Diana standing in front of the house. I walk out and stand beside her. She focuses on the passing cars and although she's next to me, she seems a million miles away.

"Is everything okay?" she asks.

"Yeah, the team is saying good-bye to Key. They should be out in a few minutes. Then we can head to Noble and find out where the Deed is," I tell her.

"Good," she replies simply, without turning to face me.

"You did an amazing job in there. You saved her life—again," I reply.

"She'll be okay. The Soak will give her all the strength she needs to resist her addiction," Diana replies.

"Why didn't you tell me?" I ask gently.

"I didn't want you to think of me as weak."

"You are a lot things, Diana. Weak is not one of them."

We had these incredible nights and made it through some really close calls. We lived in the moment and it was exhilarating. We made love in exotic places and broke nearly every rule there was. Being with her was like getting caught in a cyclone. It was crazy, dangerous, and all consuming.

And back at Julian's place, Diana showed so much courage in baring her soul. I knew she had a softer side, but I didn't know to what degree. She really amazed me. Not just me but the entire team.

So why aren't you two together?

Because the girl I want, the girl I've always wanted, is Pryor. Because I love Pryor so much I can't bear the thought of a world without her. The whole time I was going around the world with Diana I wondered about Pry.

I wondered if she had laughed that day or if someone had hurt her. I worried that her life as a Noru was getting more and more difficult. And she needed me and I wasn't around. Worse, I worried she didn't need me.

I would see her smile on the surface of the things she loved like rivers and stained glass windows. She had a way of creeping into my heart and occupying every corner of my brain. I remember kissing her for the first time; I remember it so well…

Anxiety starts to build when I think of what could be happening to her right now. I hear her screaming in my head. Then I start to question all my decisions. Should we have waited so long to get to Noble? Was it right to stay with Key? What if we are too late? What if Bishop pushed Pryor beyond her breaking point? Dear Omnis. What if Pry is in the White Room right now?

The horrors of the White Room come back to me. Things at The Center were bad, but when they put me in the White Room...that's what made me want to die.

"Silver, watch out!" Swoop says as I nearly collide into the Eiffel Tower.

"Are you okay?" East asks.

"Yeah, let's speed up," I order.

The team does as I say and five minutes later we land in a cobbled street just off the main road. We read the numbers on the buildings, looking for Noble's lab.

"Got it!" East says as he gets off his Port and heads for the blue oak door with complex carvings and clear see-through paneling on the side.

"We can't just walk in there," Bex tell us.

"You think Noble could have a trap set for us?" Randy asks.

"I don't know, but it's better we be ready for anything," Bex replies.

"He's right. Swoop, you take the roof. Bex and Diana enter through the side. Randy—"

"No, you're not containing me inside a Holder," Randy says adamantly.

While Randy protests, East looks through the side panel of the door into Noble's home.

"Seriously, why can't I come with?" Randy asks.

"It could be dangerous, you know that," Swoop reminds him.

"I don't think The Face would send us to her son if he was as deranged as his father; she's on our side," Randy counters.

"You can't be sure," Bex says.

"I'm not going in a Holder in order for us to meet with an angel; a demon, yes, but an angel? C'mon!" Randy insists.

"Randy, get in the damn Holder!" I demand.

"That won't be necessary," East says.

"Easton, we don't know Noble. He could still be working for his father. He could have a trap for us," Bex snaps.

"Noble can't hurt us; he's dead."

CHAPTER THIRTEEN
I WILL LEAD THEM

We enter the hallway of the lab and find the half angel lying face up on the staircase with his eyes frozen. The last sight Noble saw was the ceiling of his lab. Someone had blasted him with a Powerball in the center of his chest. He's been dead for a while now.

"Fuuuuuuuuuuuck!" I scream as I kick in the door and storm out.

The rage that grips me is impossible to control. I'm seething with anger and can't keep my hands from shaking. Without warning, my palm is engulfed in flames. I hurl fireballs at the empty shops on the street and the windows blow out one by one.

"Silver, stop it!" Bird yells.

"ARGH!" I scream and set yet another building on fire.

"Silver, I know how hard this is, but you have to remain calm," East says.

"This situation isn't hard, East; it's impossible!" I correct him.

"I know, but you still need to remain in control," he replies.

"Noble was our only lead. Our ONLY lead!" I shout.

"Who do you think killed him?" Randy asks.

"Bishop may have taken him out," Swoop says.

"You think he'd take out his own son so that we don't find the Deed?" Bex says.

"If his dad is anything like mine, yes," East says.

"I don't care who took him out. What matters is that he's gone and we are no closer to Pryor," Bex snaps.

"She's been at The Center for hours…" I say to myself.

"Silver, we'll find her," Randy says hopefully.

I know Randy is trying to help; they all are, but it's no use. I know what Pryor is facing. I know she's being introduced to the agony that no angel ever thought possible. And she's facing it all alone. And for the first time since this ordeal began, I am forced to deal with the truth; we may not get to her in time.

This is all happening because I allowed myself to get close to her.

I have tried to keep the guilt at bay because I know it won't help to bring her home. But now the tidal wave of blame is coming. It has been hanging in midair for hours and now it finally crashes down on me.

I sit down on the nearest steps and place my head in my hands. The voices of my team members start to fade. The streets, shops, and humans all fall away in my mind. It's just my guilt and me now.

I promised myself that no matter what, I would protect her. I stayed away so that she could be safe. I returned in order to save her from a fire a few months back, but all I ended up doing was placing her in even more danger.

I should have stayed away. I should have never kissed her. I should have known that once I felt her lips on mine, I would never be able to pull away. Now she's facing the worst moment of her life and it's because of me. I didn't just make a promise to myself that I would keep Pryor safe. She doesn't know it, but I made a promise to her father, Marcus.

He came to see me before the incident in the alley with Key. I was getting into trouble even before then. I was skipping school, blowing off training sessions, and getting into fights with just about everyone.

I was such an asshole at the time. I was angry because my mom was taken from me and I never even laid eyes on her. I was angry that my father grieved for her and felt like he wished he had her with him instead of me. I was angry at—the world. The scene with Marcus plays in my mind as if it just happened.

That day, I was in the garage out back of my dad's house, working on my motorcycle and ditching yet another day of school. My father was out of town, so ditching was a no-brainer for me. I didn't hear the First Guardian enter until he spoke.

I looked up from the concrete floor and saw him standing over me. Marcus Cane was tall, with powerful wings and seriously intense eyes, and was without a doubt one of the most imposing angels on earth. Everything about him demanded your attention. He walked like a leader and spoke like someone who had faced and defeated death repeatedly.

"Shouldn't you be in school?" he asked.

"I'm sick," I replied sarcastically as I got up from the floor and wiped the grease from my hands with the towel rag on my shoulder.

"Yeah, you're on death's door," he quipped.

"My dad's not home. He's away on a mission," I replied, hinting that there was no reason for him to be there.

"I know; I'm the one who sent him," the First Guardian informed me.

"Then what do you want?" I asked.

"I'm here because I need you to do two things for me—two things that at first may sound contradictory. Yet I need you to do them both. And be exceptionally good at both."

"Well, I have a long list of stuff to do, so maybe you can check back with me in a few months. Or better yet, try someone else. I don't know if you've heard, but lately I've been more demon than angel," I countered as I headed over to the nearby cart filled with tools.

"The two things I need from you, only you can give them to me," Marcus said.

"Then you're shit out of luck," I replied.

Before I understood what was happening, Marcus had lifted me up by my neck and effortlessly pinned me to the wall. I didn't want to show it at the time, but I was scared shitless. The Guardian looked up at me with a stern, hard glare. And when he spoke, his voice was calm yet deadly.

"You are my best friend's only son. Your mother was my second in command and saved my life more than once. That is why I won't rip your damn soul out and hurl it onto the sidewalk. But you ever speak to me in that disrespectful tone again it will be the very last thing you do. You got it?"

"Yeah," I mumbled.

He looked at me angrily for another moment and released me. I gathered myself and started putting the tools away. I was raging inside and started contemplating attacking him. But I knew it was foolish. For one thing, he could outmaneuver me, and while I was Noru, I wasn't yet powerful enough to take on the legendary Marcus Cane.

Also, Marcus and my dad were best friends. And while he's pissed off now, Marcus has always been there for my dad and me. His whole team rallied around us to make sure we were not only looked after but also protected.

Lastly, there was the matter of his daughter, Pryor. A girl I had been unable to get out of my mind. I didn't know anything about girls at the time, but I knew attacking her father wasn't the way to go.

Marcus took a moment to compose himself while I placed the tools in their rightful place. When the leader spoke again, his tone and facial expression had softened.

"You're just like your mother," he said with a hint of wonder.

"How's that?" I asked.

"You both could bring out anger in me. I think it's because I care about you both," he admitted.

I shrugged my shoulders and pretended to be uninterested. The truth was I was always curious about the First Guardian and my mom. I knew they dated, but I never got the full details. Whenever the subject came up all anyone would say was that my mom ended up with my dad because that's what was supposed to happen.

I've looked at them closely when they hung out and there didn't seem to be any animosity between my dad and Marcus, although they were both in love with my mother before she was killed.

"Aaden, I know things are hard for you right now. I've heard about the countless fights and your repeated outbursts. You father even asked me if he should leave the team so he can look after you full time," Marcus said.

"What? No, he doesn't need to do that," I replied.

"That's what I told him. The simple fact is you have decided to allow what others think of you guide your actions and that's an asinine thing to do. Rage leaving the team to be with you like you're a toddler isn't going to help because in the end, the only angel who can help you is you," he said.

"Yeah, well I guess I'm just born to lose," I countered, shrugging my shoulders again.

"No, Aaden, what you are is the second most powerful angel that ever lived. You are spiraling out of control because you are looking to the world to tell you who you are. You're a teenager, so I guess you can do that. Hell, it may be your right to do that."

"So you came here to tell me I'm great at screwing up and good going?" I asked sardonically.

"No," he said, suppressing a smile.

"Then what is it?" I asked.

"I came to tell you that while you have a right to do the whole 'finding yourself' thing, you don't have a right to inflict your inner turmoil on the ones that love you. Namely my daughter," he said, returning to his serious voice.

"What? I haven't done anything to Pryor," I replied, taken aback.

"Your reckless actions and out of control behavior colors everything she does. She's worried about the path you're headed on," Marcus informed me.

"Pryor is worried about me?" I said before I could stop myself.

"Yes, Aaden, we all worry about you because we love you and because you're important to us; all of us. But you are especially important to Pryor."

"Oh…" was all I could think to say.

Then I started thinking of all the times I dreamed of being with Pryor. Could it be she was thinking about me too? Did she have feelings for me? What were they? Was it just surface bullshit or the real thing?

I wanted to ask Marcus, but I knew he wouldn't go into details with me. And besides, it's weird talking to her dad about that stuff.

"I didn't come here to watch you zone out and daydream about my little girl," Marcus said, pulling me out of my thoughts.

"No, I wasn't thinking…"

"Aaden, I'm here to tell you that I think you will be an amazing second in command one day. You will be a force to be reckoned with in battle and in the Angel world."

"You really think that?" I asked.

"Yes, I do. But for right now, while you still insist on being out of control, I need you to do something for me," the leader said.

"What?"

"Stay the hell away from my child," Marcus warned.

"I'm not good enough for her?" I snapped.

"No one is good enough for her. I'm her father; it's my job to make sure she ends up with the angel who comes the closest to deserving her. And some day that may be you. I can accept that. But right now, you're a raving lunatic with more rage than direction; a weapon with no aim. And while I love you, I will not let you take my daughter down the wrong path."

"You want me to stay away from her. Got it. Anything else I can do for you?" I asked tightly.

"Yes, I want you to look out for her," he replied.

"What? But you just said—"

"I know what I said. You need to stay away from her because you haven't found your way and I will not have her get lost with you. But I need you to also promise me that no matter what happens, in life or in battle, you will look out for her from afar. You will protect her," Marcus said with growing desperation.

"Pryor is more powerful than I am. Why would she need my help?" I inquired.

"You have been around more than she has. Because you've been exposed to the Demon world and Pryor has been sheltered."

"Whose fault is that?"

"Trust me, Pryor can hold her own in battle. But there are things that can't be learned in training sessions or in school. She has a very strong sense of right and wrong and while her mother and I love that about her, it's also her weakness. She's young. She doesn't know just how cruel the world can be. But you do. You've lost your mother and you face scorn from both the Angel and Demon worlds. You've lived more than she has."

"So?"

"So, I need you to keep a watchful eye on her should her mother and I be unable to look out for her for whatever reason. I know she's the First Noru. I know how powerful she will grow to be. But no matter how strong and skillful she is, no matter how much power she wields, she's always going to be my little girl. And I need to know that she is being looked after," Marcus said with concern.

"Why do you trust me to do this?" I asked.

"Because I've seen how your father is when he's in love and I know you will be the same way."

"Love? I didn't say I—"

"Aaden, the first fight you got in was when you were three and the kids teased Pryor about her hair color. The first time you used a Powerball was to incinerate a wayward ball that was headed straight for her. And last week you damn near yanked another guy's wings off because he attacked Pryor."

"He had no right to touch her."

"Aaden, it was a training session," he reminded me.

"He was too rough on her."

"Believe me, I know what it feels like to want to keep the ones you love from pain. That's why I want you to promise me that you will look after her."

"What makes you think Pryor would want me looking out for her? You know how she is," I reminded him.

"Yes. She's stubborn, willful, and unyielding. She won't like you watching out for her. She hates being protected and does a great job at being independent. She trains harder and longer than any other angel her age. She's constantly pushing herself to be stronger, faster, and better."

"Exactly. She'll push away anyone who tries to look out for her," I said.

"Not you; she won't push you away."

"And why not?"

"Do you know what a Kaiden is?" he asked.

"Yeah, it's the markings a woman gets when she's pregnant," I said.

"Yes, and when the markings light up, it's because the baby is in the presence of someone it loves and is connected to."

"I don't understand," I confessed.

"Since the moment Pryor was conceived, she has been surrounded by love from everyone: the members of the team, the other Noru, her grandfather, her mother, everyone. Yet the markings on my wife's arms only lit up for two people: you and me."

"It could be a coincidence," I replied, still processing what the leader told me.

"It could be, but it's not."

"So you think Pryor and I are meant to be together?" I asked, trying to keep the hope out of my voice; I failed.

"Look, I'm not here to discuss Pryor's dating life. She's thirteen years old. She is not going to date for a long, long, long time," Marcus said in a not-so-subtle tone.

"You're here to tell me to watch out for her and keep her safe no matter what?" I confirmed.

"Yes, will you do that?" he pushed.

"Yes."

"I have your word as a Noru?"

"Yes."

"And what about the second part?" he asked.

"The part where I keep away from her? Yeah, fine, whatever," I countered.

"Look, I know I sound harsh and believe me I don't want to be like my wife's father, Julian. He put us through hell when Emmy and I tried to be together."

"I heard he was a real dick."

Marcus glared at me. I sighed and apologized for my language.

"Looking back I get why he did the things he did. It wasn't about him hating me; it was about him loving her. He wanted to protect her from the Angel world," Marcus said.

"Are you saying Julian was right to do all the things that he did back when you and your wife first met?"

"I'm saying I'm a father now and I think Julian showed great restraint by not driving a dagger through my chest when I took his only child to Hell with me. I'm also telling you that I do not have the same restraint. And if you come near my Pryor before you become the man she needs you to be, you and I will have a very serious problem," he said unequivocally.

He started to exit the garage and I called out after him.

"I was always going to look after her. She's important to me. I'm gonna be there for her," I vowed.

"You might want to start by being there for yourself and taking your ass back to flight training," he said as he walked away...

***

From that day on I skipped out on a lot of things, but never a training session. It was imperative that I be ready should she ever need me. At the time I thought if I had enough training and honed my powers, it would be enough to keep Pryor safe. I had no idea how wrong I was...

"We called The Face, she's coming to see to her son's body," Swoop says as she sits on the step next to me.

Her voice pulls me out of my flashback with Marcus. The team now gathers around me waiting to hear what my orders are; I wish I knew.

"His mother sounded so strange. Like she was on autopilot," Diana says.

"Everyone handles grief differently," East replies.

"I know The Face is hurting and we would like to help, but we have our hands full. And anyway, there is nothing we can do for her," Bex adds.

"I agree. We have to stay on task. We have to find the Deed," I reply.

Suddenly we hear a voice coming from the top of the building. A Para angel stands looking down at us. It's Hollander and a few other Paras whose names I don't know but have seen around.

Hollander orders the ones who are with him to stay on top of the roof while he gracefully flies down to where we are. He looks good considering a few hours ago I almost ended his life. His wings have repaired well, and judging from the look on his face, he's enjoying this moment. As I said before, Hollander is in charge of the Paras until Bex decides he wants to be Kon, or king, as the humans would call it.

"Look, I know you want me to come back to the Paras, but we have some important things to do so I can't leave now," Bex snaps at the Para before him.

"Your search for Pryor has been unsuccessful I gather," he says.

"How do you know about that?" Swoop asks.

"Do you really think there are any secrets in the Angel world? I forget how young your team is, Silver," he quips to me.

"Not too young to rip your damn wings off," Diana counters.

Hollander summons up a Powerball and aims it at Diana. Without any encouragement from me, the whole team places themselves between Diana and the impeding attack. This surprises us, most of all it shocks the hell out of Diana.

"It's fine, I actually didn't come here to fight. I came to help," the Para angel says.

"Why would you help us?" I ask.

"Because I am a very kind angel," he replies.

"Try again," I demand.

"Okay, okay, I can admit I'm not a big fan of the Noru. But can you blame me? It's simply too much power in one place. However, I did come to provide you with information you might find useful," Hollander says.

"What is it?" Bex asks suspiciously.

"I know you're looking for the Deed. And that it will lead you to the location of The Center," he says.

"And how do you know about The Center?" East pushes.

"We Paras have nothing to do with that place; however, there have been rumors that it's become somewhat radical in its objectives. That being said, I know where you can find the Deed," he replies.

"And you're going to tell us, just like that?" I ask.

"Well…there is a little something I want in return. After all, Silver, you weren't very nice to me earlier today. In fact you were very rude, you know, when you tried to kill me."

"If I really wanted to kill you, Hollander, trust me, it would have been a done deal," I assure him.

"What do you want in exchange for the location of the Deed?" Randy asks.

"The human gets right to the point. I like that."

"Get to it, Hollander. What do you want in exchange for the location of the Deed?" Bex says.

"I want to be in charge—permanently," he says.

"What the hell are you talking about?" I ask.

"I'm tired of being the Kon while some little boy plays school games with the Noru. I have more than proven myself. I think it's time we make my position official."

"You want to be the Kon?" Swoop asks.

"Yes, I deserve to lead the Paras. Far more than Bex does. So, if Bex agrees, I will tell you where to find the Deed and save Pryor."

"Hollander, you are out of your fucking mind. Bex can't give up his birthright," I shout.

"I have done an outstanding job as Kon. I have lead the Paras in these troubled times and I should be the one to guide us, not Bex," Hollander shouts.

"You can't even be Kon, you have to be born into it," Diana replies.

"Well what you don't know, demon, is that if a Kon feels he is unable to lead for any reason, he can give his title to anyone he chooses so long as a majority of Paras on the Board of Paras agrees. There are ten of them; I polled them and most agree that I should lead. Now all I need is for Bex to step aside," Hollander informs us.

"So long as Bex's mother is still in power, you would have to get permission from her," East says.

"No, as of today, Bex's mother has been stuck in the light and has not stepped foot on Earth for ten weeks. That automatically means she is inactive as a Kon—the power now reverts to Bex."

"Hollander, you can't do this! Bex cannot lose leadership of the Paras. He has been groomed to take over since before he was born. He trained to lead; it's his right to rule and you know it," Swoop says.

"This is bullshit! You're putting us in an impossible situation. You know Bex can't give up everything he's ever had just to get one piece of information from you," I snap.

"And how did you come by that information anyway?" Randy asks.

"You are human and I am sworn to protect you. But you would be wrong to assume that means you can speak to me any way you like," Hollander warns.

"You can't do this. Bex isn't going to give up his entire kingdom and you know that!" I yell, close to throttling him.

Soon all of us are engaged in a very heated battle of words that is close to becoming an actual battle. In all the noise and hysteria, Bex makes an announcement but we are too loud to hear what he said.

"ENOUGH!" Bex shouts.

This time we all stop talking and face him. Bex addresses Hollander with certainty and resolve.

"Yes, I will give up the Para kingdom."

CHAPTER FOURTEEN
ONCE A KING

We take Bex aside and try to talk some sense into him, but right away I get the feeling he is resolved to give away the very thing he loves the most. We remind him that so far Hollander has proven to be untrustworthy at best.

"Do you think I want to do this?" Bex asks.

"There has to be another way for us to get the location of the Deed," Randy offers.

"Maybe there is, but the fact is we don't have time to find it. We need to go get Pry and it needs to be now," Bex replies.

"Have you even thought about what it would mean for the Paras if they are officially led by Hollander?" East asks.

"He's an ass, but at the end of the day he wants what's best for the Paras," Bex replies.

"What's best for them is to be ruled by their rightful king and not this power hungry jerk off!" Swoop snaps.

"Look, I want to find Pryor too, but something feels wrong about giving away your birthright to this guy. Everything about him says 'madman' or 'madPara' in this case," Randy argues.

"You guys are acting like I have a choice, but I don't," Bex snaps.

"I don't think Pryor would want this for you. She wouldn't agree with what you're doing," Randy pleads.

"Well, she's not here. She's off somewhere facing the worst nightmare imaginable. So while this isn't my preferred route, it's the only one that leads to saving her," Bex counters.

"I don't know if you are doing the right thing or not, Para, but whatever you decide, it needs to be right now, as in this second. Standing here debating is stupid and counterproductive." Diana says.

"She's right. Bex, I won't order you to give your birthright away. The decision is up to you. But you should know that being led by Hollander could have some serious consequences later," I tell him.

"I will deal with that later. Right now is all I can think about. And right now, we need to find Pryor. Nothing else is more important than that; not my title or my life. Pryor comes first."

It's not what he says but the tone with which he says it that renders the rest of us silent. There is nothing we can say to stop Bex from giving Hollander control of the Paras. So we all reluctantly agree and head back to Hollander. Once we tell him the news, he smiles broadly and tells Bex he's making the best decision for his people.

"Can we just get on with this?" Bex says.

Hollander signals for the other Paras to join him on the ground. They encircle Bex, holding out their hands, and a small orb takes form in the center. Bex holds out his hands and the orb slices into his palm. It then travels up to Bex's wings and makes its way down his body.

"What's it doing?" Randy whispers to Swoop.

"The orb cut into Bex's palm to ensure that there are no mixtures in his blood, forcing him to relinquish his birthright. It then goes into his wings to make sure he's really the Kon and has a right to give away the Para kingdom," she replies.

The orb makes a glowing trail as it rotates around him. Every time it completes a full circle, Bex gets weaker and the symbol on the back of his neck starts to fade.

"The symbol of the number '8' sideways is like the infinity sign, right?" Randy asks East.

"Yes, it's the symbol for a Kon. In the center of the '8' there are three markings. One for each member of the Council: Time, Death, and Fate," East tells him.

Randy studies the markings on Bex's neck closer and sees the symbols. He watches, mystified, as the markings continue to fade from Bex. By the time the once king of the Paras falls to the ground from having the orb drain his powers, the markings are gone.

"The location of the Deed is inside," Hollander says as he gets down to the ground and places a flat see-through coin in the palm of Bex's bloody hand.

"What is that?" Randy asks East.

"It's called a Plate. The contents inside will gather and form a word or symbol giving us the location of the Deed. Plates are ideal to use because they will only reveal the answer to a designated being; in this case, the answer will only appear in Bex's hand," East informs Randy.

"It's been a pleasure, Bexington," Hollander says, calling the Para by his full name.

The rest of the Paras fly off and follow the guy who will soon be their new leader. We help Bex off his knees.

"I'm fine, I'm fine," he snaps as he shrugs us off.

He straightens himself out and tries to act as if what has taken place is nothing major. But all of us know better.

"I can fix your hand," Diana offers.

"No, it's fine," Bex says.

"Yes. Let her fix it," Swoop replies.

Bex is about to argue but then thinks better of it and holds his hand out. Diana uses a small blue colored vial and Bex's wounds disappear almost instantly.

"Thanks," he says, avoiding eye contact.

Suddenly Swoop embraces Bex tightly. Bex is taken aback by this and stands shocked for several seconds.

"This isn't *me* hugging you; this is me hugging you for Key. She would do this if she were here, so I'm filling in," Swoop says as she continues to hold him. He embraces her back. We try and look away to give them some sort of privacy.

"Okay, let's find this Deed thing and go get Pryor," I say once Bex and Swoop are done.

Bex looks into the Plate and waits as the information gathers in the form of smoke inside the clear coin.

"Okay, so where is the Deed? Bex, tell us," Randy says impatiently.

"Oh no…" Bex says.

"What? Did Hollander trick us? I swear to Omnis if there is nothing inside the Plate, I will kill him," I vow.

"No, he didn't trick us. We have the location of the Deed," Bex says in an uneasy voice.

"Well, where the hell is it, Para?" Diana demands.

"Mercy Island," Bex replies.

"That's good, right?" Randy asks.

We all look at each other with growing dread. Randy studies our faces and is baffled.

"I was waiting for Bex to say something like 'No Survivor Lane' or 'Good-Luck-Finding-Your-Teeth forest,' but 'Mercy Island,' that's gotta be good, right?" Randy says, filled with hope.

"'Mercy Island' is an ironic term, Randy," East says in a grim tone.

"Of course it is," Randy says, scolding himself.

"Mercy Island is—"

"Wait! I just need two seconds before I find out about the next hell that awaits us," Randy tells Swoop.

We wait a few moments as Randy composes himself. He takes a deep breath and silently curses our luck.

"Okay, I'm ready. Tell me about not-so-Merciful Island," Randy says.

"Many cycles ago, a group of angels had a falling-out with Omnis. The leader's name was Knox. Knox and his group were radical thinkers. They believed that Omnis should take away his greatest gift to humanity—free will," Swoop says.

"Why?" Randy replies.

"Knox and the others thought it was cruel to let the humans find their own way in the world. He argued that humans sucked at finding and maintaining peace. It was like they would constantly find things to wage war for: land, money, or worst of all, religion," East explains.

"Wait, Omnis is all about religion, right?" Randy asks.

"You don't get into the light based on what you believe; you get in based on your character," I tell him.

"Okay, so this Knox guy wanted to take away humanity's free will. I guess Omnis wasn't happy about that," Randy says.

"The most important thing Omnis ever created was humanity. It was perfect in that it was imperfect. Omnis loved to watch humanity learn and grow. He didn't want to take away the humans' right to choose goodness or evil. So he turned Knox and the other angels away."

"Knox was certain that if Omnis knew what humans were like when they followed blindly, he'd agree to it and take free will away. So the group rounded up five hundred humans and took them to a small island off the coast of Spain. They administered a mixture called 'Mercy' to all five hundred humans," Swoop says.

"Did the mixture work?" Randy wonders.

"It was too potent. Making mixtures for humans is very delicate because humans are very fragile," Diana adds.

"Something went wrong with the mixture and the humans died ghastly deaths. Some were exsanguinated; some faced horrid disfigurement and loss of limbs before they died. A few of them were driven insane and took to cutting their own flesh off. And in one instance with a pregnant a woman, her name was Melinda, her fetus ate its way out of her belly and they both died shortly after," Bex says.

"Wow, that's...seriously?" Randy says, turning pale.

"Yes. When Omnis found out about the five hundred dead humans, he made a deal with Time, Death, and Fate," East says.

"Omnis made a deal with Pryor's mom?" Randy says.

"No, this was before Pryor's mom took over as Death," Bex says.

"Okay, so Omnis made a deal with the then Council members?"

"Yes, they agreed to allow the five hundred humans who passed away to live on even after death on the island. The five hundred souls had free reign to rule the island and face no consequences for their actions whatsoever," I reply.

"Then Omnis gave Knox and his group a choice. They could go to Difi, otherwise known as Hell. Or they could face the wrath of the now five hundred evil spirits that roamed the island, commonly referred to as Furies," East says.

"Knox and the others went with Mercy Island," Randy guesses.

"Yes; they were never heard from again," Swoop says.

"What?" Randy asks, once again baffled.

"Rumor has it the Furies tortured the angels beyond the point of madness and got them to kill themselves. But some believe that they kept them alive so that they could have the angels there to torture without end," Bex adds.

"Omnis allowed it?" Randy says.

"He deemed the island free of his control. There are no laws on that island. There are wicked, unnatural things that roam the woods, swamps, and dilapidated structures," Diana says.

"Mercy Island is what happens when there is no Omnis. It's Hell on Earth, literally," I reply.

"The Furies are vengeful, enraged humans who hate all things. Their one and only goal is to destroy life wherever it can be found," East tells him.

"The Furies got so out of control that they wanted off the island and out into the world. Omnis could not let that happen so he locked them onto the island with the largest Holder ever made," I explain.

"So Omnis placed them in a protective dome thingy that prevents them from getting out?" Randy says.

"Yes. The base of the Holder has a meter attached to it. It measures something you will never find in a Fury—inner peace," Swoop says.

"So as long as they are pissed off and unwilling to forgive, the meter will register their anger and keep them stuck on the island for good?" Randy asks.

"Yes, but so help whoever is stuck on that island with them," I reply.

"In this case us?" Randy says as he shakes his head.

"Yes, that is where the Deed has been placed," East says.

"Fine, let's go to Hell on Earth and get our girl back," Randy says bravely.

"Randy—"

"Don't think about it, Silver! You are not cutting me out of this. She's my best friend and I am helping," Randy declares.

I can think of a million reasons why allowing Randy to come would be a bad idea. For one thing, if he dies in the process, Pryor will have my head for taking him along. Bex senses my hesitation.

"Can you stay and look after Key for us? For me?" he asks.

"You know I love Key, but she's with Julian. She's in good hands. Just like you needed to sacrifice for Pryor, so do I. Please, guys, let me come. I can stay in a Holder, I promise," Randy vows.

"Fine, but we need to get going," I reply as we take to the sky.

"You said Mercy Island is in Spain, right?" Randy says.

"It was originally, but Omnis had it moved," Swoop says.

"Where is it now?"

"No one knows, Randy. It's well hidden," I reply.

"Silver, how will we find it?"

"We're going to ask an old friend for help."

***

Moments later we arrive in Atlanta, Georgia. We land behind the trees just off the main road. As we head down the winding path, we see a large yellow and white southern style home just up ahead.

The home boasts large pillars, a wraparound porch with a swing, and a six-piece white wicker patio dining set. The land in front of the house is filled with children of all ages. They play and run around without a care.

"Wow, what is that place?" Randy wonders as we get closer to the house.

"It's a group home for Quo children. It's run by Maybelle Harper," Swoop says.

"Who is she?" Randy says.

"Mrs. Maybelle is a Quo. She's half angel and half human," East says.

"And all attitude," Bex adds.

"She owns this place?" Diana asks.

"She owns property all over the world, thanks to her uncanny business sense. She owns a large Fortune 500 company, but her passion is kids," I inform her.

"What's her power?" Randy says.

"She is the finder of lost things," I reply.

"Great, why don't we just ask her to locate Pry for us?"

"Nice try, Randy, but Mrs. Maybelle can only find things, not beings," I tell him.

"So she can lead us to Mercy Island?" Randy asks.

"Let's hope so," I reply.

"I've heard about her, but I've never seen her face-to-face," Diana says.

"She's a real trip. She used to babysit Silver," Swoop teases.

"Really? So she knows some major embarrassing stories," Randy says mischievously.

"Hey, we are not here to socialize. We just need to get the location of the island and get going," I remind them when we draw near.

Standing in the middle of the lively group of Quo children is a tall, heavyset woman with licorice colored skin, dark brown eyes, full lips, and a bright smile. She wears a designer flower printed dress and has her hair pinned up in a mop of close curls. She sees me approaching and folds her hands across her ample bosom in dismay. When she speaks, she has a southern no-nonsense tone.

"Silver Case, don't you dare step foot in my home. I mean it, you take your wings and your no-good self and get on down the road…"

CHAPTER FIFTEEN
DEVIL'S TONGUE

Randy is shocked at Mrs. Maybelle's reaction to seeing me. He whispers in my ear that I was wrong about going to see a friend. I smile back at him and assure him that Mrs. Maybelle is not only a friend but also family.

"Mrs. Maybelle, I came a long way to see you," I reply with a smile.

Her cell phone rings and she holds up her hand, signaling for me to wait until she is done with the call.

"Mrs. Maybelle speaking," she says into the phone.

Her voice has lost about ninety percent of its southern accent. Her voice is official, strong, and certain.

"Mr. Warfield, I think we have made your company a fair offer given your current situation…the fact is your suppliers have backed out, your stock holders are calling for your head, and the SEC is closing in…I hear disdain in your voice, Mr. Warfield, and that's not acceptable. So as of now we are offering you fifty million dollars less than we did yesterday…yes, I am very serious. And Mr. Warfield, have an answer for me by the end of business today or we will pull out altogether," Mrs. Maybelle says.

She then calmly hangs up her cell and looks over at me.

"And why are you still in my front yard?" she asks.

"We know you can't stand Silver, but what about me? Do I have to go back too?" Swoop asks.

"Now, you know how much I love your behind. Come on up here, sweetness!" Mrs. Maybelle says to Swoop.

She hugs Swoop tightly; she does the same to Bex and East.

"Why do they get a big welcome and not me?" I ask.

"Cause I don't like you." She reminds me with a small smile.

"Well, I like you. In fact, I've really missed you," I reply.

"You ain't no damn good," she says, suppressing a smile.

"You know you missed me," I tell her.

"Aw hell, I been think'n bout you and your crazy self, come here," she says, embracing me.

I really have missed her. I didn't realize how much until I inhaled her flowery scent. Mrs. Maybelle is the closest thing I have to a mom. When my dad would leave me with her, it only took five seconds for me to get in trouble. But as many times as she scolded me, put me in the corner, or outright spanked me, I never doubted she loved me.

I could tell by the way she treated me. It didn't matter that I was half demon. Whatever the other kids had, she made sure I had the same. And when some of the kids refused to play with me because I was a demon, she'd cuss them out. Then she'd she let me follow her around and ask a million questions.

In the Angel world she is highly regarded as a caregiver among both angels and even demons. She never really took sides. If you were a kid then she protected you no matter what. Everyone had stayed with Mrs. Maybelle at one point for one reason or another. But I got to stay with her the longest, while my dad tried to deal with my mom's death.

I stayed with her for nearly a year when I was a kid. As happy as I was, I also missed my father greatly. She could tell that I was homesick so she called my father and I remember that conversation word for word.

"Thomas, I know you're sit'n up in New York City hurt'n cause you done lost the one you love. But you need to get your pretty demon ass up and come get this boy. He needs a daddy. So shake that shit off and come do right by him," she said.

It worked. From that day on, my father never left my side. I think he was a little afraid of her; most of us are. Mrs. Maybelle is and always will be the very definition of "no nonsense." She stands before me now, examining Randy and Diana.

"And who is this li'l boy and why ain't you all fed him?" she asks.

"This is Randy. He's human," I confess.

"Hi, Maybelle," Randy says.

"Maybelle? I am your elder; we did not go to school together, young man. You call me Mrs. Maybelle," she says.

"Yes, ma'am," Randy replies.

"Now who is this pretty face skinny li'l thing?" she asks, looking at Diana.

"Um…hi," Diana replies.

"How you do'n li'l bit?" she asks.

"Ah…I'm good," Diana says awkwardly.

Mrs. Maybelle studies Diana suspiciously. She then raises her eyebrows and opens her mouth as if she's about to ask a question. But then Diana looks back at her with pure panic. And Mrs. Maybelle decides not to say anything.

"What's that about?" Bex asks.

"No idea," I admit.

"Mrs. Maybelle, we need your help," Swoop says.

"Hey, if you can't play without your powers, Davey, I will take them away." She yells at a small boy using his powers to cheat at hide-and-go-seek by disappearing.

"Sorry, Mrs. Maybelle," the boy replies.

"He's just as crooked and shady as his damn daddy was," Mrs. Maybelle whispers to us.

"How long has he been with you?" I ask.

"Davey just got here; now I love him already, but he is sure 'nough try'n me. Just like you did."

"I wasn't that bad," I protest.

"I was tempted to sell your fresh behind to a band of demons the very first day you came here," she reminds me.

"Was Silver really hard to handle?" Randy asks.

"Hard don't even begin to cover it; he set my kitchen on fire twice. He kept using his secondary power and summoning things up out of midair. I walked in my living room and I would never know what I would find. One day he conjured up a pack of penguins. The next day he summoned up a forest. It ruined my hardwood floors. And there was also the time he summoned the crown of the Queen of England. Boy, were the humans mad about that," she says, laughing.

"What's the worst thing Silver has ever done?" Diana asks.

"Well, there was the time he ran away and tried to fly back to New York on his own. Can you imagine? His wings were so scrawny at the time he could barely make it past the front porch," she recalls.

"Where was he going?" Diana says as she joins in the laughter.

"He was going to find Pryor. Seems like ever since I knew you, you been chasing after that girl. Where is she? She didn't come with you all?" Mrs. Maybelle asks.

"No," I reply simply.

"What's going on?" she asks.

"Pryor is back home," I tell her.

"Boy, you bout as good at lie'n as I am at that Face-novel things the kids love."

"Mrs. Maybelle, it's called Facebook," Swoop corrects her gently.

"Whatever you call it, I ain't no good at it and Silver ain't no good at lie'n. Come on and tell me what happened to that little girl. I know things been bad since most of your folks are stuck in the light. Now the question is, just how bad have things gotten?" she says.

We explain the situation with Pryor. She listens carefully and her smile is replaced with worry and fear. I didn't want to tell her because I knew she'd react this way. She loves us and even though we are older now, still thinks of us as her kids, regardless of our age.

Mrs. Maybelle is about to lead us into the house. That's when one of the kids points to me and shouts "Noru!" All the other kids quickly clamber to get a look at the team. They ask us to demonstrate our powers and recount battles.

"Okay, okay, you all get back to playing, leave them alone. I'll call you all in when lunch is ready," she says to the kids.

All the kids go back to playing except one little boy who refuses to go away. Instead, he stands next to Bex. The boy is about three years old and he looks up at Bex as if he were a giant. Bex looks down at him, shakes his head, and crosses his arms over his chest. The little boy does the same. Bex heads for the house and the boy follows.

"Go play," Bex instructs.

"I am," the little boy replies.

"This is Kevin. He loves him some Paras," Mrs. Maybelle informs us.

"You're a Kon!" Kevin says excitedly.

"No kid, I'm not," Bex replies as he storms inside the house.

"Kevin, why don't you follow Bex and show him your best 'Para' moves?" Swoop says.

The boy runs and follows Bex inside. I know Swoop is trying to cheer Bex up, but I'm not sure the kid is the way to go about it. Mrs. Maybelle makes the rest of us take a seat on the porch as she goes into the house to get us refreshments. I think she's doing this to keep herself busy and not think about the news that Pryor has been taken.

"Is Bex okay in there?" Swoop asks when Mrs. Maybelle comes back onto the porch with a tray of drinks.

"Them two little knuckleheads are fine. Kevin is showing Bex how to 'fight.' He is just kick'n his little arms and legs in the air every which way. And Bex is try'n to keep a straight face."

"The light yellow glass has citrus calm flavored Coy, for the team," she says as she passes it out.

"What's the brown drink?" I ask.

"That's for the human; it's sweet tea. I know how these fools can get carried away with things and forget to feed the humans who accompany them," she says, furrowing her eyebrows at me.

"Thanks," Randy says as he takes the glass and brings it to his lips.

"And who's the last glass for—the green one?" Swoop asks.

"It's for li'l bit. She needs to drink it," Mrs. Maybelle says.

"What is it?" Diana asks.

"If I tell you what it is, I will have to tell you what it's for. Do you want to have that conversation here, now?" Mrs. Maybelle asks.

"No."

"I didn't think so. Now, go on and drink. Trust me."

Diana drinks the glass of green mixture and thanks her.

"Now how can I help get that little girl back?" she asks.

"We need you to help us find Mercy Island," Swoop says.

"Silver, you know it is no place for angels. It ain't no place for anyone," she warns.

"I know, but we need to get there. There's something on the island that will help us rescue Pry. You know I wouldn't ask if it wasn't important," I reply.

"I know…okay, I will do my best. But first I need you to do something for me," she says.

"Anything."

"Be careful. The more power you all have, the more folks want to destroy you. So make sure you make it on back," she says.

"We'll do our best," Swoop replies.

"Good, because I got lots of chores for you all to do around the house," she says.

We laugh, but she is serious. And I'm certain once this is all over, we will be back here fixing things and taking orders.

***

Bex manages to get Kevin to rejoin the other kids but only after vowing to return another day. Bex tries to act bothered by his "super fan," but we know better. He has a light in his eyes I have not seen him display since, well, since we last saw Pryor.

Before we get started, Bex calls and checks in on Key. He tells us she is still resting and according to Julian she is on her way to making a full recovery. We then gather in front of Mrs. Maybelle and watch as a greyish film grows over her eyes. A few moments later she opens her eyes and tells us we can find Mercy Island off the coast of Turkey. She gives us the exact coordinates; we thank her and start to leave.

"Hold on now, you can't just fly to Mercy Island without knowing what you are getting into," she calls out.

"The truth is, we simply don't have time to do any research on where we are going. We just need to get there," I reply.

"I called up a friend of mine, Harris, he has studied Mercy Island for years. He's obsessed with that damn place. He'll be here in a few minutes. He'll tell you everything you need to know. Here he is now," Mrs. Maybelle says.

"Good evening," the old man says as he appears behind us.

"Normally, I don't let him pop in and out of my living room—it's rude. But this is a special situation so I let him go on ahead," Mrs. Maybelle says.

The old man has intense blue eyes, snow-white hair, and wears a well-worn tan colored leather jacket. He's over six feet tall and very alert.

"Oh my Omnis, he could totally be an old-man version of Indiana Jones!" Randy says, barely able to contain his excitement.

"Who?" Swoop asks.

"Okay, that's it. When we get back, *everyone* is getting cable," Randy says, shaking his head.

"Harris, Mrs. Maybelle says you know something about Mercy Island," I say to the old man.

"Yes, but before I tell you what I know, quick question: What is it about your life that makes you want to end it?" Harris asks.

"We don't want to end our lives, but there's something very important we need to find on Mercy Island. It will allow us to rescue a friend of ours," Swoop says.

"Is your friend worth it?" Harris asks.

"Yes," we all reply, while Diana remains silent.

"Okay, if you insist. Here goes," the old man says as he unfolds a hand drawn map and lays it out on the table for us to study.

"Mercy Island is surrounded by a dense, dark forest with a swamp in the center. Getting through the woods is going to be your first problem."

"Why?" Randy asks Harris.

"The island itself is very much like a living thing. The ground, the air, the trees, everything is aware. The island will see you as an invader and it will protect itself by creating whatever maleficent force to destroy you."

"That's just like *Lost*," Randy says wondrously.

We all look at him blankly. He looks back at us and once again shakes his head in disbelief at our ignorance.

"Never mind," Randy says.

"Okay, so the woods are filled with evil. Can you get more specific?" Bex asks.

"We have no way of knowing what's in the woods because no one has ever come out of it," Harris says.

"Well, that's comforting," East quips.

"However, I have something that will help you along the way," Harris says as he hands me a rectangular box made of black leather.

I open the box and find a necklace with a ruby red, teardrop crystal pendent. In the center it has the symbol of Time, Death, and Fate. Swoop takes it from me and examines it.

"What does it do?" I ask Harris.

"It's called an Inka pendent. It's a virtual Wikipedia of demons and malevolent beings," Harris replies.

"That's amazing, how does it work?" Randy asks.

We look over at Diana and ask if she would be okay with being scanned by the Inka. She declines and says she hates gadgets. I agree to be scanned instead. Swoop points it towards me; a red laser beam shoots out of the crystal and scans my body. It then creates hologram of me in the air with all my biological information.

Subject: Aaden "Silver" Case

Species: Noru (Offspring of High Ranking Guardian. Only five in existence)

Hybrid: Half Akon (Demon), Half Guardian (Angel)

Abilities: Indestructible fire, object summoning, unparalleled strength.

Weakness: Unknown

"That's perfect! It'll give us a fighting chance. Thank you," Bex says.

"Bird, put it around your neck," I tell her.

"I don't know, Sliver. Can I see it in another color?" Swoop asks.

We turn to look at her. She shrugs her shoulders.

"What? It clashes with my outfit," Swoop points out.

"She's not wrong," East adds.

"This is the only one I have," Harris says in disbelief.

"Don't listen to them, thank you so much. We really appreciate this," I reply.

"I'm happy to help. Mrs. Maybelle is always talking about all of you. I feel as if I know the whole team personally," Harris says.

"Again, thank you for the Inka; combined with our powers we should have a fighting chance," I tell him.

"What are you talking about? You know the agreement the Furies have with Omnis, don't you?" Harris says.

"Yeah, Omnis allows them to run the island any way they want," Swoop says.

"Yes, and the one thing the Furies detest more than anything are angels. That's why the first thing they planted on the island was row after row of Devil's Tongue," Harris adds.

"Damn it!" Bex shouts as he grits his teeth.

"Um…what's Devils Tongue?" Randy asks.

"It's a tree that's been outlawed in the Angel world." Swoop replies in a sad voice.

"Okay, so the island is full of this tree. What does it do?" Randy adds.

"It makes this sap that seeps into the earth. If an angel steps on soil that has 'Devil Tongue,' their powers are taken from them," I reply, trying desperately to remain calm.

"Wait, wait one second. Are you saying this tree will render them all powerless?" Randy asks Harris with sheer terror in his voice.

"Human, the moment the angels step onto Mercy Island, they will be just as powerless as you."

CHAPTER SIXTEEN
JUST A GIRL

Hearing the news that we will all be powerless on Mercy Island does nothing to deter us. The fact is we need to find the Deed and we will face whatever we need to. I convey this to Harris. He looks back at us as if we are already dead.

Mrs. Maybelle warns him that if he doesn't help us by giving us whatever it is he has that may be helpful, he will have her to deal with. Like all of us, Harris is afraid of Mrs. Maybelle and agrees to help us even more.

"I've researched Mercy Island, and given the account of angels who swear they have flown near the area, the layout is simple enough," Harris says.

"How simple?" Bex asks.

"The Port will leave you and your team on the shore. Once you get there, there is a forest, a swamp, and finally a temple dedicated to the Queen of Furies, Melinda," Harris says.

"That's the one that lost the child on the island, right?" Mrs. Maybelle asks.

"Yes. It's the only place I could think of where someone would place something of value, because it's heavily guarded."

"Thank you. Is there anything else?" Swoop asks.

"Well, I'm not trying to get on Mrs. Maybelle's bad side, so here," he says, handing over three items from his leather pouch. The first is what looks to be a small flashlight.

"That's a handy little gadget I picked up a few years back. It's every weapon, all at once. It's called Gain. It's intuitive. If you need it to be a blade, it's a blade. If you need an axe…"

"Nice! How many do you have?" Diana asks.

"I'm sorry, I only have one," Harris replies.

"We'll make it work. Anything else?" I ask.

"Just this: that island will play tricks on your mind in ways you won't believe. Stay together and don't let your guard down for a second."

***

When we arrive on the shores of Mercy Island, the first thing I notice is the silence. I thought there would be howling and various growls from different parts of the island, but there isn't. Instead there is silence—a stark, heavy, unnatural silence that covers the entire island.

The steel grey sky above us is angry and violent. There's a chill in the air, the kind that goes deep into the marrow of your bones and makes you feel like you will never be warm again. Our Ports hover on the edge of the raging dark sea. The shoreline is rocky and surrounded by glass and bone. Ahead of us stands a dense forest of decrepit ash colored trees.

"The Port won't take us past this point," East says.

"I thought maybe we could navigate through the trees somehow so that we could avoid placing our feet on the ground, but East is right, we can't use the Port in the forest," I reply.

The team jumps off the Ports and lands on the jagged shore; the Ports then disappear.

"They are programed to come back as soon as we signal for them with the device Harris gave us," I tell Randy, who looks stricken once the Ports go away.

"Okay, what now?" Swoop asks.

"If Harris is right, the Deed will be on the other side of the island. And we can't get there without going through the forest," Bex says.

"Why is it always a creepy forest?" Randy asks, shaking his head.

"Could have been worse, could have been a cave," Swoop says, reminding him of his misadventure a few months back.

"That's not helping," Randy replies.

"Okay, I know Harris said our powers wouldn't work, but let's test them out anyway."

Everyone tries to use their powers but nothing happens.

"I thought at least you and Ruin would have some power," Bex says.

"Yeah, me too. I think the sap from the trees is far more powerful than Harris thought," Diana replies.

The wall of grey trees reaches high in the air. They are frozen in a series of twisted and cruel shapes. Some of them have gaping holes in their trunks that look like faces being tormented. Others have branches that seem to be pointing their fingers at us—inviting us to begin whatever foul fate awaits us.

"Swoop, keep the Inka pendent close so we can aim it at whatever comes at us. Bex, to my right, East, take the left. Swoop and Diana, let Randy stay in the middle so you can isolate him should anything happen. Randy, do not go off on your own, do not touch anything, and if something goes wrong, I need you to place yourself in the Holder. Got it?"

"Yeah, I got it; Randy to the Holder as usual," he quips.

We walk towards the forest, but we're unable to get in because thousands of black vines spring to life and form an impenetrable barrier blocking our entrance. In the center of the newly formed barricade is a three-headed serpent with unnaturally long fangs and a hiss that echoes throughout the island.

The three heads hiss and coil wildly around each other and then lunge wrathfully out at us. We quickly step back and are grateful to find that the beast cannot extend beyond a few feet. I signal for Swoop to aim the Inka at the wall of vines and the serpent. She follows my orders and soon a 3D image springs from the pendent and out into the air.

Subject: Forest of Ash & Bone
Current Image: Gideon Vine Barrier

Summary: A beast with the head of a snake and a body constructed entirely of vines. The vines cannot be cut as they will return, stronger.

Weakness: The only way to get past the barrier is to feed the beast. It hungers for that which is most precious to the traveler.

"The thing that's most important to angels are our souls so I guess that's what it wants. I'll do it," Swoop says, getting ready to place her hand out for the serpent to bite.

"No!" I reply, pulling her back from the creature's waiting three-forked tongue. It's not that simple, Bird. How do we know it won't keep sucking your soul until it kills you?" I ask.

"Silver's right. I'll have it feed on me. Even without my powers I should be able to fight it off," Bex says.

"No, I'll let it feed on me," I reply.

"You are half demon, Silver. It will need a full angel to feast on," Ruin suggests.

"How do you know?" East asks.

"The island and everything in it stems from a hatred of angels. Bleeding them dry of their soul is the best way to go. I think a full-on angel has to do this," she replies.

"That brings us back to me. I can do this," Bex assures me.

"Feed just one of them—that way you won't get drained too quickly," Randy suggests.

"Good idea. You ready?" I ask.

Bex nods, rolls up his right sleeve, and stretches his arm out for the snakes to feed on. He gasps as the middle serpent clamps down on his wrist and begins to drain the soul from his body.

"Okay, the moment the opening is wide enough, everyone get in as fast as you can."

"What about Bex?" Ruin asks.

"I'll stay and help him detach from the snake," I reply.

Slowly we watch as the light is being sucked out of Bex's body. He's shaking slightly and trying to stay focused, but it's hard because every second the snake feeds, Bex gets weaker and weaker.

"C'mon, c'mon, c'mon!!!!" I shout angrily to the vines that refuse to part.

"Maybe we were wrong. Maybe a soul isn't what is needed to get the vines to part," East says, panicking.

"It has to be. That's the most important thing to an angel," Swoop says as she licks her lips nervously.

Bex is starting to shake even more and the glow has gone from his face. He lowers his head in pain as the snake drinks and drinks his life force.

"Bex, you have to stop, this isn't working!" I yell.

"Wait, look!" East says.

We all turn to the wall of vines and watch as they begin to slowly separate. We shout at them as if that'll make them come apart faster. We tell Bex to hold on and that we don't have far to go. However, the truth is Bex is being drained at a much faster rate than the vines are parting.

"It's gonna kill him! Can't we help by pulling it apart now that it's already loosening up?" East asks.

"No, don't touch it. If you do they might close up again. You read what the Inka said. If you try and part it, it will grow back stronger!" Ruin says.

The team begins to argue as Bex faces immense pain and is brought to his knees. Among the chaos and back and forth, Randy manages to get our attention with the tone of his voice—fear.

"Hey guys, what is that?" he asks.

We follow Randy's gaze and look up. The sky has churned and is now forming a dark massive twister comprised of over a thousand demons.

"This can't be good, can it?" Randy says, terrified.

Swoop aims the Inka at the sky while we monitor Bex.

Current Image: Swarm of dark entity known as "A Calling"

Summary: An army of dark spirits with the ability to move in and out of hell. Often summoned by evil to eradicate large groups. Contact with these beings leads to certain death as they are poisonous to the touch.

Weakness: A Calling cannot penetrate the Gideon Vine barrier.

"We have to get inside the forest, now!" Ruin shouts.

"It's not wide enough. We can barely fit our hands in there, let alone our whole team," East snaps.

"More…" Bex says, signaling for the other two snakes to feed on his other arm.

"No, it'll kill you!" Swoop says.

"Guys, the 'Calling' thing um…it's moving really fast," Randy says, unable to take his eyes off of the sky.

"We have to go, now!" Ruin pleads.

"MORE!" Bex screams.

We have no choice. We place his other hand out and the other two snakes begin to feed on Bex as well. Bex is now on the floor screaming in agony as his soul is being taken from him. The vine starts to unravel a little faster, but by now the Calling is about to land on the shore.

"We have no way to fight it. We cannot be here when it comes!" Ruin shouts.

Bex mumbles something in the midst of his pain. I get closer to the ground to hear him. When I realize what he's saying, I adamantly refuse.

"What is it?" East asks.

"He wants us to cut open his chest so the snakes can have direct contact to his soul."

"That would kill him in ten seconds!" Swoops says.

"Seven seconds; trust me," Ruin admits.

"Here they come!" Randy shouts as the swarm of demons lands on the shore, all at the same time.

I take out the Gain again, and I will it to be a knife. I then carve it into Bex's chest. The snakes now have full access inside Bex's soul. The barrier opens wide, the dark spirits land, and Bex lies dying.

The spirits form a mob and crawl over each other to get to us. They surround us from every angle. I order everyone into the forest while I try to pry the snakes off of Bex's arms. The team argues that they want to stay with us, but I yell at them to do what I say. They run inside the barrier and call out for us to hurry.

Bex has lost consciousness, and according to Diana he now has four seconds. I pry two of the snakes off of Bex, but the middle one won't let go. I reach for the Gain to cut their heads off, but it drops on the ground and out of my reach.

"Shit!" I shout as Bex's only hope slips away from between my fingers and out of my reach.

"Three seconds!" Diana screams.

I manage to extend my foot far enough to nudge the Gain over to me. I pick it up just as Bex's life is about to be taken forever.

"Two seconds!" Diana yells.

In one swift motion the Gain becomes an axe and I hack the three heads off the serpent. Seconds later the snakes come alive again. I drag Bex's body with me as the barrier begins to close. But just as we are about to go all the way through the barrier, a demon reaches out for Bex's limp body.

Thinking quickly, Swoop grabs the Gain and it turns into a torch. She uses it to wave the flames in front of the demon. It does not kill him, but it enrages him and makes him go after Swoop. Thankfully the barrier closes and puts a wall of vine between certain death and us.

We are all weak with relief to be inside the forest. We hear Bex groan, so we know he's alive. We go over to help him but we halt suddenly when Swoop places the palm of her hand over her eyes and starts screaming. She falls to the ground writhing in pain.

"Swoop, what is it?" East begs.

"It hurts! It hurts!" Swoop cries out in torment.

"The spirit demon she attacked must have made contact with her eyes. I need her to be still so I can check," Diana tells me.

"Swoop, you have to stay still so we can take a look," I reply.

While Diana looks Swoop over, she orders East to get a mixture from her pouch and administer it to Bex.

"We can't be out here in the open like this. Randy, go find somewhere for us to hide. Somewhere close!" I order.

"Okay, be right back!" Randy shouts.

"Lucky the demon just brushed by her face, but it's still harmful," Diana informs me.

"How bad?" I ask.

"If we don't get her to stay still so I can extract the remainder of the poison, she could lose her eyes—permanently."

"Swoop, you're gonna be okay, but you have to let us help you. You have to stay still," I tell her.

She cries out and begs us to get the poison out from her eyes, but she's still moving too much.

"Damn it, Bird, please, please stop moving," I beg as I take her hand.

Diana places a drop from a dark vial into Swoop's eyes and reminds her not to move.

But Swoop is in too much pain to comply. She sends out a cry from the bottom of her soul. It seems to wake the forest up and call out to all the malicious creatures that dwell within it. We hear howling and moaning coming from different parts of the forest.

"East, is Bex okay?" I ask.

"Yeah, he's ... he's weak but he's alive."

"Good. Go find Randy and a place for us to hide—quickly."

Swoop calls out again, and Diana warns me that in the next few minutes, if Swoop does not stay still, she will lose her eyes for good. Swoop sobs as the pain continues to rip into her eyeballs.

"Silver...it hurts," she says, her voice so broken it's no longer recognizable.

"I know, Bird. I know, baby. But you have to do something for me, okay? You have to think of something else. Something better than this place. Please try; for me."

"I'm with my mom," Swoop says as she tries to calm herself down.

"Good, good. Where are you two?" I ask as Diana tends to her.

"Shoe shopping in Tokyo. She lets me try everything in the store. She laughs...when we buy the same pair...boots...My mom, she has the best laugh..." Swoop says as she starts to sob again.

Thinking of something else works. Swoop is still as Diana takes care of her. I hold her hand and vow not to let her go. Swoop is always so happy and energetic it's difficult to see her hurting. And even though she pretends like she has it all together, deep down she's still just finding her way. And with all the powers she has, she's still just a girl who really, really misses her mom.

Once Diana is done applying the mixture, she applies bandages over Swoop's eyes and tells us she needs to rest.

"How much time?" I ask.

"I should know more in about an hour," Diana says as she goes over to check on Bex.

East and Randy return and together we get everyone inside the nearest hidden refuge. In this case, it's a small cave hidden deep in the base of a large rock formation. As soon as we step inside, it starts pouring freezing rain. I sigh and shake my head in disbelief.

Sometimes, I'm really not sure whose side Omnis is on...

CHAPTER SEVENTEEN
THE FAMILIAR

The rain has turned into an all-out storm. The glacial wind whips through the trees, tearing the branches off and discarding them onto the ground. Lightning carves crudely in the sky and splits it open. And the thunder announces itself with a deep baritone voice.

There are times when I think I see a shadow moving outside the cave, but I can't say for sure. What I can say with certainty is that the Forest of Ash and Bone is arguably the creepiest place on earth right now.

There are mysterious sounds echoing throughout the island, making me miss the silence we faced when we first got here. I stand in front of the cave opening and spot movement from small creatures: creatures without names and in some cases without a face. They scurry around in fear of bigger darkness out to get them. Darkness that I know we will soon face.

Inside the cave, Swoop rests against the stone wall. East covers her with his jacket and Diana instructs her to keep her eyes closed until the mixture she placed on them turns into a clear paste. Right now it's a deep purple, and according to Diana, that means Swoop is not healed yet.

Bex, on the other hand, is recovering nicely. Had he not been a Para, I think he would have died back there. Paras have stronger souls than most angels. And even though Noru are more powerful than them, Paras' souls are very strong and durable. Bex isn't ready for a full-scale battle, but his wounds are healing, thanks to Diana's mixture, and he's able to walk around the cave.

"Could I really lose my eyes?" Swoop asks Diana.

All of us exchange a worried glance. Swoop is deathly afraid the mixture Diana used won't work. She has to wait for the mixture to change color and that wait is killing her.

"Your eyes will be fine, Swoop. Stop being such a baby. We need to focus on more important things—like what kind of cell phone plan I need to get in order to call my girl from here," East jokes.

We know it's an attempt on East's part to keep Swoop from worrying. She loves a good piece of gossip, and East knows she won't be able to resist the news that he has a girl.

"What girl? Who are you seeing, Easton? I want details!" Swoop demands.

We smile as Swoop finds a new focus.

"I'm seeing Marisol," East replies proudly.

"The cute girl in the hallway you blew our cover to?" Swoop asks.

"Yeah, I was supposed to Mind wipe her but I didn't—and before any of you say it, yes, I think I did the right thing. And no, I'm not wiping her mind," East says firmly.

"It's a shame, you just got a steady girl and now Pryor's gonna have to kill you," Bex says.

"I am not afraid of Pry. I will proudly admit to her that I disobeyed her orders and that I did not Mind wipe Marisol."

"So in other words, you're gonna text her what you did from an undisclosed location and then go into hiding?" Bex says.

"Exactly," East replies.

We laugh at the look of fear on his face. He starts to go through the countries we'd most likely get lost in where Pry could find him and give him her "Do what I say" stare.

"Okay, all jokes aside, East. How serious are you about Marisol?" I ask.

He takes out his phone and shows us the screen.

"You made her your wallpaper on your cell? Damn, that's commitment," Bex replies.

"She's just so great, you know? She likes to work with a bunch of different charities and she knows how to have fun and she's so courageous.

She stands up to people for the greater good. To quote her, she hates bullies."

I tell them about the fight I witnessed earlier, when East and Marisol were at the shelter.

"She sounds like my kind of girl," Swoop replies.

"Yeah, she's also been through a lot. Her mom died in a car crash when she was a kid. She was in the car too. She had to watch as they used the Jaws of Life to get her mom out. She told me her mother lived for ten whole minutes as the blood drained from her body...You would think after witnessing that she would be bitter, but she's not. She's a fighter. In fact, I'm pretty sure she's at a rally right now trying to save something or someone."

"Maybe she can start a rally to help put your wings back on when Pryor rips them off after finding out you didn't Mind wipe her," Swoop teases.

"She sounds great, East, but I can't believe you didn't wipe her. But then again, there's so much I don't get about you angels," Randy admits.

"Oh yeah, like what?" Swoop asks.

"Like how come you guys don't ever pee?"

The whole group starts laughing. None of us expected Randy to wonder about such a trivial thing.

"What? It's a fair question!" he counters.

"Anything else you don't get?" Swoop asks, trying not to laugh.

"I don't get how there's no traffic in the Angel world. I mean, don't a group of you guys ever head to the same place all at once? And if so, who has the right of way?"

"Seriously, human, what takes place inside your head?" Ruin asks, amused.

"I guess that's just who I am. I'm a nut. And there are things I will never, ever understand: like Bex. No matter how hard I try, I just don't get you," Randy admits.

"What don't you get?" Bex asks Randy, intrigued.

"Well, you seem kind of smart," Randy says.

I suppress a smile. Swoop and East exchange glances. Ruin looks down at the floor and shakes her head slightly as if she thinks this conversation may take a wrong turn. Bex studies Randy and waits for him to finish his thought.

"Never mind," Randy says.

"Randy, you have something to say; say it," Bex replies in a calm voice.

"Okay…I don't get how you could be so reckless and so stupid. You have this remarkable angel in love with you. And that's what Key is—remarkable. She's intelligent, kind, funny, and Omnis himself could not have made her any more beautiful than she already is. You are lucky enough to have her in your life and what do you do? You wreck her! You slice her heart open, watch her insides fall out, and then stomp on it. And you shouldn't have done that because Key's amazing. She's…she's just so…amazing." Randy concludes his heartfelt rant and no one is more surprised at his words than him.

Bex looks at Randy in a way that tells me I will have to run interference. But much to my surprise, Bex doesn't attack Randy. Instead he gets up and addresses me.

"I'm gonna scout the area," he says as he walks out into the rain.

I would have ordered him to stay with us, as splitting up in a place like this is dangerous, but I know if I don't let Bex take a walk, we will have Randy's blood all over the cave. I am very familiar with the look on Bex's face. It's the look a guy gets when he is trying really hard not to pull someone's spinal cord out with his bare hands. Every time I have seen that look on a guy's face, whether the guy was human, demon, Quo, or angel, it always involved a girl.

"Twenty bucks says Bex takes Randy out before the day is over," East says.

"I have fifty that says the Para will take him out before the rain stops," Diana replies.

"I'll get in on that," Swoop replies.

I shake my head and look over at Randy. I am also familiar with the look on his face. It's the look you have when you are supposed to regret doing something but you don't. And no matter how foolish or dangerous the move you made was, you'd do it all over again.

That's exactly the way I felt when I kissed Pryor for the first time. I try not to go back there in my head because it will only make it harder to focus. Yet try as I might, I can't stop the flashes from appearing in my head. Suddenly the team around me starts to blur and their voices fade. And in my mind's eye, I am back in my room with Pryor like we were before. She had come by my room and wanted to talk. What I did was brave but mostly risky.

"I lied before, when I said I didn't know what I wanted. I know exactly what I want. I just don't know if it's what you—fuck it," I said as I reached out and kissed her.

She pulled away. I stepped back, fearing I had upset her. Feeling like a complete jerk, I apologized for trying to kiss her.

"No, I want to kiss you. I'm just not sure how," she admitted.

Then she started blushing. Silver colored blood surfaced on her cheeks.

"Pryor, am I your first kiss?" I asked.

She bit her lower lip and looked off to the side.

"Oh," I replied.

"This is so embarrassing. I better go," she said.

"No, wait," I begged.

She turned back towards me. I leaned in and whispered softly in her ear.

"When you're kissing the right person, there's no way to do it wrong," I assured her.

Then I leaned in once again and pressed her lips to mine. I don't think I've ever felt such a rush before or since. Her touch stayed with me long after she left the room.

"So, how was your first kiss?" I asked.

"Better than I ever thought kissing you could be."

"You've thought about us being together like this?" I wondered.

"Only every minute of every day…"

A cold gust of wind enters the cave and brings me back to the present. I know I should not have let my mind wander—especially about kissing Pry.

The pain in my chest tightens and spreads throughout my body. The pain isn't just coming from the virus the Center placed on my chest. It's the genuine ache that comes with her absence.

Pry, what are they doing to you?

Suddenly I want nothing more than to leave the cave. It's as if getting away will somehow help me stop missing her. I know it won't, but still, I need to get out of here. I look over at the team; everyone is resting.

I inspect Swoop's wounds, and like Diana said, they are healing but the color has yet to return to Swoop's eyes. Bex has not returned, but I'm not worried because I can see him from where we are.

I head out into the rain and go far enough that I get some space to myself and yet I'm close enough I can run back should they need me. I sit on a large rock under a makeshift awning of leaves and branches. I don't know how long it is before she comes over to me, but I feel her before I actually see her.

"Diana, what is it?" I ask.

She tries to get out of the rain by coming under the awning with me. I make room for her to sit next to me and she tells me that Swoop should be ready to go in another half hour.

"That's great, thanks for taking care of her," I reply.

"No big deal," she lies.

"Diana, I know things can get crazy between us, but you know I care about you—a lot. Why didn't you tell me you were raped?" I ask carefully.

"It's not something I talk about—ever," she whispers.

"Okay, I get that. But I'm here. If you need me, I'm here," I reply simply.

"My family was taken from me. My grandmother died and my mom shortly after. They were my world. I bounced around from one place to the next. I finally ended up with a distant relative, a cousin who I had never met before. She was nice enough to take me in. It wasn't a big place, but I had my own room and I was thinking about going back to school."

"What happened?" I ask.

"Her fiancé couldn't stop looking at my breasts."

"I'm sorry."

"I tried to ignore it for as long as I could, but I knew it was only a matter of time before he acted on his urges. So I told my cousin."

"She didn't believe you?" I wonder.

"She did—at first. Then a few weeks later he convinced her that I came on to him. She kicked me out. I was homeless for a while, but it wasn't too bad. I found a way to make it work. I went to different shelters, worked odd jobs, I survived."

"Did you manage to find somewhere to stay permanently?" I ask.

"I found what I thought was my saving grace. I was working at a country club. I took out the trash and cleaned up for a few bucks. That's where I met Sebastian Jr. He was handsome, rich, educated, and for some reason he liked me. I felt like Cinderella. We dated for a few weeks."

"Did you love him?" I inquire.

"Yeah, at first I thought it was just because he had money, but as time went on, it was more than that. We laughed a lot and watched a million sunsets. He smelled like pine trees and fresh snow. I remember thinking I wanted to wake up to him every day. I remember thinking maybe I had found a new family of my own."

"Did he feel the same way?" I ask carefully.

"Yes. It was love. It was perfect. Then he said he wanted me to meet his dad, Sebastian Sr. I knew how important Sebastian's dad was to him. So I gathered every dime I had and bought this dress from a thrift store. It was a knee length blue wrap dress. There was a jacket that went with it perfectly but I couldn't afford it. The cashier got tired of me gawking at it and she bought it for me. It cost five dollars."

"Did you get to meet his dad?"

"I did. A few days later we went to his house for dinner. They had things I'd only ever seen in movies: high ceilings, a crystal chandelier, and a marble staircase. It was like being inside a dream. His dad seemed to really like me. We talked and even joked around. Then about an hour later, I found myself alone with Sebastian Sr. He'd sent his son on an errand."

"Diana, what happened?"

"Sebastian Sr. told me how pretty I was and how good I looked in the dress. Then he locked the door. I tried to wrap my head around it but I couldn't. These are rich, upstanding people. They're not lousy drunks in a trailer park. Surely he won't do something so cruel and savage. I was wrong. It turns out rapists are from all walks of life. I screamed so loud he slapped me. But I didn't care; I fought him as hard as I could. And I kept screaming because I knew sooner or later, my boyfriend would come for me."

"There was no one else in the house?" I ask, growing angry.

"No one came for me. Sebastian's dad grabbed me by the throat and threw me down. My head hit the floor so hard I felt like my brain was rattling inside my skull. In throwing me down, he'd knocked a glass of water off the table and onto the floor. I could feel the liquid all around me. There was also a slight scent in the air but I couldn't make out what it was."

I want her to go on because I feel like she needs to get this story out, but I don't want to push her. So I wait quietly as she gathers herself.

"He ripped my panties off and shoved them in my mouth. He grabbed my thighs and spread them apart. I begged him to stop, repeatedly. He told me to shut up or he'd use his belt. He said I was lucky to have him pick me for this honor. I tried to talk to my body and convince it to let him in because he was going to insert himself anyway."

Her voice is far away and filled with fear. It's as if she has brought herself right back to that moment. It's like she's not a powerful demon anymore but a human girl with nowhere to run.

"But the body isn't logical. It doesn't understand rape. So no matter how hard he tried to enter me, my body closed up. Finally he had had enough of trying," she continues.

"Did he stop?"

"No. He found something to loosen me up: a beer bottle. He jammed it inside me and..." She's having trouble keeping her voice steady.

I want to touch her. I want to hold her and make it better, but being touched by a man, human or angel, is the last thing she needs.

"After that, my body didn't resist. It couldn't. He came barreling inside me like a freight train. He pounded into me over and over again. It felt like he would be inside me forever. He was a virus and he infected every part of me."

"Did you at least get him arrested?" I ask.

"No."

"Did you tell his son what he did?"

"No."

"Diana, that bastard raped you. What did you do?" I push.

"I died."

Damn...

"That's your Core?" I reply.

A Core is the story of how someone becomes an angel or a demon. That is if you were not born that way.

"Yes, that's my Core. Turns out the liquid I felt under me was coming from my head. He'd cracked my skull. I bled out with him on top of me. But the whole time I was being raped, I never shed a tear. Not one. But then as I was dying, something actually brought tears to my eyes. I finally placed the scent that had been looming just outside the door—pine trees and fresh snow."

"Your boyfriend was out there the whole time?" I demand.

"The whole time. He was just behind the door. I don't know if he planned it or if he was too afraid of his father to help me. But as I lay dying, I just hoped for one thing. I wanted to eat that coward's heart out. I literally wanted to bite down on its meaty red flesh and pull it apart. That's how I got to suck the life out of people; it was my last thought," she says.

Often when a human becomes an angel or a demon, they are given their power from their last thoughts before death. Diana's ability to suck the life from her victims has always made me curious as to how she died.

"I tried to be something different after I died. But I died in a flame of rage. I hate everything and everyone. Including myself. And I try not to think about it. But the truth is, I could never be good. Because to be good, you have to follow Omnis and do what he says. And I can't. I can't follow

Omnis because he let me get raped. He let it happen. And I won't forgive him. I'll never forgive him…" she whispers.

Tears spring to her eyes. They are the same color as her blood: black. I have never seen a demon cry. I didn't think it was possible.

"Diana, I'm so sorry," I reply as I hold her close.

She sobs and shakes in my arms. I hold her as tight as I can. I look down at her and for the first time, I can see the human she once was. The frightened girl who found herself alone, brutalized, and betrayed.

She looks back at me, broken. We lean in and close the gap between us. Our lips part and seek out a familiar touch. The kiss is slow, tender, and seeking…

CHAPTER EIGHTEEN
THE MOMENT BEFORE

It's only when Diana and I pull apart that we notice him standing there, watching us. He glares at us and stands perfectly still, rooted in his anger. I don't know how long he was standing there but I know he saw everything, which makes a bad situation that much worse.

"What is it, Bex?" I ask.

"Swoop is asking for the demon," he replies coldly.

"Yeah okay, I'll go check on her," Diana says.

She looks back at me before she goes. She has something she wants to say, but she knows this isn't the time or place. So, she heads back to the cave.

"Was that all?" I ask Bex.

"No, Silver, that's not all," he replies.

The rain has started to die down, enabling us to get a good view of each other. Even the wind has managed to calm itself. It's as if the whole forest is vested in the conversation about to take place and it doesn't want the weather to interrupt the sound quality or visual.

"You pushed Randy to say what he had to say, so now it's your turn, what the hell is it?" I ask.

"You saved Key from a year of certain agony and for that I will always be grateful. And when it comes down to it, I will place my life before yours because you did that for my girl. But you hurt Pryor, and there is no limit to how far I will go to take you out."

"You really think I would hurt Pryor?" I snap.

"Yeah, Silver, I do. I think it's easy to hurt a girl like her because she's naive enough to believe a guy like you can fight his dark side and win. But I've seen your dark side—we both know that's not true."

"Bex, you haven't seen my dark side, but keep pushing…" I ask.

"You blame everyone else for actions when the truth is it's you that makes the decisions. You could have stayed away from Pry but you didn't. That's not The Center's fault. That was you. You could have at least warned us that The Center was out to get her and we would have taken steps to protect her, but you didn't. Instead you do what you always do—you let your dick guide you."

"Are you done?" I ask.

"No."

"Bex, trust me; you are done."

I march back towards the cave and with every step, fury gathers inside me. It's not anger towards Bex but rather supreme rage at myself. I am a grade "A" asshole right now. The only girl I want is being tortured and tormented and I pick now to kiss someone else? Who the fuck does that? *ARGH!!!!!!!!!!!!!!!!!!*

How the hell could you do that, Silver? How could you kiss Diana? What the hell were you thinking? She's already under the impression that you two have something together and now you go and lead her on even more by kissing her? Seriously, could you be a bigger jerk?

Fuck me…

I enter the cave and find the team is gathering their things to go deeper in the forest. I check on Swoop; the mixture over her eyes is clear and, according to Diana, healing very nicely.

"Can you see clearly?" I ask.

"It's still a little blurry, but I don't want us to waste anymore time. We need to get to the Deed," Swoop replies.

"And what about you, are you back to full strength?" I ask Bex.

"I'm good. Let's go," he says shortly.

We leave the cave and venture out deeper into the woods. The good news is that the rain has stopped completely. The bad news is nightfall has completely set in, and we have almost zero visibility. So as we make our way towards the river, I take out the second object Harris gave us: a portable light source called Iso.

Iso looks like a small glass marble and hovers just above our heads. Without it, we would have had to wait until morning because it's impossible to see anything at all. As we make our way, Diana leans in and speaks to me in a whisper.

"Can you please stop?" she says.

"Stop what?"

"Reprimanding yourself—and don't say you're not because I know you, Silver, and I know what you look like when you are taking on blame."

"I shouldn't have let that happen," I confess.

"All you did was comfort me. What's so bad about that?"

"Diana, you know what's bad about it."

"Why do you have to do that? Why do you have to step on every nice moment between us?"

"I don't want to hurt Pry. She's important to me, you know that."

"Yeah, I got it, Silver. But while you're walking on eggshells to ensure her happiness can you not stomp on mine? We saved each other's lives countless times. We made love in every conceivable part of the world, in every possible position."

"Diana—"

"When the nightmares you had about The Center brought you over the edge, and nearly robbed you of your sanity, I was there to help pull you back. And just now I was more honest with you than I was with anyone in my entire human or demon life."

"That doesn't mean we should be together, Diana."

"No, but it does mean that after everything we've faced together, you shouldn't be shocked when we reach out for one another. And you damn sure shouldn't look so guilty about one kiss. Did I miss something, because as far as I know you and the redhead aren't dating, right?"

"No," I reply tightly.

"Then why are you walking around here looking like you backed the car over the family kitten? Seriously, enough with the damn guilt."

"Why is it so important to you that I'm okay with the kiss?"

"It's not the kiss. It's the moment before when you held me against you. It was…nice. And it's okay if it wasn't nice for you but stop ruining it for me," she says as she marches ahead.

"You think Marisol's okay?" Easton asks us.

"We're in the Forest of Ash and Bones and you're worried about your girlfriend, who's probably in line at Starbucks right now?" Swoop replies.

"She doesn't like Starbucks. It's something to do with low wages for employees. Anyway, she won't touch the stuff."

"Does she know about your addiction to dark peppermint mocha?" Swoop asks.

"No. 'Mocha' and I are forced to hide our love," East teases.

"You drink three of those things a day. How do you hide it?" Bex asks.

"I pour it into generic coffee cups that say 'Coffee' on the side; like an animal," East says, giving voice to his "shame."

"Hey, stop," I order the team.

"What is it?" Randy asks.

"Shhh…" I reply as we gather and scout the dense wooded area.

There is no creature behind us or in front of us, yet I can't help but feel like we are being followed. Bex echoes the same sentiment although he too can't see any possible threat. We keep going but I remind the team to stay together and to be on high alert. We now walk in silence and try to make as little noise as possible.

Suddenly, Easton signals for us to look over to the right; there we see a pair of bright blood colored eyes in the black forest background. I order the team to halt. Bex signals us to look over to the left; we now have another pair of red eyes focused on us.

I can't tell what the creature is yet and therefore can't decide what weapon we will need. I take a chance and will the Gain to turn once again into an ax. Suddenly a third set of eyes appears in the darkness. In a matter of seconds we are surrounded by nearly fifty sets of bloody eyes. That's followed by a series of menacing growls and sneers.

"Swoop, what does the Inka say?" East asks.

"I can't point it at them because I can't seem them. We have to wait for them to come towards the Iso. That way they'll be in the light," she says.

"By the time they do that, we could already be dead," Randy replies.

"Everyone stay close together and don't make any sudden movements. Swoop, get ready to use the Inka the moment they are close enough," I order.

"An additional ten sets of eyes just popped up on my right," Bex says.

"Same here," I reply.

"We need to move now!" Diana says.

"No, we need to know what we are up against first. There's no telling how they will react," I tell her.

"Come on, step into the daylight so we can see you," East says.

"I got it," Swoop says as one of the creatures makes a slight move forward and is suddenly bathed in light.

The creature has the body of a rotted out pitbull and the needle-toothed jaw of a piranha. Its tail is long with a pointy spike on the end of it. From where we stand we can make out the stench of decay.

Current image: Eway Snatchers

Summary: A breed of proficient pack-like hunters. They surround their prey and attack when given the signal by their leader. Their jagged teeth contain a toxin that paralyzes its victim, allowing for the pack to devour at will.

Weakness: The skin of the Eway is hard like that of metal, but the underbelly has a spot often exploited by its enemies. However, given the ferocity of these beasts, running is often the first and wisest option.

I calmly make eye contact with the rest of team, and then give them the signal to run. We charge ahead at top speed and the Eway are right behind us. They let out a series of horrifying sounds as they chase us through the woods. The more we run, the more determined they are to catch us.

We weave in and out through the trees, hoping to throw them off, but it doesn't work. They are still right behind us. Swoop shouts a warning to Diana, but it's too late. An Eway comes up the side and pounces on her. Diana falls to the ground and tries to keep it from biting into her.

I turn to help her, but an Eway leaps out and knocks Randy into the muddy ground. Bex shouts to me that he has Diana and I run over to Randy who is trying to escape the Eway by climbing up a tree. Meanwhile, East and Swoop have been encircled by a dozen Eway with no way to escape.

I tackle the Eway chasing Randy and wrestle it to the ground. The beast aims its sharp tail at my chest. I move quickly, but not quick enough. The Eway manages to insert its tail into my lower right side. I swear and groan as the pain works its way down my body.

Seeing that its prey is hurt, the Eway goes to strike me again. I quickly will the Gain to turn into a knife, then I slice its underbelly. The creature whimpers as its guts spill out from its underbelly.

I order Randy to stay up in the tree where he is as I try to get up and help the others. Swoop and East have been able to injure a few of the Eway that were surrounding them with the help of heavy branches nearby. But they are still outnumbered and in need of aid.

I hurl the Gain at them and East catches it. He turns the Gain into a sword; he cuts it through the air and manages to take three of those bastards' heads clean off. A few yards away, Bex tackles the Eway by snapping their necks. As I run over to help Bex and Easton, I shout to Diana to get Randy and Swoop to safety.

We have managed to kill a good number of them, but the leader sends out a howl into the air and within seconds a new surge of Eway come running towards us.

"We can't fight them all, we need to go!" I order.

The three of us start running towards the river along with the other team members; the Eway follow. I have no choice but to use the last item

Harris gave us—an orb the size of a ping-pong ball that liquefies anything within its blast radius. It's called a Sparrow and I wanted to save it for the temple, but at this rate we won't even make it there. So, I hurl the orb into the midst of Eway.

As soon as the orb lands on the ground, it explodes and a wave of smoldering fire engulfs the forest behind us. What we didn't expect was that the wave would keep expanding.

"It's headed straight for us—Go! Go! Go!" Bex yells.

We all bolt towards the river to avoid the oncoming blast. It's too late; a bright auburn burst of light goes off and sends us all hurling helplessly through the air. We land on the edge of the riverbank.

"Everyone okay?" I shout as I place pressure to my side in an attempt to stop the bleeding.

"Yeah, we're good," Swoop says.

Diana, Bex, and East signal that they are unharmed.

"I'm fine. Let's go again," Randy jokes as he hangs his head, exhausted.

Diana tells me she's out of vials to stop the pain, but she still has a vial to stop the bleeding. I insist she save it for the others because while no one is in mortal danger, everyone on the team has wounds. Instead she uses a liquid bandage to seal the hole in my side although she worries it won't hold.

"Diana, it's fine, for now. We are almost there. All we have to do is get on that bridge and cross this river. Then we'll get inside the temple, find the Deed, and rescue Pry," I remind them.

"Why is the river doing that?" Randy asks.

We all look towards the water and watch as it begins to whirl around in a giant loop. A twister has formed in the middle of the water, leaving a massive cyclone in the center.

"I'm pretty sure I'm gonna regret this, but Swoop, what's in the river?" Randy asks.

Current image: Anhabay River (Also know as "Stew River")

Summary: This is in fact the most dangerous river in the known world. The river feeds on a special kind of emotion: untapped anger.

If the traveler crossing the bridge has an unexplored hatred or rage towards someone or something, the river will exploit that weakness. It will create images and sounds that only the traveler can see and hear. Every time the traveler's anger rises, a piece of the bridge will disappear.

The End Game: The river's goal is to make the traveler so furious and blind with rage that the bridge disappears altogether. The traveler is then hurled into a raging vortex and is never seen again.

Weakness: The Anhabay River is perfectly harmless to those with calm minds and spirits. Ironically, those who often show their rage and anger are also safe as that anger has been expressed. This river is dangerous only to those who hide their emotions from others. If a traveler is about to die on the bridge, it is said their only chance is to name the source of their anguish. Most travelers cannot bear to reveal the name of the person or thing they hate the most even with death looming below. Hence the Anhabay River's endless list of victims.

"Yup, I regret asking; oh so very much," Randy says to Swoop.

"When we get on the bridge, we could just make a run for it," Diana suggests as we make our way towards the water.

"Are you looking at the same bridge I am? That thing is like a thousand years old. If the wind blows, the bridge could fall, let alone if we run across it," Swoop says.

"I agree with Bird. We need to go slow and be careful," Easton replies.

"How far across is it?" Diana asks.

"About four hundred feet," Bex says.

"And um...how high?" Randy wonders.

"I'm guessing about three hundred feet," I reply.

Randy swallows hard and the color drains from his face.

"You okay?" East asks.

"Yeah, it's just that it didn't look that high from where we were. Now close-up…" Randy's voice cracks.

"I'm sure you can do it, Randy. Just pretend my girlfriend is on the other side waiting for you. Seriously, you'd be able to help her, right? You wouldn't freeze up like a coward, would you? How would that play out to Key if she were here?" Bex asks, obviously getting Randy back for his earlier comment.

"Fine, I can do this. In fact, I'll go first," Randy offers.

"Yeah, that's not gonna happen. You follow us," I order.

"You don't think I can do it?" Randy pushes.

"Yeah, I know you can, but the fact is heights are natural for us and even without our wings we have better balance than humans," I reply.

"Fine, whatever," Randy snaps.

I glare at Bex for being a prick and challenging Randy.

"Come on, happy thoughts, people," Easton says as we step onto the shaky wooden bridge that seems to stretch out forever. The panels are narrow and no more than two feet wide. They're worn out and many are missing, leaving wide gaps between them. The handrail isn't a rail at all. It's just a few cords strung together. One good shake and the bridge will overturn and cast us out into the darkness below.

"Um…maybe Silver should skip this part," East jokes.

I ignore him and we take our first step forward. The bridge shakes slightly. Again, I order everyone to pause and focus on something that will calm them. We take another step and the bridge shakes slightly harder. Swoop talks Randy through every step and although the wind is whipping through us and the water below is greedily waiting to consume us, so far we are all okay.

It feels like hours have gone by but in actuality it's only been a few minutes. We are now heading towards the middle of the bridge. East moves his head slightly as if trying to dodge something. I'm guessing it's some kind of bug by his ear. I call out and ask if he's okay and he says "yes."

Moments later, East starts talking to himself. We call out to him, but he seems to be in a sort of trance; he sees something before him and whatever it is, it's upsetting him.

"East, it's just the river, you have stay calm," I shout.

"No, that's not true!" he shouts to no one.

Two of the wooden panels under our feet disappear. If Swoop didn't quickly readjust herself, she would have been thrown down into the water.

"East, you have to snap out of it!" Bex says.

"No, it's not true!!! It's not true!!" East screams at the top of his lungs.

"I'm gonna try and walk back over to him," I tell Bex.

"No, you could make it worse. We have to talk him down from right where we are," Bex replies.

"East, who are you seeing? Who's there?" Swoop shouts.

"GET AWAY FROM ME! STAY AWAY FROM ME!" East demands to no one.

Four more panels disappear. The team is rocked by the sudden lack of support and we nearly fall forward. We hold on to the side rail, knowing at any moment we could be thrown to our death.

"East, c'mon man, talk to me. Who do you see? Who's there with you?" I plead.

"I'M NOT AFRAID OF YOU! I'M NOT AFRAID!" East vows as he throws punches at the air wildly. He starts to motion as if he has his powers, which tells me he's really out of it.

The bridge is rocking back and forth from both East's movement and gaps caused by the vanishing panels. Yet, the river is determined to heighten East's rage.

"I'LL HATE YOU! I'LL HATE YOU!" East yells as he lunges at the imaginary figure before him.

Every panel on the bridge vanishes. We grab hold of the rail as a last-ditch effort at staying alive. We all manage to hang on. Now, we desperately dangle on the end of the fragile ropes, three hundred feet from a watery grave.

"I WILL KILL YOU I SWEAR! I SWEAR!" East vows as he lets go of the only thing standing between him and certain death…

CHAPTER NINETEEN
QUEEN OF FURIES

I use the Gain so quickly I don't know what I willed it to be until it actually forms into the object: a whip. I use it to wrap around East and pull him up just as he's about to hit the water. Now East is dangling at the end of my whip, but he is far from safe.

Normally I can support his weight, but the wound I suffered earlier is reopening, causing a throbbing pain at my side. Holding on to East becomes more and more difficult. It's not a matter of *if* I drop him; it's simply a matter of *when*.

Knowing that I am about to let him fall to his death, I have no choice but to try and hurl him towards the shore. Throwing him is a huge risk because he could miss the landing and he could get sucked into the void despite all my efforts. But there's no time to debate with myself. I have to the take the risk and hope I can swing East far enough to get him to safety.

I force myself to forget about the wound on my side that is now spewing blood and the burning pain that comes with every passing moment. I gather all my strength and send Easton flying onto the shore. I pray to Omnis my friend makes it.

He doesn't.

Well, at least not fully. He lands just short of the shore, on the rim of the vortex. He's holding on by inserting his hands in between two small openings embedded along ridges of the riverbank. He reminds me of a fly trying to save itself from the pull of an industrial vacuum.

Knowing he is running out of strength and will soon be forced to let go, East takes a chance and reaches for the whip that's tangled around his waist. He turns it into a pick and shoves it into the wall of earth before him. He pulls himself up slowly. Every step is dangerous and could very well be his last. Still East fights to stay alive by slowly climbing away from the void.

When he gets to safety, he signals for Swoop to swing herself over to him because she is the lightest of us and is very flexible. Swoop manages to twist and contort her body enough to get past us and on to the land. The two of them band together and with the help of the Gain, which they turned into a grappling hook, they are able to help all of us on to the shore safely.

Exhausted and weak, we all kneel down on the soft ground to get our bearing. The pain at my side is now at an all-time high and I groan as I press my hand against it to stop the bleeding. Diana drags herself over to me and tries to apply the vial of pain relief she had from earlier.

"No...save it for the team," I instruct her.

"You're part of the team. Now, move your hand so I can make the pain stop," she insists.

"I forgot you were so pushy," I tease as I remove my hand from the wound.

"You know that's what you love about me," she quips as she tends to me.

"Is everyone okay?" Bex asks.

Randy has wandered a few feet away from us and turned his back to us.

"Randy, are you alright?" Swoop asks.

He nods "yes," but he doesn't turn around.

"Hey, look at me. What's wrong?" I ask.

He shakes his head "no," signaling he will not turn so we can see his face.

Worried now, I signal to Swoop to go check on him while Diana applies the mixture to my side.

"No, I got this," Bex replies as he takes off towards Randy. When Bex walks up to him, Randy turns his face away, ashamed.

"What's going on with Randy?" I ask Diana, who has a better vantage point.

"They're looking at something on the ground—oh," Diana replies, wincing.

"What is it?" I ask.

"I think the human threw up—a lot."

In the beginning Randy is mortified at what he's just done and signals for Bex to go away. Judging by his expression, Randy is waiting for Bex to make fun of him, but that doesn't happen. Instead Bex spots a broken jar at the base of a nearby tree, filled with rainwater. He takes the jar over to Randy and holds it up and slowly pours in into Randy's hand. Randy washes his face, hands, and feet. Bex whispers something to Randy and Randy nods, looking grateful.

The two of them head back to us. I wouldn't say they are best friends by any means, but for the first time since Randy's outburst they aren't throwing icy stares at each other.

"The temple is just up ahead; we should get going," East says, sounding somber.

"Really, that's it? You don't want to tell us what the hell that was back there?" Diana asks.

"I don't have to tell you anything," East reminds her.

"Easton, we're worried about you. What happened on the bridge? Who were you talking to?" Bex says.

"It doesn't matter," East counters aggressively.

"The hell it doesn't. We almost died. We should know the reason behind it," Diana protests.

"I'd kind of like to know too," Randy says gently.

"Why? It's over now. What does it matter?" East snaps.

"It matters because everything in the Angel world is connected to some kind of crazy emotion. Who knows what's waiting for us at the temple? Maybe it's a 'chainsaw of guilt' that chops your arm off if you have unexpressed guilt.

"Or maybe at the entrance of the temple there's a three-headed monkey who will pull out your soul through your nose if it finds unexpressed sadness. Hey, it could be a circus clown with a screw loose who will cut your damn head off if you don't reveal how you felt about the last round of American Idol!

"The point is, keeping emotions hidden away causes crazy damage in your world. So I don't want to get personal, East, but you need to share because I like my head where it is," Randy concludes passionately.

East looks around at all of us and sees that we are all waiting for him to reveal his hidden anger. I know he'd like nothing better than to stop this moment from happening. I know that feeling all too well. Yet sometimes there's no escaping it. Sometimes everyone needs to get a look at your demons.

"The image on the bridge was my father, Frank," he says, avoiding eye contact.

"I knew you didn't like him but…do you really hate him?" Bex asks.

"No. I don't hate him; at least not that I can remember. He's just always unhappy with me. No matter what I do, it's wrong."

"Dads are…weird. They are always harder on us than they should be," Swoop replies.

"No, this is different. He hates me. I overheard him saying it to a friend of his. He actually hates me. I learned that when I was nine, so from then on I tried to piss him off to get back at him. I guess I had defied him one time too many; one night he had enough."

"East, what did you father do to you?" Randy asks.

"He broke my arm. My mom was out of town. When she came back I told her that I fell off my Port while I was fooling around."

"Is this an everyday thing with him?" I ask.

"No. He only hit me that once, but you know what's crazy? I kind of wanted him to do it again. That way I'd know he sees me. You can't hit something that's not there. So if he beat the crap out me, then I'd exist in his eyes."

"Easton…" Swoop says as she embraces him.

"Is your father stronger than you?" Diana asks.

"No, I have more powers and he's always hated that too," East replies.

"If you're stronger why don't you fight back?" Diana pushes.

"Ruin…getting someone to hate you takes no work at all. But just getting a guy like my dad to smile at me…" East begins but can't finish his thought.

"Okay, fine. I guess. But if you need me to suck his miserable life from his useless body…well, I have some spare time later," Diana offers.

"Um…thanks," he says, uncertain how to respond.

"You have to do something about this, East; you can't keep living this way," Bex says.

"I spend most of my time with you guys. That's my escape," he admits.

"Okay, well, I never thought I'd agree with the demon over there, but if Frank hurts you again, they will never find the body," Swoop says.

"You have a dark side; I like that," Diana replies with a smile.

We laugh and gather our things and head to the temple. While we walk, I go over to East and speak to him low so as not to be heard by the others.

"If you need a father you can always borrow mine. He'll drive you nuts. He's overprotective, opinionated, hotheaded, and prone to hugging you in public. But all in all, it's pretty okay," I offer.

"Your dad isn't okay. He's awesome. And thanks."

As we walk down the muddy pathway to the temple, I reflect on my life with my father. The thing that's always impressed me about him is also the thing that's pushed us apart—his love for my mom. On one hand, I hated that he grieved for so long and it seemed like he didn't want to be around without her. But on the other hand, there is something about their uncompromising love that I always admired. I thought that's the kind of love I want to have with Pryor.

Then maybe you should stop kissing other girls in the rain…

***

As we venture towards the temple, something flies by us, leaving a trail of dark smoke.

"What was that?" I ask.

"I don't know. It was too quick for the Inka to recognize," Swoop replies.

Without warning, another being flies above our heads. It flies so fast we are once again unable to make out what it is. I signal to the team and we race towards the temple. The faster we run, the more dark entities there are whipping around us. Thankfully our destination is in sight.

The Temple of Furies is made up of burnt colored clay. It has two rooms on either side of it and one large room that serves as the epicenter. There are carvings on the walls that depict the tragedy of Mercy Island and its inhabitants.

The temple is dilapidated and on the verge of collapse. A mammoth sized tree springs from its center and invades its doors and windows with its thick branches. The root of the tree has grown so much it's actually lifted the temple up from its foundation. The temple now hangs several feet in the air.

We make a mad dash for the entrance, but we are halted by the beings from overhead that have landed and are now standing before us. They have landed on the ground and now surround us from every angle.

They have dome shaped heads, hollow sunken eyes, and veins bulging out from underneath their translucent skin. Their unhinged jaws are pulled apart by their nearly three-inch jagged teeth. Swoop slowly aims the Inka at the beings now only a few feet away.

Current image: Mercy Island Furies
Summary: Revengeful dark beings who were once human and now forever roam Mercy Island seeking to eliminate all signs of angel and human life. They are led by their leader, Queen Melinda, the most powerful among them.

Powers: Furies have the ability to move objects, invade the body of their victims, and to control their movements. They can also tear into flesh with both their fangs and their voices.

Weakness: Omnis has granted the Furies of Mercy Island immortality. They can never die. However, they can be rendered motionless for a short time by rubbing the sap from inside the Gagu plant into one's body. The Gagu plant looks much like an aloe vera plant except it is carnivorous and only open when human flesh is present.

"I think I saw the Gagu plant on our way here," Diana whispers to the team.

"We'll split up and distract them and you go back to get the plant to make them motionless," I order.

Half of the team goes right while the rest of us head left. The Furies split up and take off after us. One of them waves his hand and sends Bex and Swoop flying backwards through the trees. They slam into a large rock and slump forward.

I run to help, but a Fury with half her face missing intercepts me. She slashes into my flesh by opening her gaping mouth and emitting a shrill noise in the air. I cry out in agony as my previous wound is once again carved into.

The pain going through me is so bad I drop to the ground and the Gain falls out of my hand. Luckily East is able to grab it in time and wills it to become a harpoon. He shoots it at the nearly faceless Fury. It spears her in the gut and rips what remains of her insides out. She slumps down to the ground.

"She will get back up in a minute, we need to go!" East says as he helps me to my feet.

"Swoop and Bex..." I reply weakly.

"I've got them," East promises me as he helps me lean on a tree out of the immediate line of fire.

He then turns the Gain into a net and casts it over the group of Furies surrounding Swoop and Bex's bodies. Knowing he can't stop them for long, East rushes over to Swoop and Bex and tries to revive them.

I make myself get up and search for a makeshift weapon. I find a heavy branch with a point sharp enough to cause damage. I send it flying across from me where a Fury is slashing Randy's arms and legs with its voice. The makeshift spear sinks into the skull of the Fury; it falls face-first at Randy's feet.

I go over to him as fast as I can, take out the Holder in my pocket, and get ready to place him inside the bubble-like prison.

"Silver, no!" Randy protests.

"We don't have time for this; get in the damn Holder, now!" I demand.

"No, you don't understand. Diana can't get the plant to open up. She's a demon. The Inka said the Gagu plant opens for human flesh. Silver, I'm the only one who can retrieve it," Randy reasons.

"East is half human, that may work," I shout over the roar of the ongoing battle.

"We can't take that chance. Please, let me go get the plant. I can do this," he swears.

"Okay, go with Diana. Go, hurry! I'll cover you," I shout.

Randy heads back the way we came in search of the plant. A Fury spots him and takes off after him. I leap into the air and tackle it. I land right on top of the creature. It goes to open its mouth but I gag it with my hand.

"You Furies need to learn when to shut the fuck up." I rage as I slam its skull into the base of the tree repeatedly. The Fury is knocked out, but within seconds it starts to come to life again.

Come on, Randy, we need that plant!

A few feet away Swoop and Bex have been revived but now have to help East, who is being torn open by a circle of Furies and their deathly sounds. I spot the Gain where East must have dropped it and throw it at Bex, who is closer.

Bex wills the Gain to become a sword and cuts through the air, slicing his blade into the midsection of the surrounding Furies. He pulls Easton out from the middle and carries him to safety. Unfortunately he takes his eyes off of Swoop, giving the Fury behind her a chance to invade her body and control her movements.

Swoop, now possessed by the Fury, grabs the Gain and wills it to become a machete. She swings it at Bex's unsuspecting head.

"Bex, duck!" I order as I run towards them.

Bex drops to the floor instinctively and misses decapitation by a fraction of a second. I reach Swoop in time and tackle her. She falls backwards but comes up ready to fight. I'm not sure how to lure the Fury from inside Swoop's body without hurting her.

Thinking quickly, I grab on to the nearest Fury and aim it at Swoop. I then pull its arm out of its socket; that causes the Fury to cry out, which then cuts into Swoop's flesh and mine. I'm bleeding and Swoop is too, but so is the Fury inside her. It flees away from her body quickly.

"I'm sorry; I had to get it out of you," I tell her.

"I'm okay. I'm okay," she says as she presses her hand against the large gash now carved into her chest.

"This is a bloodbath; we can't hold them off for too long," Bex says.

"I'll make a run for the temple," I reply as I lean against the tree and try to stand up straight.

"No, you won't make it. You're hurt badly. You can barely stand," Bex reasons.

"None of us will make it. There's too many of them at the entrance of the temple. We won't make it inside before we're killed," East says.

"Well, we need to do something. We have to get that damn Deed!" I rage.

The rush of emotion causes the bleeding in my midsection to increase. The team is right, I'm in no condition to take on the rest of the Furies, but I'm also not about to sit here knowing the only thing that can help Pry is just beyond that door. I order the team to cover me while I stumble forward, headed for the temple.

"Wait, they're back!" Swoop says.

I turn around and follow her gaze. Randy and Diana are waving their green sap-stained hands in front of a group of Furies. They are quickly rendered still. Randy runs towards us as Diana attacks more Furies with her now powerful palms.

"You did it!" Swoop says gratefully.

"Yeah, you know; no thing," Randy replies, trying to smile through the pain.

I look down and there are two fingers missing from his right hand. He's sweating profusely and the color has drained from his face.

"Randy, no…" East replies.

"The plant was hungry, really hungry," Randy says, blinking back tears.

Randy gives each of us a piece of the plant and we rub it on our hands.

"If we want what Randy has done to matter, we need to go inside the temple now. Otherwise his sacrifice will have been for nothing," Bex reminds us.

"Wait, shouldn't we tend to Randy's arm?" Swoop asks, concerned.

"We will as soon as we get out of here. But right now we have to go; we don't know how long the Furies will stay still," I reply.

"I'm fine, Swoop. Let's go."

Swoop nods reluctantly. I signal to Diana that we are headed to the temple and stand by just in case the Furies start moving again.

"I don't want her out here alone. East, stay with her while we go inside and get the Deed."

We race towards the temple. The Furies go to attack us, but we quickly raise our hands before them and they too remain motionless. We run inside the temple and search for the box. The search only takes minutes, but for us it feels like days.

"Got the Deed!" Bex says.

I take the dark box from him and examine it. It has all the complex patterns we were told about. The circular seal on it is intact, meaning no one has yet to pry it open. I say a quick prayer to Omnis and look at the bottom of the box. There are small digital numbers blinking. They are coordinates to the location of the Deed's maker.

"We have the location of The Center!" I reply, weak with relief.

"Good, let's go get our girl back," Swoop says as we run out of the temple.

We run past the Fury "statues" and call out for Diana and East.

They run towards us; together we race past the temple and make for the shoreline. That's when we see her—Melinda, Queen of the Furies. She sent her Furies ahead to kill us but waited at the shore just in case we made it out of the temple alive. We know it's her because she's more powerful than the others; when we raise our hands up, the sap does nothing to stop her. She continues to fly towards us.

Melinda's skin looks like it's made of porcelain with cracks rippling throughout her face and body. Her long raven hair floats wildly around her and a scarlet colored mist engulfs her slim frame. There is a crudely cut hole where her belly and a fetus should have been. Inside the hole is an infestation of maggots and worms.

Melinda waves her hand casually and sends the whole team flying into the air. Bex goes to tackle her, and she throws him up against a large tree; blood oozes from his temple. East wills the Gain to become a hatchet and hurls it at the center of her forehead. It lands and splits her head open.

Melinda laughs sardonically.

She then pulls the weapon from the middle of her forehead, opens her mouth, and consumes it. We watch, stunned at what we've just witnessed. Melinda lets out an earth-shattering cry and all of us scream as our skin starts to tear open.

Melinda enjoys our agony so much she stops yelling and comes closer to us. It seems she wants a front row seat to our suffering. At this point we will die before we leave the island; determined not to let that happen, I desperately search for a weapon.

Randy whispers in my ear that he has more sap with him. I remind him the sap does not seem to be working on the queen.

"Maybe if we force her to ingest it instead of just waving it in her face like the other Furies. She may be resistant to a few smeared drops of sap, but maybe she'll react to a concentrated amount, placed directly inside her," Randy says, placing numerous aloe vera-like pieces inside my hand.

"This is a big risk," Bex replies as Swoop is sent flying into the air by Melinda. We rush to help Swoop, who has badly twisted her left arm.

"Look, we don't have a choice. Bex, you distract her. And we'll tackle her and get the sap into her mouth," Randy says, as if he's the leader.

I have no issue with that at all; anything to get the hell off this Omnis-forsaken island.

"Randy's right. It's our only chance," I reply.

Everyone agrees. I give Bex the signal and he positions himself in Melinda's path.

Pissed that he would be so brazen, she calls for Bex's body to be lifted several feet in the air. She toys with him by twisting and turning his body at will without ever having to go near him.

I signal to the team and we all smash into the Queen of Furies and beat her to the ground. She is stronger than us but together we are able to keep her down long enough to shove the Gagu leaves in her mouth. The plant has no effect on her.

She gets up even more pissed off, and from the look in her midnight soulless eyes, we know she is about to kill us all. She opens her arms wide, ready to bring our lives to an end but then she stops, frozen mid-strike.

"I was right! It worked! She's not moving," Randy says, nearly in tears.

"Randy, we will throw you a big ass 'thank you' bash later; right now, let's get the hell away from this place," East says.

We run to the edge of the shore and I summon the Ports. They appear instantly. We hop on to them and just as we are about to take off a Fury zooms past us. It knocks Diana off her Port. As we float up to the sky, Diana goes tumbling back down to Mercy Island.

"DIANA!!!" I cry out, as if some piece of my soul has been taken from me.

I demand that Bex and the others keep going as I jump off my Port. I land not far from Diana's body. I run to her, but I'm too late. Melinda is now free of the sap and grabs hold of Diana's shirt. She yanks on it and drags Diana's squirming body across the rocky shore.

I watch, horrified that this is the last time I will see Diana alive. I reach out to help her again and Melinda waves me away, casting me out into the water. Melinda grabs hold of Diana; she struggles but can't break free of the Queen of Furies' grip.

I use the last bit of strength I have to swim back to the shore towards Diana. I emerge out of the water and find Melinda studying Diana intensely as their hands touch. Melinda looks deeply into Diana's eyes. She sees something in there that shocks her.

Suddenly the rage that was on Melinda's face begins to soften. Not sure what's happening, Diana pulls her hand away. Melinda does not fight to get Diana's hand back. Instead she allows Diana to take several steps away with no retaliation.

I reach out for Diana and am able to get to her with no interference from Melinda. I call for the Port and it appears. We get on and start to take off, expecting the queen to attack at any moment, but she doesn't. Instead a glow appears on her face and spreads throughout her body.

She makes eye contact with Diana and we watch the impossible happen: Melinda the Queen of Furies smiles. Her body then transforms into a burst of light. And as Diana and I take off on our Port, we watch Melinda's newly formed spirit leave the island and ascend…

***

Despite what they promised, the team did not leave without us. Instead they hovered above and waited for us. When we catch up to them, I demand that we go straight for The Center.

"No," Swoop says.

"What? We have to go get Pry," I remind her.

"We are all injured, we have Randy with us, and it won't matter if we get to The Center if we are too weak to help Pryor escape," Swoop says.

"She's right. We need to make a stop—a quick one. We need to get some supplies so I can fix you guys up and Randy will need more than a few mixtures to get his fingers back," Diana says.

"Yeah, okay. We'll drop Randy off so the Healers in the Clinic can fix him. Meanwhile we will load up on supplies," I tell her.

"Randy, are you okay with staying behind?" East asks.

Randy is not paying attention. He is too busy studying Diana as she wraps his bloody hand in bandages.

"Randy!" East says.

"Oh, sorry. I wasn't listening. I just can't get over it," he says as he studies Diana.

"It's no big deal," Diana replies.

"Yes it is! You are learning to be good and stop your evil demon ways. That has given you inner peace. And when Melinda touched you, she tapped into that inner peace. She is a free spirit now because of you. That's so damn cool. C'mon, admit it!" Randy pushes.

"We don't know for sure that's what happened, but if it is, then yeah, whatever," Diana replies dismissively.

"C'mon guys, that's cool!" Randy pushes.

"He's right. It is kind of cool," East says.

Diana smiles slightly but does not say anything. She and I exchange a quick look and she turns away bashfully.

The team is as quick as they promised to be. We gather the supplies Diana needs and drop Randy off with the Healers at the Clinic. The whole time Randy was with us, he was in shock. He never really processed the fact that his index and middle finger were gone. But once we get to the Clinic it starts to sink in and he panics. The Healers sedate him and as he closes his eyes he makes me promise to bring his best friend back alive. I vow to do just that.

The team is not one hundred percent better, but with the help of Diana and the other Healers, we are strong enough to travel. And now that we have our powers back, our bodies can withstand more pain than before.

We get on the Ports and program them to take us to The Center. And as I look around at the faces of the team, I know the moment I have been dreading has come. I turn to my team and address them with a pained, somber voice.

"It's time you all know exactly what happened to me at The Center, and what has been happening to Pryor..."

BOOK III

PRYOR REESE CANE

"Sometimes to self-discover you must self-destruct."
— *Robert M. Drake*

CHAPTER TWENTY
THE WHITE ROOM

I miss my skin: the part that used to be attached to the right side of my face. I also miss the bones that were once inside my wings; I miss my wings. They don't let you keep your wings here in The Center. In fact, the only thing they let you keep here is the thing you want the least—your life.

They inject you with something called Nuvo. It's a mixture that allows you to stay alive no matter what horrific thing is happening to your body. Normally this would be a good thing, but given where I am, I prefer death to this. Well, to be honest, death is not a preference it's a luxury. One that I am certain I will never have.

I'm lying here on the floor of this floating glass box; the scorched remains of my blistering hands and feet are bound. It's overkill really because the fact is, bound or not, I can't run away. They have broken my leg. Honestly, it's hard to remember which torture came in what order.

Was I burned first, then cut open, or was it the other way around? They injected a liquid version of a bone saw into me, called Enda. Once inside you, it seeps into your joints and snaps your bones in half like a twig. You can actually hear your own bones breaking from the inside. So did the Enda come first?

It could be that the Barum came first. It's a pale grey mixture that is inserted inside your eyeballs. It burns at first but then it cools off. It lets you think that the hard part is over; it's not. A few moments after Barum enters your eyes, it travels down to the rest of your body and it leaves behind heat.

Or what starts out as a warm feeling. It quickly escalates to a raging fire inside your body.

Your blood begins to overheat and it starts seeping through what's left of your skin. Unable to withstand the impossible temperature, your skin drips onto the floor. You are being baked from the inside and you can't scream because your vocal cords have melted away.

No, wait! I think it could have been the Susu that came first. It's a machine that uses a laser to slice you open, digs into your insides, and takes a portion out to be analyzed. It's like some kind of twisted ice cream scooper; it hollows you out one big scoop at a time. Is that the first thing they did to me?

Damn it, I have to stay focused and remember. Recalling how this all began will help you to know that it's not forever. There was a beginning and there will be an end. It's the only way you will survive this. Don't you want to survive this? What the hell happened to you in the beginning? What did The Center do to you first?

Oh, yes! I remember now. The memory of what took place the night I was taken plays out in what's left of my fragile mind. I see it all so clearly; it's as if it's happening right now. The first thing, the *very* first thing they do is introduce me to the darkness…

I am home waiting on Randy so we can watch a movie together. Then I get a call from The Center. They have Randy. They place a dark vial on a Port and send it to me. I am instructed to drink the vial or there will be severe consequences. So I drink the mixture and I wake up in a special kind of hell.

I am engulfed by darkness from every angle. It seems to coat both my mind and body. There is no way of knowing how long I was knocked out for. It feels like it's been days, but it could easily have been minutes. When I open my eyes, I'm trapped inside a glass box suspended in midair. They have stripped off my clothes, put me in a white hospital gown, and removed my shoes.

I take a closer look at my surroundings. The room is white, sterile, and freezing. There are shadows walking around just outside the door. I pound on the glass with every ounce of energy I have but it doesn't break. I scream and shout for what must be hours, but no one comes in.

Finally, just when I am about to give up hope, someone enters the room.

He's a Para angel. He's elderly and has stark white hair, reading glasses, and wears a white lab coat.

"Who the hell are you and why are you keeping me here?" I demand.

"I'm Dr. Bishop. It's a pleasure to meet you, Pryor. I have heard a lot about you," he says, as if we are meeting each other for Sunday brunch.

"I don't give a shit who you are, let me out of here!" I rage.

"I can't do that," he replies.

He takes out a glass casing the size of a small cellphone and presses down on one of its many red colored buttons. Without warning, a series of strong sliver coils spring from behind me. They wrap around my shoulders, arms, midsection, thighs, and legs. The glass cage opens up and the coils place me on the shiny white floor, in front of Dr. Bishop.

"There, is that better?" he asks.

"Where am I? What have you done to Randy? If you hurt him I swear—"

"Now, now, Pryor. There is no reason to worry about the human. I assure you he is alive and well."

"He better be. Now what the hell do you want with me?"

"First, I'd like to welcome you to The Center. This is the place where we do some truly amazing things," he says.

"I know exactly what you do here. You torture innocent angels like Aaden, and when I get out of here you'll need to run—fast." I warn him as I struggle to loosen the coils that bind me.

"Silver was a great specimen. He helped us learn more about the Noru. That's the goal of The Center: to know as much as we can about our enemy."

"We are not your enemy, you freak!"

"Not yet, but that day will come. And when it does, we need to prepare. We need to learn as many ways as possible to destroy you should the need arise."

"We are not dangerous. We're angels just like you."

"Oh come now, I think we can all agree that the Noru are far superior to Paras. Your strength, your abilities, and your very nature allow you to outperform us on every possible level," he says in awe.

"Yet you're stupid enough to try and contain me," I point out.

"We do what we must in the name of preservation."

"We have never harmed any of you!" I shout.

"Not long ago you lost your temper and nearly demolished all of New York City," he points out.

"I didn't mean to do that. I just found my brother's dead body, you asshole!"

"Yes, well, meant to or not, your kind is a liability; a threat that must be neutralized. I wish we didn't have to do this. But for some reason angels insist on mating with ones outside of their species. And that makes for these super-powered mistakes, like yourself."

"When my team comes for me, they will have no mercy on you," I roar.

"Yes, I have no doubt of that. In fact that's what I am counting on. You see I have programmed a Deed. As you may know, it's essentially a bomb. It will go off should Silver reach an unprecedented level of anger. I have no doubt he will find your location, as he can be a very determined young man. But once he sees you, he will reach the level needed to activate the Deed. And when that happens, all of you will die."

"Why not just kill us?"

"I need more data on you, and by the time Silver finds us, I will have all the information I need. And again, I myself am not a violent angel. I would never kill. I deconstruct angels in the name of science. In the end it is Silver whose actions will kill your kind. He had a choice, may I add. We told him to stay away from you. We needed to know that this intermingling would stop but he refused. In the end I think this is best."

"You really are out of your mind," I reply as I shake my head in utter disbelief.

"My ex wife used to say that. In fact you know her, she teaches at your school I believe. Anyway, she'd say it in jest, but I think she really thought that. Well, I will prove her and everyone else wrong. Noru are dangerous and should be destroyed."

"You were married to The Face?" I ask.

"You know she actually loves that name. She jokes about it," he says, laughing.

"Did she do this? Is she helping you?" I demand.

"Oh no, she'd never do a thing like that. She's a kind woman but limited in her thinking. No, but I do however have help. I have an Apprentice."

"And who is that?" I ask.

"Someone who I have arranged to come by and meet you soon. You won't see my helper's face. It's better that way."

"Why?"

"In case we need to activate plan 'B.'"

"You might as well tell me because I promise your plan 'A' will fail."

"I doubt that, but since you won't live long, I think it's only fair you know. With all that we learned from our time with Silver, I have developed a mixture called Balance," he says, holding up a vial so I can see it up close.

"What is that?" I ask, already dreading the answer.

"It's a mixture that does the impossible. It strips Noru of their powers. I only have a pint of it made, as its ingredients are scarce. But rest assured, I will make more. Because I'm certain more of you will come into our world.

"Once we learn all we can about you, I hope it will help us perfect Balance. Right now its major flaw is that it takes several minutes to strip Noru of their power. We are working to accelerate the process. Now, enough talk, Noru. It's time."

"Time for what?"

"Exploration. We are about to subject you to a series of medical procedures, mixtures, devices, and general discomfort. But rest assured this is all in the name of science and discovery. And don't worry; you won't miss them all that much."

"What? I won't miss what?" I shout.

"Your wings."

***

What followed was so horrific, parts of my mind refuse to accept that it happened at all. The glass box folded itself and turned into a gurney made of the same material. The same coils kept me in place while Bishop injected me with the first of many mixtures. The torture had officially begun.

"Now, my dear, I'm inserting you with Frost to understand just how cold your body will get. You need to know this: the coldest substance in the human world is liquid helium. It's rather nasty. It will flash freeze your flesh in a fraction of a second. This mixture I'm putting into you is liquid helium mixed with a special advancer. In other words, there is a good chance you might lose a body part or two. But it's only going to last a few minutes. We need to freeze you because we need to get to your soul, without harming it. We wouldn't want your soul to die and have you leave us before we were done with you"

The needle pierces into my skin and the liquid enters my body; I feel a cold unlike anything I have ever felt before. It's a kind of cold that your body does not understand and cannot process. I scream and scream over and over again for him to let me go. My cries fill the spaces in my head and bounce around the room.

I catch a glimpse of myself in the reflection of the exit door. That's when I realize I'm screaming inside my head. My body is actually frozen. I am being held prisoner inside my body.

They use the Susu; the laser carves into the glacier that they have turned me into. They cut into the ice on my chest and take a chuck of my skin off along with it. A tube then springs out from under the gurney and attaches itself into the hole in my chest. The tube sucks out a glowing orb from inside my chest cavity.

That's my soul...

Bishop studies the orb and speaks to his minions about what he sees. I can't think long enough to form a sentence. I don't know how I'm able to live with my soul outside my body. All I know is that I am empty. I feel nothing.

"That's a very strong soul you have there, Noru. Now that we have seen it, we are going to warm you back up and see just how much your soul can take."

They then warmed me back up so that they could proceed to the next experiment. That's when I first saw it—the Enda vial. The vial that snaps your bones in half while it's inside you. They insert it into my leg and it makes its way around my body randomly picking which bone it will snap in two.

"AAAAAAAAAHHHHHHHHHHHHHHHHHHHHHHHHH…"

I'm crying blood. I'm shaking. The bone rips through my body and sticks out from my leg. Can't understand how this much pain can exist. Can't grasp the agony coursing through me. The Enda makes its way into my wings and snaps off every bone it comes in contact with.

"NOOOOOOOOOOOOOOOOOOOOOOOOOOO!!!!!"

I bang my head against the glass gurney in hopes of knocking myself out, but it doesn't work. I bang my head harder and harder still. I split my forehead open and keep going. His minions hold my head down and inject me with something so that I am wide awake and unable to even close my eyes.

"AHHHHHHHHHHHHHHHHHHHHHHHHHHHH!" I rage as my torment worsens.

The last thing I recall before my mind can no longer process is the Enda latching on to the bone that holds my wings together. It binds it until I hear a snap.

"Aaaaaaaaaaaaaaaaaaaaaaaaaaaden!!!" I cry.

In my head I'm floating out into a never ending void of anguish. I don't know how much longer this goes on. I can't tell time. I'm in hell; there are no clocks in hell.

***

When I open my eyes, I find myself back in the glass box. Everything hurts—my fingers, face, toes…everything. But when I look across the room, all the hurt goes away and I am left with only one emotion: unmitigated sadness. There, hanging on the wall like a cheap poster, are my wings.

They ripped my wings away…

I won't cry. I refuse to give that Bishop bastard the satisfaction of seeing me weep out of sadness. Maybe I can't control crying out in pain, but I will not weep for him or anyone else!

It's okay, the team will come for you. They will save you. He will save you. Aaden is coming. You just have to hang on…Pry, hang on.

Once again the coils spring up and restrain me. The box forms a gurney and the next step in "discovery" begins. They inject the Barum behind my eyes and set me on fire. The agony of having your blood boil inside you cannot be put into words. There simply is no way to convey the torment that is making its way into you.

My blood cooks inside me so much it bubbles up to my scalp and singes my hair. The roof of my mouth slides down my throat. I should be dead. But Bishop will not allow that kind of mercy.

Once again, my mind cannot process my agony with words. Instead images flash into my mind: In the first image, the devil himself is breathing fire into my mouth. In the second, the world's hottest peppers are ground up and placed inside my eye sockets. The final image before Bishop finally allows me to pass out without reviving me is lava dripping into my skull.

***

"Did you get any information from her?" *a voice asks.*

"Oh yes. We've learned a lot about them. How much they can and can't endure. This will help us to make our Balance mixture even more effective. Based on the testing done here, we should have no problem with future Noru," Bishop says.

"That's wonderful. I am honored to be a part of this."

"And I am honored to have you as my Apprentice. Please stay and watch our test experiment. We have tested her body and broken it. Now it's time we tested her mind."

"It is time for the White Room?" the voice says, excited.

"Wonderful, then you'll stay?" Bishop asks.

"Certainly," the Apprentice replies.

I pop my eyes open, desperate to get a glimpse of Bishop's helper, but I'm too late. They have both left the room. The only thing I know about his helper is that I have heard the voice before. But I can't place when or where. But then again, I can't really depend on my senses. For example, I swear as the Apprentice walked away, his scent wafted through the air and he smelled like almonds.

Almonds?

I'm going crazy. It's not just my body like Bishop said. The Center is getting ready to mess with my mind. I remember the terror that filled Ruin when she spoke about the White Room that Aaden had been in. She wouldn't go into details, so I have no idea what's about to happen…

***

Bishop must have knocked me out because I wake up and find myself in a different room. There's the sound of a machine roaring to life in the background, but it slowly fades. This room I am in is also white but in a totally different way. It's a warm glowing white that fills me with hope and peace.

I'm on the gurney, but my restraints have been lifted. I look around and there are windows that look out onto the beach. My body is broken, so making it to the window seems next to impossible.

What the hell?

My body is back to normal. There isn't a scratch on me. I examine my body in disbelief. How did this happen?

No, this is some mind game, right?

I walk over to the window and see the ocean laid out before me. There's an angel standing on the sand; he's facing away from me and has silver wings. Before I can stop myself, I call out to him. Aaden turns around and smiles back at me; he gestures for me to join him. I look around for a door—the second I see one, I run out towards the water. But for some reason the door takes me right back to the room.

I try another door, but no matter which one I try, I end up back inside the same room. I call out to Aaden; he grows angry that I am taking so long. I ask for his help and he smiles, but not at me. There's a group of girls who appear out of nowhere and surround him. He laughs with them and together they walk off.

"Aaden!" I shout repeatedly.

I don't understand...

I walk away from the window and look around. The room now has more than a dozen doors. I know this is a trick that The Center is playing on me. I decide I'm going to stay right where I am. But then I hear someone call me from outside the window.

"Carrot! Carrot! Come play!"

"Sam!" I shout as I run to the window.

My little brother stands in front of the ocean with his red hair and freckles. He flashes me his biggest smile and begs me to come to him. I don't care if it's a trick or not, I run out of the nearest door. Yet again it leads me right back to where I started. This happens with each door I try.

I look out the window and call out to Sam. I want him to know that I will find a way to get to him no matter what. But when I look out the window, Sam isn't alone. There are demons flying down towards him.

"No! Run, Sam, run!" I scream.

But he can't hear me. Instead he just keeps waving to me while giving his back to the demons. I yell for him to turn around, but he won't. I pound on the window and try to break it, but I can't. The demons land and tackle Sam to the ground.

"NO! Leave him alone! Get away from him!"

They feast on Sam's flesh as he calls out my name and begs me to save him.

"NO! Please don't hurt him. Hurt me please; you can hurt me! Not him. He didn't do anything! Please!!!!"

I slide down to the floor, curl up in the fetal position, and place my hands over my head to drown out the screams. It doesn't work. For the next few minutes all I hear is my little brother's cries. Then silence. Sam is gone. Again.

***

My memories are all played out now. I'm back to the present now and out of my head. The White Room happened earlier today. It broke me just like Bishop said it would. He stands before me making notes as he studies what's left of my body.

"I see you decided to open your eyes and join us. How did you like the White Room? I hope you enjoyed it, as you are headed for yet another visit," he informs me.

I hear the same machine I heard before. It roars to life and Bishop tells me it's the sound the generator makes and that he needs it to fully operate the large device that runs in the White Room.

The Apprentice was here. I don't see him but I smell almonds again. I close my eyes and think of nothing. I don't think about being rescued or taking revenge on Bishop. I keep my eyes closed because I don't care anymore. Sam is gone. I know that it was just an illusion to begin with, but it still hurts. It hurts more than anything The Center has done to me so far.

Hearing Sam laugh and call my name and then having that sound taken away from me is beyond cruel. I didn't understand what true evil was until now. I don't care about getting out of here. Here or somewhere else, it's all the same to me.

I don't know how Aaden stayed here for a year. It's been days and I give up. Do you hear, Omnis? I give up.

Like some cruel cosmic joke, the moment I give up, help comes bursting through the door. I watch as Aaden and the rest of the team battle Bishop and his minions. I watch as if it's a movie and there is nothing I can do to change the outcome.

In the heat of the battle, Aaden looks over at me, strapped to the gurney. He sees that my body has been burned and broken. He then sees that my wings have been cut off and placed on the wall. I know what's going to happen even before Aaden does.

He's angry; the kind of angry that turns his eyes full-on "demon." His wings are now black as the night sky. The team sees this happening and tries to stop Aaden from losing his temper, but it's too late. The Deed in Aaden's hand starts to open. All The Noru are going to die.

Bex grabs hold of Bishop around the neck but he won't stop the Deed from going off. The way a Deed works, once it's open fully, there's no stopping it. The box continues to open. Aaden's ire grows every second. Death is guaranteed.

Bex, seeing that Bishop will not give in, hurls him at the wall and runs to try and stop the box from closing up by force. The twins try to get over to me, but Bishop's underlings intercept them. Bishop gets up from the floor and starts hurling Powerballs at the team. The box is almost open all the way. This is the last I will see of my team; my family.

Suddenly Bishop stops what he's doing, goes over to the box, inputs a code, and the box closes. He then grabs the blade from one of his minions and slices his own throat. The team and I look on shocked, not sure what's going on. That's when I see him.

He enters through the double doors of The Center with commanding, undeniable grace. He wears a long black utilitarian coat that's fitted at the top and flows out at the bottom. He walks with poised certainty. Although we are surrounded by dangerous chaos, his movements are not hurried, but calm and controlled. And as our eyes meet, I detect something familiar in his chiseled face. He has the same perfect cheekbones, lips, and jawline as my father. There is no doubt in my mind; Malakaro is here. He heads over to me on the glass gurney.

He's come to kill me.

I'm pissed off. It's not that I'm going to die that bothers me, it's not being able to fight on my deathbed. Even if I don't win, I want to know that I at least tried to kill this murderous son of a bitch, Malakaro. And now he gets to finish what The Center started and I don't get to so much as hit him?

He looks down at me; I fight to remain calm. I don't want him to see the panic in my eyes. I don't want that to be what he remembers about me. I want him to remember the scorn and hatred I have for him. I want him to know that I loathe him in a way that can never be undone. He killed my brother. My Sam. And I want him to see that while what he did changed me, it did not break me.

He places his hand on the side of my face gently and strokes my cheek with his thumb. Not sure what's going on, I stay still. Malakaro leans in close and whispers something in my ear. Tears fill my eyes and run down the side of what's left of my face. Malakaro then releases me from my restraints and gracefully takes off into the night sky.

Seeing that I am now free helps Aaden control his temper. His wings begin to revert back to their original silver color. As he rushes over to me, he sends a fireball towards the direction of the lab equipment where the Balance vials are being held.

"It's gonna blow, move it!" Aaden shouts to the team as he scoops me up in his arms.

The team dives for the snowbank just as The Center goes up in flames behind us.

I look around and find that I was being held deep underneath a snowy mountain range. The snowflakes fall down from above and gently land on me. I expect them to hurt since everything that has touched me these past few days has caused extreme agony. I flinch, but the snowflakes prove harmless.

My body can't cope with what has been happening, and now, without being injected with mixtures to keep me awake, it begins to shut down. I'm in Aaden's arms when the darkness starts to roll in. He tells me he's sorry it took so long. The team asks me what Malakaro whispered in my ear but I don't reply. I can't.

Aaden holds me close and says that I will be all right. He says that the Healers will heal my face and that I will be okay.

If only he knew how wrong he was…..

CHAPTER TWENTY-ONE
THIS GIRL, PRYOR

I drift in and out of consciousness. I have no real concept of time or how long I've been in the trauma center. When I am awake and aware, I hear a beautiful song fill the air with a haunting melody. I'm not sure who's singing, but I want them to sing forever. Aside from the song, I hear other things. Things I don't care about: bits and pieces of conversations around me.

"As you know, they have torn her wings from her. That was enough to horrify myself and the other Healers on staff, but once you brought her wings for us to take a look at…what we found was even more disturbing."

"Just tell us; what have they done to her wings?" someone asks.

"Silver, stop snapping at the Healers, they are trying to help," a female voice says.

"Sorry, Bird, I just…"

"I know. Me too. But let's hear the Healer out," this "Bird" being replies.

"As I was saying, we took a look at her wings and every bone inside them have been smashed."

"So that's it? Pry may never fly again?" the male asks.

"Fly? Silver, she has a fractured skull, a severe infection from the incision they made under her chin down to her abdomen, portions of her spine have been removed, and her right leg is broken in two places. Fly? This girl will be lucky to walk again."

223

"I don't give a shit what you have to do; you just fix her!" He rages at the Healer.

"Silver, please."

"Bird, I can't do this, okay? I can't just stand here and—argh!!!!!!!!"

I hear the sound of heavy objects hitting the ground.

"Get Silver out of here, now!" someone says.

"Bex is right; you need to take a walk," the female known as Bird replies.

I'm guessing they make him leave because I hear the sound of footsteps getting farther away from me.

"I'm sorry. I am not trying to upset your teammate," the Healer says.

"It's not you, it's just…it's been hard on all of us," a different male replies.

"As a fellow Para, I understand your frustration; I do. But I want to be realistic about the situation. In addition to what I said to Silver, there are other things wrong with the First Noru."

"Okay, what else?" the Para asks, sounding pained and haggard.

"Her collarbone and both wrists have been broken. And even if we are able to reconnect her wings, they have severed the connection between her shoulder blades that control them."

"Please do what you can; she's not just the First Noru to us, she's a friend. We need her—desperately."

***

Again, I'm not sure how long I have been in this bed, but the pieces of information I gather from the rare moments I am awake aren't all that encouraging.

"The more time goes on, the more difficult it is for them to put her back together," a Healer surmises.

Ha! Put me back together? Silly Healers. I'm broken in places they can't get to, let alone fix. "Put me back together?" *Ha!*

"What happened when you tried to attach the wings?" someone asks.

"I told you, Silver, first we have to create synthetic bones to hold up her wings, since all of hers were destroyed. Then we will see if reattaching is even possible," the Healer replies.

"It's already been four weeks! How much longer?"

"As long as it takes. If she wasn't a Noru, if her parents weren't a First Guardian and a council member, she would have been dead by now."

"Well they are, so you remember that," he warns.

"There is no need to threaten me," the Healer replies.

"If she doesn't make it, I'll do more than threaten you. So you make sure she survives this. And do not tell anyone outside of this team that she is here," he warns the Healer again.

"Yeah, yeah, I already got that speech from the Para," the Healer replies.

"What did he say?"

"Oh you know, the usual. If any Healer dares speak a word about The First Noru's condition, he'll shove our wings down our throats and gut us alive."

***

From yet more stray pieces of conversation, I gather that I have now been in the Trauma center for nearly two months. They were able to reattach my wings but it took another two weeks to get me to communicate with them. By the time my wings are fully functioning, I have spent a total of twelve weeks in the hospital.

"Why can't you regrow her wings like you guys did my fingers?" someone asks.

"The bones of angels are far more complex than that of humans."

"Okay, fine, but her wings are back where they belong, she can fly, and her wounds are slowly closing up. So why isn't she talking? Why doesn't she say anything?" I hear someone say as I open my eyes. It's a human boy speaking. He's the voice I heard singing to me. I so wish he'd do it again.

"She's slowly on the mend physically. Mentally, she is still very much in shock. She's distancing herself from everything that's happened to her," the

Healer says. The human looks back at her with deep regret and misery. He can barely stand to look at the bed where I lie.

I am mostly awake now although I'd rather not be. Whenever I open my eyes, someone is there, sitting beside my bed. I know them from my life before the torture. But know I can't really put together who they are.

There are two sisters who are always looking down at me, worried. I don't know how I know they are sisters but I do. I also know that the human who comes to see me feels close to me, but I'm not really sure what our relationship is. There's a Quo who comes to visit me also. He has a nice smile but his eyes are sad. Then there's the Para. He's tall and handsome. But he looks so serious.

And finally there's the half demon. He is always there, no matter what. When I wake up he's the first face I see. He's also the saddest. But his sadness is different, more personal. It's as if he is somehow to blame for what happened to me. There's guilt in his eyes. Yes, deep-rooted guilt.

***

As my stay here nears three months, the Healer begins to see far more progress. Although I have not spoken a word, my body is showing signs of coming back to life. How ironic that the more alive I am, the more I wish I were dead.

The angels who come to visit me want me to sit up, make eye contact, and move my lips. All these things require far more effort than I care to make. There's a heaviness inside me that weighs me down. It makes even the simple act of blinking too daunting. So doing the things they want me to do is simply impossible.

I know they are here with me, but it's like they are thousands of miles away. It's as if I'm looking at them through a telescope. I can see them but I can't reach them or connect because they are too far away. Or maybe it's me. Yes, I think it's me. I'm far away from them, from my team.

I know I've been rescued, but I'm still in hell in my mind. I see the sunlight streaming through the window but I can't feel the warmth from the sun on my skin. I know my wings are now reattached to me and that they work, but I can't process the fact that they are whole again. I can't process that I too am whole again.

Am I whole?

How could I be if I can't be present? The angels call my name often, hoping for a response; so does the human. I don't reply. It's not my body— I am healed, or at least my body is healed. I don't reply because I can't find the desire to talk to them or anyone. What I want more than anything is to slowly fade from view.

I want to not be here anymore. I want to stop living and all that comes with it. I want my wings, skin, fingernails, hair, veins, and bones to stop existing. I want my eyes to stop registering images and fade to black. I want the delicious feel of nothingness to surround me and reach inside the deepest part of me.

There's a sadness that injects itself into my soul and spreads throughout the shell that is my body. It coats the spaces between my eyelashes, under my fingernails, my toes, and the lining inside my lips. Sorrow, misery, and melancholy form a haunting refrain in my head and play on repeat.

There's only one thing I know for sure as I stare out the window: I will never feel happiness again. I will never feel anything other than this hopeless despair. How long will Omnis keep me in this misery? Why didn't he let me die in The Center? Why won't he let me die now?

They have filled my room with framed pictures from someone else's life: some girl with red hair like flames and purple eyes. Pryor did things. She flew in the air. She laughed. She had a baby brother. She had concerns. She had hope. She's gone now; long gone.

I'm left here, trapped in the body of a girl I can no longer connect to. They are sad that she's gone. They want their old Pryor back. Every day they try a new way to reach her. The twins read to me from what must have been my favorite books. The human being shows me photo albums of the girl with my face. She's having fun with him. In the pictures she's carefree and hasn't been tortured. I hate her.

The Para comes to my hospital room and holds my hands. He tries to warm them up but he doesn't know the cold is coming from inside me and that I will never again be warm; silly Para. And then there's the half demon that comes to see me every day. He's the first here and the last to leave my room. Most nights he sleeps on the chair across from my bed.

The half demon is the most distraught of them all. He misses the Pryor girl he knew. He wants her back more than anything. He's never going to get her back because she's not here. She left me in her body but she's truly not here. I sit on the windowsill waiting for death and find that once again it has missed its appointment with me.

I don't know what time it is as I don't care enough to turn and read the clock in my room. Time doesn't matter all that much; nothing does. I can tell a chunk of time has passed by watching people from my window.

There's a human crossing the street, running for the bus. She is always running for the same bus. She runs to it and later she runs from it and goes home I guess. I wonder why she bothers running. I wonder how long it will take her to realize everything is meaningless and that sooner or later, death will claim her.

She's so lucky.

There's a spider that sits across the room and every day she travels and returns to check on her eggs at the center of her web. She does her job dutifully. Pryor had a job. She was supposed to be strong and protect her team and family. She failed spectacularly.

The spider is smarter than that Pryor girl and probably stronger.

Somewhere between the human running to the bus and the spider's return to her web, the half demon sits on the windowsill beside me and speaks to me. From the sound of his voice he really liked Pryor. He may have even loved her.

Silly half demon...

"It's been nearly three months, Pry, and you have yet to say one word to us; to me. Please, say something. I know you're in there. Please talk to me," he says, heartbroken.

I continue to look out the window in search of the human who should now be running for the bus. I can't find her.

"I know what you're going through; believe me. I know you want to die, but you are not getting away that easily. There's a list of things I want—need to do with you. There's a lake in Tanzania that turns the animals into statues. I figure we can take Randy there and freak him out.

"Also there's a small village in Russia where every year these like eighty-year-old ladies with blue hair gather, strip naked, and run—voluntarily—into a frozen lake. The look on their faces when they first hit the water is priceless. And the crazy thing is they are actually having a good time. And then we can stop off and see blue lava flow in Indonesia; it's so bizarre, but really beautiful…

"Okay, Pry, the thing is there are lots of places I have thought about going with you. There's a million moments I want us to have together. But the one that matters most to me is the one where you wake up in my arms.

"It kills me to know that you are here but your mind is still somewhere lost in the darkness. I know that place. You won't survive there. Please, come back. The year I was away from you, I'd find myself missing you and I thought nothing could be worse, but I was wrong. Having you near me but not being able to reach you…that's a hell even a demon like me can't face." His voice is thick with emotion and he strokes my hand.

Where the hell is the human on the bus? Damn her, she missed it. She missed the bus—again.

"Pryor, do you hear me?" he asks.

I wonder if the human will make the next bus.

The half demon hangs his head, hurt and frustrated. Later, I have another visitor. This one is a full demon. I know him but his name escapes me at the moment. He looks into my vacant eyes and brushes my hair away from my face.

"Pryor Reese Cane, you can't stay locked up in your mind, kid. You need to cut the crap and come back to us. You got it?" he says firmly.

The human is back! She makes a dash for the bus.

"Pryor! They need you. I need you. You're my family. You can't stay away. You have to fight to return to your senses. Your parents…it would kill them to see what's become of you. You're all they have left, kid. You have to fight to come back," he says.

The human gets on the bus.

"I'm gonna be honest, it's not just that the team needs you to come back; he needs you. Pryor, you are the Omnis in my son's world. You are his everything. If you don't come back…I don't know how he will go on without you. I lost his mother and that broke me. I don't want him to feel that kind of pain. Save him; save my son…"

The bus pulls away. The spider returns to her web. The full demon kisses me on the forehead and leaves the room. While I'm turned away, someone comes into my room and mumbles something about cleaning up. I don't reply, I just stare out at nothing. It's only when I turn back around I realize that the cleaning lady has actually cleaned the entire room; including the spiderweb.

I don't remember striking the cleaning lady or going berserk and screaming at the entire staff that I would kill them all for destroying the web. The Healers restrain me and inject a mixture into me that forces my eyes to close.

When I open my eyes, I find the Para is looking down at me. He gently makes me sit up and face him.

"The Healers said you got very upset about a spider's web," he says.

I remain quiet and look over where the web used to be. He follows my gaze. He opens his hand and there's a small envelope inside it. On it is the spider's web. It's still attached.

"The cleaning woman used a broom and dust pan. She swept it right off the wall and it landed in the dustbin on top of this envelope. We're gonna have to leave it on the envelope because it's so fragile, but it's still intact. You want to help me get it back up there?" he asks.

I nod and he is suddenly overcome with emotion. He gasps as if he were a human who had been holding his breath for half an hour and now he can finally exhale. He places his hand in front of his lips to hide his shocked expression.

"That's the first time you've responded..." he says as he pulls me towards him and hugs me. He whispers that he knew I was in there somewhere. He composes himself and together we carefully place the web back on the wall.

The Healers agree that even though I overreacted to the web being destroyed, the fact that I care about anything, even a spider, means I am regaining my sense of purpose. They think I am getting reconnected to what it means to be an angel. They send me back home to New York City.

***

When I enter Pryor's house they watch me. They watch to see if she will return to the empty shell she left behind, but she doesn't. They exchange looks of disappointment and concern between them. They should stop looking for Pryor. It would make them happier to expect that she's gone. I do.

They place my things in one of the rooms and the human points out that it's my room. He tells me what memories are attached to what item on the dresser. He starts with the picture again. The twins rush to get my mixture medications.

The Para fusses with the room temperature, determined to find what he refers to as "the perfect balance," because Pryor is always too hot or too cold. I want to point out that she doesn't care about the temperature since she is no longer with us but that requires words.

The half demon is having a hard time. I can see that because he looks pained and exhausted. Whoever this girl was, she mattered to him more than he could ever express. The same can be said of the Para. The two of them rarely exchange words, but they seem to suffer the same profound loss.

They place all my things in "my" room and remind me that they are just outside the door should I need them. Then they leave me alone in her room. It's like being left at ground zero of an explosion. The remains of someone who is no longer there surround me.

I don't know where to place myself as everything here seems like sacred ground. Someone once loved used to live here. How dare I touch her things? How dare I sit on her bed or touch her picture frames? Who am I that I should be where a leader once stood?

The Quo slowly opens the door and looks in. He tells me that I have been standing still, in the same position, for six hours. Judging by the sound of his voice, this information seems to cause him great pain. He gently brushes the side of my face with his hands. His touch is warm. He too cared about this Pryor girl.

Suddenly, I hear a sound traveling up the steps—it's a loud roar and it's getting louder. It's the machine. They are going to put me in the White Room!!!

"Pryor, it's just the can opener!" the Quo tells me.

I don't listen, I rage against him and as the others enter the room, I battle them too. I kick, scream, claw, bite, and punch my way free. I run down the steps, terrified they will get me. I can't let them get me. I can't let them get me. I bolt for the door and the half demon catches me.

"NO!!!!! I can't go in that room! Please...don't make me go...ahhhhhhhhh!" I sob into his chest.

"Okay, we won't go in that room ever again," he promises.

"NO, YOU'RE GONNA MAKE ME GO BACK. I WON'T GO BACK. I WON'T GO BACK!" I cry.

I rant and rave for what seems life forever and then I feel my body go limp. He picks me up and scoops me into his arms. He takes me upstairs. At first I think we are headed for the White Room, but then I don't hear anything. And even if it was the White Room, I'm too weak to protest. The half demon whispers to me and says my medication is kicking in and not to fight it. There's something so strong and certain about the half demon. There's something solid about him, something...safe.

"Don't let them get me..." I mumble as I give in to the oncoming darkness.

***

The next time I open my eyes, I find that the half demon was true to his word. He did not leave my side. He placed me on the bed and stands protectively beside me.

"I told you I wouldn't leave you and I meant it."

I nod, but don't say anything.

"We need to bathe you and get you out of those clothes. Do you want me to call the girls to help you do that?" he asks gently.

The thought of him leaving me causes a rush of panic. I shake my head "no."

"Are you sure you want me to do it? I am okay with it, I just want you to be comfortable with me undressing you," he says.

I nod "yes."

Someone knocks on the door. It's the twins. The half demon tells them what he's about to do and they object.

"She won't let anyone else do it. I'm not using this as a chance to get a peep show going," he says, clearly offended.

"Silver, we know you're just trying to help Pry. The reason we said we'd do it isn't because of you, it's because of Pryor," the smaller twin says.

"Key, what is she talking about?" he asks.

"Right now Pryor is lost somewhere inside her mind, but if she was here, this isn't what she'd want. This isn't how she'd want you to first see her naked. She doesn't want you to think of her as some helpless nutcase."

"I don't think that at all. You know how I feel about her!" he snaps.

"Yes, but this isn't about you. It's about Pryor. And she would want the first time you two are…you know…she'd like that to be under a different set of circumstances. Don't rob her of that."

"Swoop's right. Aaden, let us bathe her. We'll watch over her. You can stand nearby should she need you, but stand where you won't see anything. She'd want it that way."

"Okay, I can do that," he says as he turns and addresses me.

"The girls are going to bathe you and I will be right here if you need me. I won't go anywhere."

"Promise?" I ask.

"Yes," he says, relieved to hear the sound of my voice.

Once again he keeps his word. The females help me out of my clothes and into the bathtub. They are bathing me, taking care not to make contact with the scars that have yet to heal. The whole time, I am looking towards the mirror that reflects the image of the half demon as he waits for me. We make eye contact and it's the first time I actually want to wonder about this girl, Pryor. Does she know this half demon's sole purpose on earth is to watch over her?

When the girls are done, they help me out of the tub, dry me off, and help me put on pajamas. The half demon thanks them. I try to smile but I'm not sure how. When they leave, he tucks me under the covers and stands over me. I don't need to ask if he will stay; somewhere inside me, I know he will.

***

When I wake up this time it's not the half demon who's looking down at me but the human. His eyes are puffy and slightly swollen.

"I'm sorry, I turned on the can opener earlier. I didn't know it would…" The human's eyes fill with tears.

"Randy, it's not your fault. Pry just needs some time," the half demon replies from a few feet away.

"I know you've been through a lot, but I need you back, Pry. You said you would never leave me. We're best friends. You can't go back on your word!" he shouts, suddenly angry.

"Randy, stop screaming at her," the half demon counters.

"No! It's time for her to hear the truth. You're the First Noru and you cannot just sink into oblivion. It's not fair to the team or to me. And you know what? You're being a shitty sister! Sam is dead and you promised to avenge him and now you're hiding inside your head!"

"Sam…" I mutter as flashes of a sweet-faced redheaded boy flood my mind.

"Yes! Sam. He loved you and he was taken away and you have to come back and make that right. If you don't come back because of how much we love you, then come back because of how much you hate Malakaro; he had Sam killed," Randy says.

Randy! He's my friend; my best friend.

The half demon looks at me closely.

Aaden.

Aaden!

"Pry, are you okay?" Aaden asks.

"They killed him. They killed Sam," I reply.

"Yes, they did. Now we're going to fix that. Someday we'll make sure they pay," Aaden replies. I address him for the first time with complete clarity.

"No, Aaden, now. Everyone pays; now."

CHAPTER TWENTY-TWO
WHITE MEAT

I gather everyone in the living room. When I descend the staircase, they watch, mystified that for the first time in months I'm not a basket case. I seem like my old self, well on the outside anyway.

"I wanted to talk to all of you because there's a few things we need to clear up," I tell them in my official voice.

"Sure, whatever you need. We're just glad that you're getting around," East replies.

"You look so much better, Pry," Swoop says with a smile.

"Thanks. First we need to discuss this team," I reply.

"What about us?" Randy says.

"First, Randy, you're not a part of this team. I am not saying that to be cruel. You are my best friend and I love you. But members of this team get hurt. And I will not permit that to happen to you. I need you to go; please."

"Wait, you can't be serious," Randy says.

"She's not. Pry, tell Randy you're just kidding," Swoop urges.

"I don't think you guys get it. Do you know what Malakaro said to me right before he 'rescued' me?" I ask.

The whole room waits with bated breath as I finally reveal the foul words Malakaro spoke to me at The Center.

"He said, 'I need you to stay alive to watch the show. I need you alive to experience the razor sharp pain that comes from knowing people around you are dying for no other reason than the fact that they were loved by you.

And they *will* die, Pryor: your teammates, your friends, and your lovers—anyone who means anything to you. They will die slow. They will die often. And they all die with the same final thought. If only they never met you, perhaps they would have been spared…'"

I look across the room at Aaden. He's enraged by the words Malakaro spoke, but more than that, he's worried for me. Randy reaches out to embrace me but I pull away.

"Randy, I need you to go home. Now."

"But you can't send him away. He's the Blue Rose Heir, remember?" Key says.

"Yes, but Malakaro doesn't know that. Randy can just go on living his life normally. In fact, us being in his life is the only thing that could give him away," I reply.

"Pry, I don't want to—"

"Randy, please," I say to him. Hurt, Randy walks out of the house.

"Pry, why would you do that?" Aaden asks.

"Because I want him to be safe; hanging around us is not the way to achieve that," I remind him.

"We can keep Randy safe," Key says.

"Really, like you guys kept me safe?" I snap.

"Pryor—" Bex begins.

"I'm not done. The next thing on our list is the demon."

"If you want me out then I will leave," Ruin informs me.

"Wait, that's not what Pryor is saying," Aaden says.

"Actually, that's exactly what I'm saying. Thank you for all your help, Ruin. Should there come a time when we can return the favor, we will. Until then, please get your things and get out of my parents' home," I order.

Ruin glares at me. She then looks at Aaden and goes upstairs to get her things.

"You have no right to do that, Pry. Not after everything that girl has sacrificed to help us," Aaden counters.

"I'm sorry, but maybe you haven't heard. I was kidnapped and tortured by a group of angels that were supposed to be well... angels. They were supposed to protect us and guard us against evil. Instead they tuned on us; on me. They split my body open and mutilated my damn wings. And now, well, I have to say I'm a little short on trust. And whatever little I have will not be given to a demon," I inform him in a firm voice.

Pissed, he shakes his head and goes upstairs after Ruin. I turn my attention back to the team. They look at me and show me that they are displeased with my stance on the Ruin issue. That's okay because I'm their leader before I am their friend. And I will keep them away from whatever I deem unsafe, like it or not.

"Now, I've been given all the updates and I really am not happy about the way things are with this team," I continue.

"Maybe you should get some rest. You aren't acting like yourself," Swoop says.

"Yes, and I dare say that's an improvement," I reply.

"Pryor, you really need to take some time before you can lead us again," Bex suggests.

"No. I am taking charge of this team. Now," I counter.

They all exchange uneasy looks but they all stay silent. I turn my attention to Easton.

"I've been told that you did not Mind wipe the human girl, Marisol. Is that true?" I ask.

"Pry, I didn't want to take away the hope she had when she learned that there were angels in the world," East pleads.

"What about her skin?" I ask.

"What?"

"You have a problem taking away her hope but how do you feel about her skin being taken away from her? How about her ribs being snatched from inside her body? Are you good with that? Because that's what Malakaro's going to do to any and everyone we love. He's going to deconstruct them one piece of flesh at a time. What they did to me at The Center is nothing compared to what my dear bother has in mind for us. Or the people who dare to love us. You love this girl, then save her from you—from us," I order.

"You think that could really happen?" East asks.

"She may get taken by Malakaro, she may get taken by another secret group like The Center. Who knows? That's the whole point. We have no idea who or what is out there with the intent to harm us. That's why we can't open our doors or our hearts."

"Pryor may be right—about Marisol. You don't want anyone to find out how much she means to you," Swoop warns him.

"Go and wipe her mind. East, it's the only way you can protect her," I reply.

"Yeah, yeah, I guess," East says as he gets up and heads to the door.

"Oh, and Easton?" I call out.

"Yeah?" he says, sounding troubled.

"I lead this team. You follow. That is your job. When I tell you to Mind wipe someone, you damn well better do it. Is that clear?"

"Yeah," he says under his breath as he exits.

"And I hear you have given your kingdom over to Hollander. Is that true, Bexington?" I ask.

"Don't feel bad about it. What matters is that giving up being Kon helped get you back. And really don't thank me; I'm just glad you're safe," he says.

"I wasn't planning to thank you. I was planning on asking what the hell you were smoking when you gave your kingdom to a jerkoff like Hollander!"

"What? I did it for you," he pushes.

"Yes, and it was a dumbass move. Now we have the biggest power hungry asshole in the Para world running things."

"I don't care about that. I care about you," he says, growing angry.

"I'm one being; you cannot put one angel over your kingdom. If you do, what kind of king will you be? You let Hollander play on your emotions. I need you to grow a brass set of wings and give Hollander this," I say as I hand him a small flat crystal the size of a quarter.

"What is this?" the Para asks.

"It's a Plate. There's a message inside only he can read. Take it to him; tell him it's from me. And tell him if he does not release the kingdom to you, I will be down to headquarters at first light. And as the humans are finishing up their morning coffee, I will be standing over him watching as the last sign of life fades from his eyes."

"Pryor, you can't bluff Hollander like that," Bex replies.

"Who the fuck said I was bluffing?"

He looks back at me, worried and on edge.

"Do I need to make this an order because I will." I warn him.

He shakes his head and walks out to do as I instruct. I look to the twins, who now remain before me.

"Swoop, I need you to stop all your DJ gigs," I tell her.

"What? No! Why?" she asks.

"Because it keeps you out late nights and I want everyone inside at a reasonable time."

"Pry, that's not fair. You know how much I love what I do," she pleads.

"Being a DJ is not what you do. It's a hobby. And the time has come for it to end."

"No, I'm not giving it up. Music is the only thing that's mine. It's the only thing that belongs to me," she protests.

"There's a DJ app on iTunes. You'll be just fine," I reply.

"Why are you acting like this? Why are you being such a bitch?" she yells.

"What is it in my voice that makes you think I am in the mood to be tested?" I ask in a deadly tone.

"Swoop shouldn't have to give up her music just because you want her to," Key says.

"Well, she can always count on you to take her home, if you're not high and drunk, that is," I counter.

"Pryor, don't!" she warns.

"You are the third strongest Noru in this room and you have the self-control of a two-year-old human! How dare you take drugs knowing how much we count on you?" I rage.

"Leave her alone. She was going through a hard time," Swoop says, taking her sister's hand protectively.

"Well, that just makes it all better, doesn't it? I don't give a shit what your reasons are, Keyohmi. I ever catch you in the vicinity of drugs and you're off this team. Do you understand?"

"You have no right to talk to us like this," Key replies bitterly.

"I did not hear an answer to my question, so I will try again. You will not touch so much as a bottle of Coy so long as you are on this team. Am I clear?"

"What is wrong with you?" she asks.

"AM I CLEAR?"

"YES!"

I turn my attention back to Swoop. She silently agrees to stop being a DJ and staying out all night. Ruin marches down the steps and storms past us. She heads out the door and Aaden glares at me as he takes off after her.

A short while later, I put my jacket on and head towards the door.

"No one leaves the house without notifying me first. I will be back," I tell the twins as I place my hand on the doorknob.

"Where are you going?" they ask.

"To meet the Board. It's time we came to an understanding."

***

I meet him a few blocks from my house, in a seedy alley with no lights. I knew he would be on time because I told him if he was late he wouldn't get paid. And the one thing Spider loves is money. Spider is a Pawn. That means he's a human who services evil, yet he still has his soul. Most Pawns are slaves and captives, but not him. He's too damn slippery to ever be contained. And while many in the Angel world want his head on a spike, the fact is he's very useful.

Spider is arguably the Angel world's greatest thief. He's only slightly taller than me. He has stringy dirty blonde hair, a thin frame, and a few stray hairs he's been trying to convince people will someday grow into a full beard.

"Do you have what I asked for?"

"I'm Spider, baby," he says, slightly hurt that I would even ask.

"Good, hand it over," I reply.

"You know, I'm surprised you came to me. I mean, aren't you angels all 'holy' and stuff? What are you doing with a thief?" he asks.

"I need to associate with beings I can trust," I tell him.

"Wow, and you trust me? You know, that warms my heart a little," he admits with a sly smile.

"I trust you to be money hungry and sneaky."

"Well, I try. You know, it's not easy nowadays. Even the humans are getting more savvy about personal security. I was at a friend's house just the other day and he put a padlock on his refrigerator!"

"That's amazing."

"I know, right? I mean, who secures their deli meats and apple juice?" he says.

"No, I mean it's amazing that you have a friend."

"Well, I do. And I have an opening for one more. So…you wanna be my *friend*?" he asks suggestively.

"I can't be with you, Spider. You're just too much man for me. I mean you have three…four…oh no, five hairs on your chin. I don't think I could handle you," I quip.

"For your information, I have seven hairs and there's an eighth one coming in."

"Honestly, why don't you just drink a mixture to grow hair?" I ask.

"Because that would be mendacious."

"Did you just say 'mendacious?'" I ask, perplexed.

"It means 'deceitful' or 'underhanded.' I got me one of those calendars; you know the ones with a new vocabulary word for each day? And today's word is 'mendacious.'"

"So this is you trying to educate yourself?" I ask.

"Well yeah. I figure I can't be hustling forever. Someday I'd like to steal a nice little home somewhere and start a family with…"

"Swoop," I add.

"Well yeah—it can happen," Spider says quickly.

Spider has been deeply infatuated with Swoop ever since I can remember. He goes to all her gigs and waits for her backstage. Swoop never has the heart to tell him she's not interested. So she smiles and plays along. But over the years, his infatuation has grown.

"I promise to tell her that you asked about her. Now, give me the information I need," I reply.

"Okay, okay. Here it is; the location of the Board. I got it by digging around in the trash bin of the—"

"Save that story for later. I gotta go," I reply as I rush away from him.

"Hey, tell Swoop I can't wait for our next meeting. It's gonna be *auspicious*; That was yesterday's word!"

***

I stand in the center of London's financial district and look up at the skyscraper before me. Inside are the most powerful members of the Angel world. Or at least what remains of them here on earth. They form the Board. Their job is to protect us since we are the strongest angels ever created. I only know one of their members, Uncle Rage. I know he's on assignment and won't be there. That makes what I'm about to do much easier.

I get on the elevator and get off on the twenty-third floor. I walk past the human at the reception desk and head straight for the frosted glass double doors with the silhouette of wings flapping in the air. I enter the large conference room and find ten impeccably dressed angels and The Face. Judging by the looks on their faces, they weren't planning on me walking in. And I am not a welcome sight.

"I'm hurt; did my invitation get lost in the mail?" I ask.

"Ms. Cane, this is a closed meeting," the angel with the gray hair at the head of the table says.

"Well, I'm opening it up," I reply with a smile.

"This is highly irregular," the Para with the pinstripe tie says.

"Don't worry, this won't take long," I promise them.

"You are not allowed in these meetings. How did you even know where to find us?" the only female member asks.

"I did a Google search," I quip.

"You cannot be here. We have important matters to discuss and we are not opening our meeting to you. We are here to ensure your safety. We are not, however, obligated to tolerate your insolence!" the Para at the head of the table informs me.

"See, here's the thing: the Board had one job. Just one. That was to keep the Noru safe until our parents returned from the light. How's that going?" I ask.

"We know there have been some setbacks…" the female says.

I look over at her with great disdain. I then address the group.

"I was sliced open and gutted. Is that what you mean by 'setback?'"

"Ms. Cane—"

"SHUT UP!" I snap at the Para with the pinstripe tie.

The group glares at me and silently warns that my outburst could have consequences.

I look each and every one of them in the eye and don't back down. When I open my mouth to speak again, I sound more like my father.

"For the past few months we have been told what to do and what not to do by the Board because we believed you were all looking out for us. However, I have a hard time believing that The Center could have existed right under your noses and you missed it. I have come to two conclusions: the Board is either filled with ineptitude or treachery. So, which is it? Are you guys morons or traitors?"

"Now see here, Ms. Cane!" the Para on my left says as he raises his hand to attack me.

I am faster and far more pissed off than he is, so before he can even think to strike me, I have drained nearly half of his life force from his body and he lies on the floor in pain. The rest of the Paras go to help him and I warn them that I will kill their friend if they so much as move an inch towards us. The Face pleads with me to rethink what I am doing. I pay her no attention at all.

"All we have ever wanted to do was help the Angel world and protect humanity. That's what we were raised to do. But instead of celebrating how powerful we are and will come to be, some of you have come to see us as a threat. We have done nothing to earn your fear or your hatred. Yet some of you plot and conspire to destroy us.

"We have had enough of your so-called 'protection.' From now on the Noru will protect ourselves. In fact, the only being whose opinion we will take under advisement is Mrs. Greenblatt. She is the person that my mother appointed to look out for us, and she is the only one we will turn to guidance. And even then, the final decision on what we do and don't do will rest with me. I am the First Noru. I will ultimately decide what is best for my team.

"And I want all of you to pay very close attention because I am only going to say this once. If anyone at this table even *associates* with an angel or demon that means us harm…I will crack your skull open like a coconut and feast on the white meat."

I angrily release the Para, turn on my heel, and head for the door. The leader calls out after me.

"You think you can tell us what to do? You are sadly mistaken. You may be Marcus's daughter, but there are more of us Paras than there are of you, Noru," he spits.

"My only concern is my team. They are my family. And if I have to slaughter every single Para on Earth to ensure their safety, so help me Omnis I will. Oh, and for the record, I'm not coming to you as Marcus Cane's daughter. Or even the daughter of Death. I am coming to you as the sister of a sociopath; push me, Para, and you will learn exactly how *very* alike Malakaro and I are."

CHAPTER TWENTY-THREE
BEFORE I AM AN ANGEL

I am so engrossed in the Muse I am reading, I don't even hear Aaden come in. I'm guessing he's been leaning in my doorway for a while now, just looking me over. I pull myself away from the journal and address him.

"What is it?" I ask.

"I heard about your visit to the Board."

"And?"

"Well, don't you think it's something we needed to talk about before you went ahead and did it?" he replies.

"No."

"I'm gonna need a little more," he says, trying to control his temper.

"The Board is full of shit. They are more harmful than they are useful."

"Agreed, but they are representing the Paras. You can't just dismiss them," he insists.

"All I did was tell them that we will take care of ourselves. And Bex represents the Paras. Not the Board," I argue.

"You heard Hollander returned Bex's birthright back to him?"

"Yeah, it's trending on Twitter."

"Yeah, hashtag #LongLiveKon. Hollander is making believe he never even tried to take the title from Bex."

"I told you. Hollander is an asshat. He would find a way to spin it so the whole thing was just a 'misunderstanding.'"

"What did you put in that Plate that made him give up that easily?" he asks.

"We signed a contract, my father and I. Ever since I could sign my own name, every year I agree as the leader of the team that I will not form an alliance against the Paras. It's a safety precaution because we are so powerful. It was no big deal since none of us ever wanted to go to war. But today I sent him a note reminding him that I had yet to sign the contract this year."

"I'm just glad he agreed to step down. Thankfully he didn't announce becoming Kon to anyone outside of his circle. A few more days and the news would have been everywhere," Aaden says.

"That's one fire out. Now, another springs up," I reply.

"What is it?"

"It's my father's secret journal. Spider stole it off a demon named 'The Gentleman.' They were at some club—he turned away and Spider swiped it. He texted me and told me about it."

"How much did he make you pay?"

"It was free if I agreed to make Swoop go out with him."

"Does Swoop know about this deal?"

"No, I thought I'd wait until she doesn't hate me."

"Its gonna be a while," he replies.

"Yeah, I know. Take a look at this," I tell him as I hand the book over to him and show him the highlighted passages.

"So your father knew about Malakaro the whole time?" he wonders.

"Yes. He even met with him—three times. I still don't know how I feel about him walking away from his own flesh and blood."

"Pryor, you read it. Malakaro was evil from the start. Your father had to keep you and Sam safe. He did what he thought was best," Aaden says.

"I keep reading about their meeting over and over again. I keep hoping that I will find some clue as to how to destroy him, but there's nothing."

"You've been through so much right now, can't we just table the 'killing of Malakaro' for today? There's other things going on."

"What things?"

"For starters, you threw out the one person who has repeatedly saved our lives during this whole mess."

"You mean Ruin?"

"Yes, that's exactly who I mean. Pry, she was vital to us rescuing you. And when you were in the Trauma Center, she provided the Healers with information that helped them combine the right mixtures to heal you. You can't just discard her."

"I don't know that I can trust her. I know she has helped but we were betrayed, Aaden. We have to be careful who we let into our lives," I caution.

"Who 'we' let into our lives or who 'I' let in?" he ventures.

"Excuse me?"

"I don't think you're being hard on Diana because she's a demon. I think you're sending her away because she's my ex."

"Did you really just say that to me?"

"Well, Pry, what else am I supposed to think?"

"You know what, think whatever the hell you want."

"This is stupid. You are being completely unreasonable. Diana belongs on the team just as much as anyone else."

"Before you question my motives, I think you should examine your own, Aaden."

"What the hell does that mean?"

"It means maybe you like having Ruin around because you like having her fawn all over you. You like knowing that she is mad about you and would do anything for you. But this isn't a harem, Aaden. It's a team and I am not going to place some girl on my team just to boost your ego."

"That 'girl' is the reason we are not going to two funerals today. She deserves your respect."

"Fine, tomorrow I will erect a statue in her honor."

"You are being impossible right now!"

"Why are you fighting so hard for her? And why the hell didn't you fight that much for—never mind."

"No, finish your thought," he dares me.

"Forget it."

"You don't think I fought to be with you?" he asks, stunned.

"I don't want to do this. Let's just stop right here."

"Hell no! I want to hear it from your lips that you don't think I fought for you."

"Did you, Aaden? Did you really?"

"What the hell do you think we were doing in that forest?"

"That's not what I'm talking about. The Center took you and they made you promise to never see me again," I reply.

"Yes, and I broke that promise."

"After a year! It took you a whole year to miss me. It took you a whole year to check on me and to…I never would have stayed away from you that long," I counter.

"Bex says I'm wrong because I should have never come back to the team and you are standing here telling me I'm wrong because I left in the first place? Argh! I can't win with any of you!" he shouts.

"All I know is when it came time to choosing sides, you did what The Center asked you to do. You stayed away. It's like you were on The Center's side."

"DID YOU REALLY JUST SAY THAT SHIT TO ME?"

"Yeah, Aaden, I did! And if that wasn't bad enough, now you are standing here taking Ruin's side. It's like no matter what happens you are never with me. You don't have my back!"

"DON'T YOU EVER SAY THAT SHIT TO ME!" he rages as he slams his fists on my dresser and splits it in two.

Shocked by his action, I am rendered still and for a moment neither of us say anything. Our silence is layered with tension and mutual frustration. When Aaden speaks again, his voice is low and thick with emotion.

"You can accuse me of a lot of this, but…you *really* think I don't have your back? Pryor, I belong to you. Before I am the second in command, before I am an angel or a demon, I belong to you. For you to stand there and say…" He gasps, dumbfounded, and heads for the door.

"Look, I know you're mad, but don't go," I whisper.

"It's not just me, Pry. The whole team is angry with you. You made Swoop come in the house."

"It's getting dark."

"It's not even 6:30 yet."

"Well, it gets dark early this time of year," I remind him.

"Pryor, c'mon."

"What? Am I wrong for wanting to make sure everyone is accounted for?"

"You can't keep them under lock and key. You know that."

"Okay, so you hate the way I'm managing my team. I got it."

"They aren't just your team members. They are your friends and you're being really insane right now."

"What did I do that was so bad?"

"For one thing, Randy has been trying to get in touch with you for hours. He finally called me and asked if you were still aboard the crazy train," Aaden says.

"Really? So you two talk about me behind my back?"

"Pry, you know it's not like that."

"Then what is it, Aaden?"

"You were really hard on them, Pry; especially Bex. He was trying to help you," he points out.

"And?"

"And he was trying to save you; we all were."

"Giving control of an entire kingdom to that asshole was a stupid move. He needed to know that," I inform him.

"Well, now he does."

"Good. What else?"

"It's time for you to take your mixture," he replies.

"No. I don't need it. I'm fine."

"Pryor, you are not fine."

"I'm not having this argument with you. I'm not taking the fucking mixture! Now, what else?"

"You need to go see Randy."

"No," I reply shortly.

"Why?"

"Because I have business to take care of and I don't have time to watch Star Trek for the hundredth time."

"Okay, what about Star Wars?"

"This is a joke to you?" I rage.

He sighs heavily and studies me.

"Pryor, you can't go on like this."

"Like what?"

"Like everything is okay. It's not. Given what Malakaro said to you…it's okay that you feel the way you feel. You can say it out loud."

"There's nothing I need to say."

"That's bullshit and you know it!" he pushes.

"The only thing I know is that you mismanaged my damn team. They should have gotten to the center much earlier but you allowed them to get distracted. Key became a junkie on her way to being a full-blown Tic. Bex gives his damn kingdom away. Randy gets mutilated and Swoop is almost killed. You ran my team into the damn ground. Now I am back and you will do whatever I say. And right now that means getting the fuck out of my face," I yell as I turn away from him.

"No."

"Aaden, get out."

"You think acting like a jerk is going to push me away? Well it's not. You can do or say whatever you want, but it won't matter because I'm going to help you through this, like it or not," he demands.

"I don't need your help. Just leave me alone!" I bark.

"I know exactly what you're doing. You're trying to push us all away so that you won't get any of us killed. But it's too late, Pry, we already love you. And we will stand with you no matter what. Pry, let me help you."

"No! You can't help me. You left me to Malakaro. You let him put his filthy hands on my face and I hate you," I snap.

I can see him wincing as my words pierce his armor. I know my words hurt him and that's exactly what I want. I want him to get pissed off and storm away. I want to be by myself. That way there will be no one for my brother to murder just to get to me. But instead of giving up, he locks the door and stands before me, unwilling to follow my orders.

"The first step is admitting what you have yet to admit since you've been back," he says.

"I don't have anything to admit. Now get the hell out of my room."

"No, I'm not leaving until you say it. When I left The Center I tried everything to avoid having to say how I felt out loud. I found a million ways to try and run from it. But when I finally spoke the words out loud, it set me free. It let me know that what I felt was normal. Please, Pry, say it."

"I'm not playing with you; get out," I warn him.

"Saying it doesn't make you less of an angel or less of a Noru. And it *certainly* doesn't make you less of a leader. Pry, we will not think less of you. Say it!"

"NO!" I vow.

"I'm not leaving this room until you say it."

"Aaden, I swear to Omnis I will kill you," I reply, shaking my head furiously.

"Fine, that's what you're gonna have to do because I'm not leaving."

Enraged, I shove him repeatedly, but he won't leave. I try to use my powers but nothing happens. I am too out of control to tap into them. So I pound my fist against him over and over again.

"I'm not leaving; you have to say it!" He swears.

"Get out!!!!" I roar.

"Say it!"

I turn my room upside down and hurl everything that's not nailed down at him. He doesn't fight me, he just blocks my blows and he keeps trying to hug me. I am engulfed with anger, so much anger I break the mirror, grab a sharp fragment from it, and slice into his chest.

The glass also cuts into my hand but I don't care. The wrath I feel is too much. It's more than me; so much more than me. My legs won't hold me anymore. I slam myself against the wall and slide down to the ground. I hate myself for not being stronger. I hate myself for not keeping the pain at bay. And each teardrop that escapes my eyes adds to my self-loathing.

How could I be so damn weak? How could I let him control me like this? What kind of leader am I? How could I be so pathetic? How could I let him break me?

I slam myself into the wall and slink down to the floor. The weight of the past few days finally comes down on me. I rake my fingers through my hair and try to pull my hair out from its roots. I'd rather feel that pain than the pain that is about to descend on me.

"Pry, stop," he says, removing my fingers from my scalp.

"No...don't make me say it. I don't wanna say it," I beg.

"It's okay; say it."

"No, I can't. I'm supposed to be...I have to be...strong." I sob.

"You can do this, baby, please, say it."

Suddenly there's no way to avoid the tidal wave that's coming for me.

"Aaaaaaahhhhhhhhhhhhhhhhhhhhhh..." I cry out loudly as my body rocks back and forth. I gasp in complete despair as the sobs escape from the depths of my soul, where I had buried them.

He sits on the floor beside me and pulls me firmly into his arms.

"Aaaaaaaahhhhhhhhhhhhhhhhhhhhhh." I moan as my body shakes violently.

"You can say it, baby; say it to me. Say it to me," he begs.

"I'm scared of Malakaro. I was so scared...he'll kill you all."

"I know...I know," he says softly as he places his hand behind my head and strokes my hair.

Aaden stayed with me. I mean he literally never left my side. I cried from sunup to sundown and he never let go of me. And when I could cry no more, and the flashbacks of The Center threatened to take me captive, he would hold my hand between his and kiss it repeatedly, knowing his touch brought me back to the present. When I closed my eyes to Recharge and The Center would invade my dreams and I'd wake up screaming, I'd find myself right where I was before: ensconced in his strong, patient embrace.

We would go hours without speaking and yet with each passing moment I was renewed. He didn't use words to tell me that I would make it past the trauma. He told me with the smallest actions.

He told me he cared about me by covering me up with a blanket while I Recharged. He spoke of how much he believed in me when he held my hand for hours, never letting go.

And when I woke up screaming from a particularly horrific nightmare about the White Room, he wrapped his arms around me tightly from behind and let me weep without judgment. That was his way of saying he would always, *always* be there for me.

And just now, when I open my eyes after finally getting some rest, he leans in from behind, pulls me close, and kisses my bare shoulder. His kiss is…simple, soft, and sincere. The kiss tells me something I have wanted to know all my life, something that gives me strength beyond measure: Aaden Case loves me.

CHAPTER TWENTY-FOUR
THE NEW GIRL

I wake up to find that even as he Recharges, Aaden still holds on to me. The early morning sunlight streams through the window and bathes his remarkably sculpted body. I don't remember him placing me on my bed or laying down next to me, but I'm glad he did.

Suddenly I'm very aware of the fact that his arms are around my waist. It's different from last night. Last night his touch offered comfort, safety, and a promise of continued support. But right here and now, his touch isn't safe, it's very dangerous. It's not the kind of danger you run from because it will hurt you, but rather the kind of danger that thrills and beckons you.

"Good morning," he says.

How the hell can he make a simple greeting sound so damn sexy?

"Good morning," I reply, clearing my throat.

"Did you Recharge okay? It took a while, but you finally stopped having nightmares, so I guess I drifted off. I'm sorry."

"It's fine. I mean what were you supposed to do, watch me every single minute of the night?" I ask.

"Yes," he says with certainty and conviction.

Dear Omnis, I want this angel so bad.

"I Recharged well; at least well enough."

"Good. You really needed it."

"I remembered something in one of the flashbacks I had about The Center—something about the Apprentice."

"Do you know who it is?" he wonders, now very alert.

"No…but I remember a smell…almonds."

"The Apprentice smelled like almonds?"

"Yeah, I know it's silly, but it's the only thing that has stayed with me about this guy. Bishop would talk to him but he never answered back. He would just do what was asked of him. And once when he came towards me, I remember smelling almonds."

"Don't worry about it now. This guy has probably gone into hiding. That is, if he didn't die in the blast."

"Yeah, I guess. It's just I really would like to put a face to the guy that wants us dead so badly."

"I know it's next to impossible, but you have to try and live in the present. Every trip you take back to that 'house of horror' takes a little bit of joy away from you."

"You're right. No more talk about the Apprentice," I promise.

"Glad to hear it."

"Look, Aaden, about what I said last night—"

"Forget it, it's done. We can move on."

"You know I didn't mean it, right? You always look out for me. If it hadn't been for you and the team…"

"I know. Don't even think about that now," he says.

"This room is a complete mess. It kind of looks like my relationship with the team right now," I reply sadly.

"Yeah, you have a lot of work to do with them."

"Well, I better get started. Hopefully they will understand why I was such a bitch."

"If they don't, you might want to bring along some incentive for them to forgive you: cash, major organs, and for one particular member, Comic Con tickets," he jokes.

"Randy…I was so awful to him."

"Yeah, you were. But it came from a good place."

"Doesn't matter. I have to start making it up to him and the others," I reply as I leap out of bed.

"I think everyone's downstairs."

"Okay, I'm starting my 'sorry I was such a tool' tour. First stop, downstairs."

"Good luck."

I open my door to leave, but instead I pause to take a moment and address him.

"Aaden, about you and me. I mean 'us.' I…well…"

"Hey, after you fix things with the team, you and I will talk. We have time."

"We won't just talk. We'll…get on the same page about…everything."

"Deal," he says with a sly smile.

***

The first team members I run into are the twins. They are gathering their things in the living room, getting ready to head to school.

"Hey, can you guys wait a sec?" I ask.

"What is it? Are we not allowed to leave the house at all now?" Swoop snaps.

"No, it's not that," I reply.

"Make it quick, Pry, there's a drug den I'm late for," Key spits.

"Okay, I deserve that," I reply.

"No shit," Swoop says.

"You guys risked everything to save me. I should have been grateful but instead I was a jerk. I just kept replaying Malakaro's words in my head and it made me crazy. I was wrong to hold on so tight. But I really do love you both so much. I don't want anything to happen to any of you," I confess.

"If we allow Malakaro to change who we are and how we run our lives, then he's already won. You can't let him play with your mind like that, Pryor," Key scolds.

"You were mean, rude, and controlling. I don't need that. I already have Key for that," Swoop jokes. Key playfully jabs her in the side.

"I'm sorry, guys, really I am."

"Well, I don't know that I can forgive you. I am an angel with integrity. My forgiveness isn't something I give lightly," Swoop says in a firm voice as she heads for the door.

"Miu Miu black leather mesh peep toe heels," I shout.

She doesn't turn around but she also doesn't leave, so I know I have her interest.

"And I'll throw in the new Manolo Blahnik stretch lace boots—in both black and zinc metallic." I offer.

She rushes over to me and hugs me.

"Okay, I love you again," she gushes.

"Key…" I call out as Swoop heads off to school.

"I don't need shoes, thank you," she snaps.

"How can I make it up to you?" I ask.

"I know that taking drugs was stupid and reckless. I was going through a hard time; I still am. I was feeling bad enough about not being able to help in the forest, and then you go and reprimand me like a damn child."

"You're right. I should have been more supportive. I know things have been difficult for you. I really did just want to keep you and the others safe," I promise her.

"I know. It just hurt to hear what you thought of me. I know I let everyone down and maybe I deserved to be scolded like that, but it still really sucked."

"I know you're still pissed at me, but just tell me that our friendship isn't over. And that eventually you'll forgive me," I reply.

"You know I will. It's not just you. I put everyone at risk and you're right, it was an awful thing to do," she says.

"We can't change what's happened. We have to move on from it. How are you feeling now?" I ask.

"Good. I haven't used since I had the Soak back at your grandfather's house."

"That's good. I'm so proud of you."

"But, Pry, every day is a day I might go back to taking drugs and that really freaks me out," she admits.

"My mom said when my dad was using, he had a trigger. Something that always pushed him to want to zone out. For a while that trigger was her, so she had to give him space. I think if you find the thing that's pushing you to use, it will help."

"I already know my trigger," she says as she signals to Bex, who stands on the landing.

"Hey, Key, you ready to go?" he asks.

"Yeah, yeah," she says with a reluctant smile.

Bex comes down the steps. I call out his name but he ignores me, takes Key's hand, and walks out.

Okay...

"Can you move, you're in my way," East says behind me.

"Hey," I reply as I turn to face him.

East is not himself. He's pensive and clearly angry with me.

"East, did you wipe Marisol's mind yet?" I ask.

"I tried but it didn't take. I think it's because of how I feel about her. It clouds my abilities. But don't worry, boss, I will try again," he says sardonically.

"How do you feel about her?" I ask.

"Does it matter?" he barks.

"Yes, it does. So tell me."

"She's got like all these reasons to hate the world but she doesn't. She's always fighting for the underdog and she's passionate about it. I love that. I love her," he says sincerely.

"If you promise me that she will not tell anyone about us, not a single soul, then you don't have to Mind wipe her."

"Seriously?" he shouts with excitement.

"Yes."

He picks me up without warning and gives me a big bear hug. I yell for him to put me down, but he only agrees to do so after I promise to have Marisol over tonight for coffee and Coy with all of us.

"I can't wait! Pry, this girl is...wow!"

I can't believe what I am witnessing; Easton is in love...

***

When we get to school, the first thing I do is go to Randy's locker and wait for him. He sees me and turns the other way. I run to catch up with him as the crowd of students floods the hallways.

"Can I have just three minutes?" I beg.

"Why? You couldn't make time for me, and now, maybe I can't make time for you."

"Randy, please. Give me three minutes."

"What do you want?"

"I'm sorry for kicking you out of the house. You are a member of the team and we are lucky to have you," I reply.

"Are you done?"

"No. You went through great lengths to help in the forest, you nearly died trying to help, and you sang to me when I was in the Trauma Center. I never thanked you. That was wrong. Thank you, Randy, for being my friend."

"Your three minutes are up," he says as he starts to take off. I go after him.

"I'll make it up to you. I'll sing for you like you did for me," I suggest.

"Oh, so in addition to discarding me, you want to torture me too?"

"Hey, I don't sound that bad."

"Pry, when you sing, cats cry. Birds jump to their deaths. Humans all over the world beg Omnis to take their lives," he says.

"Okay, but I've gotten better. Now when I sing, I'm on key," I remind him.

"When you sing you are on every key," he teases.

"Well, fine. I suck at singing and singing right here in the open would be a complete embarrassment. But I'd still do it because that's how much I love you. Please say you forgive me."

"I don't know…"

"Randy, I will sing, right here and now," I threaten.

"You really made me mad," he says.

"Okay, I have the perfect song for that—" I open my mouth wide and prepare to sing.

"No! Please. I can't let you torture the other students. I can't have their deaths on my head."

"Then you forgive me?" I ask.

"Yeah."

"Thank you," I reply as I hug him and playfully force him to hug me back.

"But, Pry, you need to know two things: one, I will not be pushed aside anymore. I mean it. If I'm on this team then I'm on it. No more 'send the human away' stuff. Got it?"

"Got it."

"And there's one more thing: Ruin."

"What about her?"

"You weren't there, so you don't know to what lengths that girl went through to make sure we all got out of there alive. She was amazing. Even Swoop said so. You need her; we need her," Randy insists.

"Well, that may be, but I sent her away. She could be on the other side of the world by now," I reason.

"Yes, or maybe you can just turn around and check out the new girl coming out of AP English," Randy says, signaling behind me.

I turn and follow his gaze. I spot a group of students coming out of class. Among them is a beautiful demon with long dark hair, flawless skin, and seductive red lipstick.

"What? When did this happen?" I ask.

"Earlier this morning. Silver asked The Face if she could attend this school. At first The Face said no, but then Sliver reminded her that Ruin can either be an asset or a threat. So, she is letting her stay and keeping an eye on her."

"He really can't live without her," I say to myself.

"No, that's not what this is. I think he gets her. The two of them have a history."

"Great. Now his history is walking down the halls of my school."

"Pry, Silver is fighting so that Ruin has something she never had before—a place she belongs. Do you really want to be the one to stop that from happening?" he warns.

"No. I just...okay. You're right. Anyway, she should be able to go to school anywhere she wants," I reason sadly.

"It doesn't mean he wants her over you."

"We spent the night together," I reply.

"What? You and Silver—"

"No! We didn't. We just talked. But Randy, I love him. I want to be with him."

"Did you tell him that?"

"No, but I will. Later today."

"I'm happy for you two."

"What about you and Key? I heard how you stood up to Bex for her. Does she know?"

"Yeah, East told her. She called me to thank me."

"That's great."

"Yeah, but she loves Bex. And I think the two of them are going to last forever..."

CHAPTER TWENTY-FIVE
OWIN

Aaden has been on my mind all day. And while it's important to fix the team, I really would like to know where we stand. But then again, maybe I already know. I mean, first he calls on Ruin whenever he needs help and now he brings her to our school. Maybe it's one of those relationships that never really end. That would suck so hard. What if I ask him and he says they are in love and that he wants her? What do I do then?

Get over it, like a big girl, Pry.

Yes, that is exactly what I would do. Or at least try to do. If Aaden feels that his place is with her, then that will be that. I will be mature and go on with my life.

I wonder how many times I have to say that before I start to believe it?

"What are you so deep in thought about?" Aaden asks.

"What? Oh, sorry. I was…drifting."

"Anywhere interesting?"

"Nowhere fun."

"How's your first day back?" he wonders.

"Interesting. I ran into Ruin."

"Yeah, The Face pulled some strings and got her in. Is that a problem?"

"Nope, it's great. Great!" I lie.

"Have you given any thought about maybe letting her join us?" he asks.

"You know, my whole day doesn't revolve around Ruin," I snap.

"Okay…so that's a 'no,' right?"

"Aaden, I…"

"C'mon, Pry. She's good for the team," he pushes.

"Yes, I got that, okay? Message received. Hashtag 'Silver loves Ruin.'"

"The girl that's been running through my mind all night and all morning wasn't Diana," he says as he gives me this intense smoldering gaze.

"You asked her to come to this school, right?"

"Yes, but it's not for me. It's for her safety. There are demons and Kasters out there angry that she helped us. And there's also Malakaro, who may not yet be done hurting her. But that has nothing to do with you and me."

"It's just…I don't know where we stand," I admit.

"Yeah, this talk is overdue. After the coffee and Coy thing East is forcing us to have, how about we take a walk and figure some things out between us…"

Us…

"Sounds good," I reply.

"Gotta go. Since The Face did me a favor by getting Diana in here, I promised I'd try and actually attend one of the classes I'm supposed to be taking," he says as he walks away.

He said "us."

***

I don't think I'm the same girl I was the night I first learned about Malakaro. I think finding out your half brother is pure evil and that you're supposed to kill your best friend in order to save the world…well, that changes a girl. Then there was my wonderful stay at "Casa De Torture" courtesy of the lunatic Para, Bishop. After going through all that, you are forced to zoom in on the things that matter.

And right now, what matters is that the team has the best members it can gather. Ruin is a skilled Healer and she would be invaluable to the team, like Randy said. I am going to do what's best for my team and ask her to join us.

Now, having said that, I am going to hate every single second of this. In fact I'm pretty sure I would pick The Center over the kind of pain that will come from the next few minutes of being in a room with Aaden's ex. Do it quick so it can be painless, Pry.

Yeah, right. Like that ever works.

I walk into the now empty classroom where Ruin sits reading a book. As soon as she sees me, she quickly hides it so I don't see the cover.

"I didn't mean to interrupt," I tell her.

"And yet here you are."

Please let her have evil intent so that I will have a reason to beat the crap out of her.

"I came to tell you that I appreciate your help these past few weeks. We could not have made it without you. Thank you."

"Fine, anything else?"

Yeah, you're way too close to the angel I love and you need to back off.

"I would like to have you on the team—unofficially."

"So does that mean I don't get a uniform?" she says sardonically.

"Screw this. If you don't want to join us then fine, but at least I can tell Aaden that I asked," I reply as I turn on my heel and start to walk away.

"Wait! Silver spoke on my behalf?" she asks.

"He said a few things," I mumble.

"Okay, I will be on your team. You guys suck at making mixtures and well, at staying alive," she quips.

"Whatever," I reply flippantly.

"There is one condition."

Condition? Is she for real?

"What is it?"

"I want to stay in the house, like everyone else."

"We could just rent you a house close by. Or we could buy you one."

Hell, I'd buy you a mega mansion if it keeps you away from my damn house.

"No, I want to be in the house with everyone else. Please," she says.

"Yeah, okay," I reply as I walk away.

Omnis kill me now.

***

"I've been waiting for you," I tell him as he walks up to his locker.

"There's no need. You said what you had to say to me already. Don't you remember? It went something like 'Bex, you're an idiot. You can't rule over anyone. You're lucky I allow you to be part of my team; you're a loser,'" Bex says bitterly.

"I know I was awful to you. You know I didn't mean any of it. I'm sorry."

"How many times have you said that today?"

"About fifty."

"Well, you don't have to say it to me because the fact is you may have been right."

"No, I wasn't."

"Do you know what the crazy thing was about deciding to give up being Kon for you was? It was an easy decision. Honestly, the easiest one I've ever had to make."

"I don't know what to say," I admit.

"Don't say anything. The fact is I am always…there are angels in my life who love me. Angels who don't relegate me to the sideline every time a half demon decides to grace us with his presence. And instead of welcoming that kind of love into my life, I go and…"

"Bex, I'm not throwing you aside."

"Yeah, you are. And I'm grateful because it's time I took stock of life and stopped reaching out for—what's not good for me."

"Bex…"

"It hurt, alright? I have always wanted to lead. I was raised to guide an entire race of angels; angels that matter. Powerful, enlightened beings, and I threw that away to help save you. And when you get back you spend all your time with him or scolding us."

"Bex, I know I was wrong."

"And what's even worse is that knowing what I know now, if I had the chance to do it all over again, I would still give up being Kon. I would give it up for you…"

"Bex, what is it you want me to say?"

"Nothing. Don't say anything."

He gets a text and looks down at the cell phone in his hand. He reads the message on the screen and looks up, concerned.

"What is it?" I ask.

"I have to go."

"Tell me what's going on."

"It's Para business. And yesterday you told all the Paras, *my* Paras, to kiss off."

"I only aimed it at the ones who were behind The Center. You know I didn't mean all of you."

"I can't do this now. I have to go," Bex says as he takes off.

"I think I know where he's going," The Face says from the doorway of the main office.

"Where?"

"He's going to choose a new steward to watch over the Paras."

"Bex removed Hollander as steward? Good," I reply.

"Hollander wasn't removed. He was killed."

***

I sit across from The Face in her office and she explains that Hollander was found dead in his home. A Soul Chaser had been placed at his feet.

"I didn't do it," I protest.

"I know that," she replies calmly.

"Do they know who did it?" I ask.

"Hollander had enemies. He earned them. For example, there was a young man, a Quo who was under attack. Hollander saw the attack happening but did nothing to help because he was hoping to use the boy's death as a way to gain more power. He used that boy's life as a bargaining tool so he could become Kon."

"Noble…Hollander witnessed the attack?"

"Yes. He let my sweet boy…my baby…" Her eyes fill with tears but she blinks them back.

"How do you know?"

"There was a witness. She was a Pawn and they are reluctant to talk, but once she did, she admitted to seeing the whole thing. Hollander could have helped my son but he didn't," The Face says with deep regret.

"Do they know who killed him?" I ask.

"Someone who could not stand for that kind of cruelty. Someone who knows it was the right thing to do…" she says as she looks off into the distance.

Crap.

"Mrs. Greenblatt, did you…?"

"Did I what?" she asks, back to her official tone.

For the first time since I've known her, I can see past her rules and rigidity. She's not just a disciplinarian, she's someone's Mom. And she just lost her child. And even though she will mostly likely never say it out loud, she thinks of us as hers.

I think she killed Hollander. In fact, I'm pretty sure of it. And the truth is, after everything that's happened in the past few days, I'm okay with it; one less evil to take down.

Wow, Pry, dark much?

"Ms. Cane, what were you saying?" she asks.

"Never mind," I reply.

"Good. Now, about your emotional outburst yesterday…"

"I meant it; we are only taking advice from you," I reply.

"The Board has no choice but to let you go on as you see fit so long as at least one adult is overseeing your activities."

"Good," I reply as I start to leave.

"My first official piece of advice was given to Silver, and I sincerely hope he takes it."

"What did you say to him?"

"I know the two of you are...getting close. And he did just help rescue you. And often dramatic rescues lead to...relations."

"You mean...sex?"

"Yes, that is exactly what I mean. And well, I had a talk with him about that subject. I reminded him that you are only fifteen and too young to have sex with anyone right now," The Face replies.

"How could you say that to him? Do you know what you've done? Now when he looks at me, he's gonna see a damn kid."

"That's exactly what he should see," she replies.

"When I said we would listen to your advice, I didn't mean about my love life," I bark.

"I think I can say with certainty that your mother would agree with me when I say you are too young to have a 'love life.'"

"Oh, but I'm not too young to have my family get ripped away from me?" I ask.

"I know you have been through a lot. And I know I'm not your mother, but the fact still remains: you are only fifteen, and you are not ready."

"Well, I wasn't ready to watch my flesh melt off my bones while my wings were being broiled from the inside! Sometimes things happen, ready for it or not," I remind her.

"I am not giving you permission to sleep with that boy!" she snaps.

"You know what, maybe you're right. Maybe it's wrong for a normal fifteen year old to have sex. But there is nothing normal about us. So yes, we have sex sooner than we should. But there's another thing we do sooner than we should—die," I reply as I storm out of her office.

"Hey, I'm gonna bail on the coffee and Coy thing Randy told me about. I have something to do," Ruin informs me as she approaches me in the hallway.

"You wanted to be part of this team? Well, meeting each other's girlfriends and boyfriends is part of it," I reply as I head to my locker. She follows me.

"I have something I need to do. So you'll just have to go on without me," Ruin says.

"I know you're new to the team, but this is important to East. He's crazy in love with this girl."

"I don't think it's love."

"Would you know love if you saw it?" I quip.

"Would you?" she counters.

"Okay, what's the problem? You don't like Marisol?" I ask.

"I don't really know her. East just pointed her out to me in the hall earlier today. But for the record, I dislike most girls."

"Of course you do," I reply, shaking my head.

"I'm just being honest."

"Well, East says she's amazing. They are mad about each other," I shout back in Marisol's defense.

"Maybe, but I don't trust her," Ruin replies.

"Yeah, yeah, I know—she's a girl."

"Well, that and the Owin she wears," Ruin says.

"What's that?"

"It's a mixture that you use to stop someone from wiping your mind."

"I've never heard of it," I reply.

"Yeah, most Healers don't use it because it's a pain in the ass to make and the smell clings to you. Who wants to walk around smelling like almonds all day?"

Almonds...

"Oh shit! We gotta go!"

CHAPTER TWENTY-SIX
THE CHOSEN

Ruin and I hide behind the shrubs out back and sneak a peek into the house. Standing there, in all her demented glory, is the Apprentice: Marisol. She's in the center of my kitchen surrounded by some kind of force field.

At her feet lie Swoop, Key, Aaden, Bex, and East. They are face-up and motionless. There's something unnatural about their stillness. A wave of dread unlike any I've known before washes over me.

"They're not moving; she killed them. She killed everyone," Ruin says in a state of shock.

"No, no, they are still alive," I reply desperately.

"How do you know that?"

"They're still alive because I need them to be, okay? Now stop getting emotional on me and summon up some of that inner demon."

"Okay, okay. We can't do anything to her with that force field around her. How do we get rid of that?"

"The force field consists of energy. We don't have a way to drain it from her, but maybe we can overload it somehow."

"There was a downed power line not far from here—add that to your powers and her force field should be weakened. Well, at least long enough for you to get a good shot at her," Ruin says.

"You can't carry a live wire, you'll barbecue yourself," I point out.

"Aw, I didn't know you cared," she quips.

"How are you going to get the wire?"

"I have a vial that can protect my hands from shock. It's not enough to help me get past the force field, but it's enough to help me get the wire over here. You need to go in and keep her distracted."

"Yeah, killing me should be very distracting," I reply.

"Silver wasn't moving at all," Ruin says to herself as sadness seeps into her eyes.

"I don't know what she did to them, but I'm sure they are alive. Thinking differently isn't going to help us," I point out. She nods and runs off to find the wire.

Telling Ruin that she doesn't need to worry keeps my mind off the fact that I am terrified that my team is in fact dead. I push that thought as far away from me as I can because it's just not something I can handle.

I enter my house, and even if I hadn't seen what Marisol did in the kitchen I would still know that something was off. The house is too quiet. I live in a house full of teenaged angels; there should never be silence. Swoop should be blasting music. Key should be tinkering with mixtures in the kitchen. The guys are normally training, talking to girls, or in Randy's case, playing video games.

"You're late," she says.

"What did you do to them, you psycho bitch?" I shout as I bend down to the floor to check on them.

"Do you remember the team telling you about one of the nastier creatures they ran into in the forest called Eway? Well, Eways have fangs that paralyze you. Bishop found a way to extract the poison from the Eways' teeth and put it in a mixture. He was good with things like that, but then again, look who I'm telling. You witnessed his genius firsthand. All I had to do was lace their drinks. One minute we were all joking around and the next…"

I raise both hands in the air to strike. The power springs from my palm and leaps into the air, headed for her. It hits the force field and bounces the surge back towards me. I duck just in time to avoid my own blast.

"What is that around their necks?" I ask as I frantically search my mind for a way to get past Marisol's force field.

"See that thing that looks like a crystal dog collar, it's called Skin. It's a delivery system that inputs chemicals into your body at a preset time. You see how it's glowing? Well, once it has delivered the mixture I filled it with, the glow will be gone. It's a great little invention."

"And what did you put inside it?" I ask, fearing the worse.

"Duh, I put Balance into it. Did you think that The Center kept all its supply in one place? Now, that would be dumb, wouldn't it?"

"I don't get it, Marisol. Why are you doing this? East loves you," I plead.

"Easton is the sweetest guy. I am fond of him too. But us girls can't let guys distract us from our true purpose, now can we?"

"What is your purpose? I mean really, what is it you want from us?"

"For starters, I want you to tell me where the last member of your team is."

"Randy isn't here, he's not a part of this," I reply.

"I meant the demon. Where is she?"

"She's not part of my team. She was helping us out for one mission. She got what she wanted."

"Liar! I saw her in school today."

"She just came to collect her pay. She's gone," I spit.

"That's a shame. It would have been nice to have her join us," Marisol replies sincerely.

"I don't understand. How do you even know about The Center?"

"I found Bishop online. He was ranting and raving about how strong all of you would be someday and how there had to be precautions taken to deal with it. I befriended him and he told me about The Center. I thought it was a great plan. Study the Noru and find ways to eliminate them should you all cause trouble."

"So you and Bishop were what, best friends?" I ask, pissed and perplexed.

"He had a huge ego. I stroked it, and soon he was laying his plans out to me. I was a very necessary part of his backup plan. All I had to do was gain access to the group and get information. And man, I learned so much about this team from Easton."

"What was the point of it all?"

"If he failed, I was to continue his work."

"So that lunatic Bishop was your mentor?"

"More like a tool I used to get what I needed. You see, Bishop formed The Center so he could destroy the Noru should the time come. I, on the other hand, have a different goal," she informs me.

"Oh, and what is that exactly?"

"I don't want to take out the Noru; I want to take on the entire Angel world."

"You seriously want to kill all of us off?"

"No, that would be cruel. I don't want to take your lives; just your powers," she replies with a deranged smile.

"Great, so all of this because you think you can handle our power inside your system? That won't work," I explain.

"I don't want your powers. I just think you all shouldn't have any. No one should have powers. It's unfair to the rest of us."

"You're really bat shit crazy, you know that right?" I ask.

"After my mother died in that cruel way, after she was nearly severed in half in the car accident, I was inconsolable. That's why my ex boyfriend was able to beat me—I didn't care about anything, not even myself. Then that night I met East, the night he saved me from getting pulverized by Zack, I was reborn.

"When I found out that there are angels right here on Earth, I was beside myself. That night I slept sound knowing Omnis had sent angels, real honest-to-goodness angels to help humanity. But then in the morning, another thought occurred to me: if there were angels all around us, why is this world so damn shitty? I mean, there's starvation, war, diseases, and so much more.

"I thought maybe Omnis had made angels the same way he made us: helpless. So I spent every waking moment learning about the Angel world.

And it turns out not only did Omnis use all his creativity on you angels, he granted an infinite amount of power to you.

"You angels weren't just loved by Omnis—you are his *chosen creation*. He has given all of you so much power! And all of that power was to be used to help humanity. Instead what do you all do with it? Party. Fuck. And fight each other.

"I couldn't understand why Omnis just stood by and let you all get away with running wild. That's when I realized the awful truth: Omnis is just as culpable as all of you.

"This whole time I've been saying how much I hate bullies and it occurred to me that the biggest bully of all is Omnis. He enjoys watching humanity suffer. He loves knowing that we are down here drowning in a pool of blood and piss. Omnis is in fact the biggest bully of all.

"That is why he has to be made to pay. I am going to take away that which he holds most dear: his precious chosen angels. I'm not just talking about the Noru; eventually I will take every angel down. Once your team drinks the Balance, you will lose all your powers. And that will be the beginning of the end. In time, you angels will be like us: powerless.

"You see, it's very simple really. Omnis is like my ex, Zack. He had all the power. And I've come to learn that when one being has all the power, they always, always take advantage. So since I can't give all of humanity the kind of power your team has, I'm going to take that power away. You see, Pryor, either all of us have power or none of us do…"

"I really don't want to kill you, but since you are the Apprentice, I fear I don't have a choice," I warn her.

C'mon, Ruin. Where the hell are you?

"Yes, I'm sure if you could get to me things would be very bad for me right now. But just so you know, I believe in this cause and if it came down to it I would die for it if I had to."

"I'll remember that," I promise her.

"It looks like there's only a few more minutes until the mixture is in their system completely. Now all I need is for you to take that pretty device next to you and place it around your collar so that like them, your powers will cease to exist."

"Why the hell would I do that?"

"I wanted to get Randy, but we missed him, so we had to settle for the next best thing: Randy's father. So, you can try and play hero if you want, but I touch this button on my phone and Randy will have lost both his mother and father," she says as she pulls out her cell phone and plays a video of Randy's dad fixing dinner.

"How did you get like this?"

"Well, it turns out when you've been bullied by the best, you learn a few things. Put the Skin around your neck or I will blow the human up."

"You said you care about humanity, so why are you blowing up an innocent dad? He never did anything to you," I point out.

"No, but in every war there are casualties. I'm willing to sacrifice so that the ones who come after live in a balanced and just world."

"It doesn't work that way. Marisol, humans can achieve great things."

"Yes, if we had power like yours but we don't, do we? No! Instead we just grow old, get sick, and die like some cosmic joke. Well, now it's our turn to laugh. Put. It. On."

I reach over and take the device on the table beside me. Placing it around my neck will render me weak from the moment it makes contact. Yet I can't refuse knowing Randy's father's life is at stake. I've known him for a while now and he's boring and tells awful jokes. But he's kind, loves Randy, and has always been there for him. Randy would die if something happened to his dad.

"I am not going to tell you again," Marisol promises.

As I slowly reach for the collar-like device, I see Ruin through the window behind Marisol. She quietly snakes the live wire through the open window. I give the signal and Ruin bursts through the door with the hose in her hand.

"Now!" I yell.

Before Marisol understands what's happening, Ruin turns on the hose. When the water meets the live wire, the force field fails. The shock catapults Marisol across the room. She drops her cell phone. I run over to take it while Ruin frees the others.

"Oh crap! The fall activated the bomb in Randy's house. Get on a Port and get his dad out, now!"

I scramble to finish what Ruin started, releasing the rest of the team. I'm so focused on helping them I don't notice Marisol coming up behind me. By the time I do, it's too late. She jabs a needle into my neck and injects its contents into my body. In a matter of seconds I am unable to move.

She stands over me, her flesh exposed and peeling from the live wire. Her crazed stare reveals the madness in her soul. I watch helplessly as she grabs the nearest knife from the table and goes to plunge it into my chest.

East grabs her from behind and pleads with her as he wrestles the knife from her hand. The knife goes flying to the other side of the room. East quickly comes to my rescue, or at least he tries to—Marisol leaps onto his back. She is now in full psycho mode. Having no other choice, he throws her off of him and she lands near the window.

The other members of the team are finally free of the poison and the collars around their necks. They help me sit up and Key shows me a text from Ruin they all received. She tells us the bomb went off, but she was able to get Randy's dad out in time.

"We need to get Marisol to the hospital before—" I don't get to finish what I am saying because I realize for the first time what actually happened to Marisol. She didn't just land by the window; she landed on top of the live wire for the second time. This time there was no force field to absorb the shock. The Apprentice is dead.

***

East Mind wiped Randy's father so that he doesn't even remember being saved by Ruin. The official story is that there was a gas leak in the building. While Randy is grateful that we were able to save his dad, he was devastated we couldn't save his apartment. It's where he lived with his mom before she left them. Now it's just a pile of ash. But on the bright side, one thing did survive. Randy's other best friend—Mr. Frog.

A few days later, we all attended Marisol's funeral, although East said we didn't have to. The only one who wasn't there was Bex because he had to appoint a new steward to replace Hollander. The service was beautiful, filled with her friends and family. East asked to be left alone with the coffin so we respected his wishes and headed home while he said one final goodbye to his first love.

We don't see East until later that night. He's up on the roof looking at the skyline. I've never seen him this crestfallen before. I know the look well. He's missing her so much it pains him. He's so deep in his thoughts that he doesn't realize I'm there until I speak.

"The service was nice."

"I guess," he says distantly.

"I know it hurts right now, but we're here for you. Just let us know how we can help."

"Help? Have we actually ever helped anyone, Pry?"

"What do you mean?"

"Marisol was right; we have all this power and we waste it. And when it comes down to it, she was a human being. It was our job to make sure that she lived, and we not only failed at that but we killed her. Since when is it okay for angels to kill humans?"

"We don't kill innocent humans if we can avoid it. But Marisol wasn't innocent. She would have killed you to get her way."

"You should have let her kill me. At least she would have been alive. She was human and we owed her that."

"East, this is coming from your grief."

"So what if it is? That doesn't make me wrong. She died at seventeen. I mean, what the hell?"

"We tried to get her to put the knife down and she wouldn't," I remind him.

"She wasn't evil. She was just an idealistic kid with a black-and-white point of view. She didn't deserve to die."

"Neither did you."

"I'm a part of this team and have been for years. I know what comes with that. There's danger at the end of every corner. I was prepared to die if need be, but she wasn't. We should have saved her. I should have saved her."

"East, you were paralyzed," I remind him.

"No, before that. She showed signs of rage and anger. I ignored them. If I had been able to pick up the signs maybe her family wouldn't be in mourning now," he says.

"I don't see how you could have known. I mean, none of us did."

"Yes, but I should have. I failed her."

"East, you didn't. You tried to help her in the end but you can't force someone to accept your help. I know you're hurting, but I promise it will get better. It's late and you need to Recharge. Let's go inside," I say gently.

"I can't go inside."

"Why?"

"Because every evening I stand on this roof and at 7:03, she calls me. It's stupid really. It started out as a joke. She happened to call at 7:03 p.m. two days in a row; and on both days I could hear a cooking show in the background. So I'd ask her what the chef was making.

"It's one of those traveling cooking shows. The chef goes around the world and makes exotic things with the help of the natives. The first time she called me, the chef was making alligator stew and wild rice. The next day it was bacon ice cream. So every day at exactly 7:03, she calls and before she even says hello, she tells me what was on the menu.

"She'd call and say, '7:03; Monkey brain and red chili pepper sauce.' And she'd sound so excited. She swore she'd travel the world and eat everything on the chef's menu. The smallest things gave her the most joy.

"I didn't realize that I'd gotten used to the calls or that they had become the best part of my day. When 7:03 comes, I believe that I will get a call. I know I won't, but somewhere inside...I am still expecting it. It's 6:45 now; can you stay with me? I don't want to be alone when..."

I take his hand in mine. We don't speak. We simply look out at the gleaming New York City skyline before us.

6:53 p.m.

East closes his eyes. I gently stroke his hand.

7:00 p.m.

East's lips start to tremble. I hold his hand tighter.

It's 7:03.

East looks straight ahead. He's as still as a statue. His cell phone is silent as is all of New York City. The only sound comes from the weeping half angel beside me who just received a silent confirmation: his first love is gone.

CHAPTER TWENTY-SEVEN
THE BEST PART

Marisol did have an affect on us. She was right about us getting caught up in other things and forgetting the humans. While we fight evil on their behalf, it's not the only way to help. So, the team and I get reacquainted with the best part of being angels: charity work.

When we were kids, all the team and I wanted to do was learn to use our powers. We yearned to prove ourselves. And show our parents we could be great and powerful just like them. Yet our first lesson as angels wasn't about battle; it was about being of service to humanity.

We were all made to choose charities that we felt connected to and then we would spend weeks providing that charity with our help. We weren't allowed to use powers. We had to get our wings dirty, so to speak.

I can't lie—at first we all thought it sucked and we tried to beg, lie, and scream our way out of it. But in a matter of days the humans became more than just assignments; they became our friends. We got to know them not just as Omnis' creations but also as individuals. Getting the team back to that mindset took almost no time at all. The person who enjoyed helping the most was East; it was his way of honoring Marisol. For us, it was a good way to honor our parents, whose absence we were feeling very deeply.

The twins helped build homes in Haiti, East and Bex helped get food to the homeless, Randy and Ruin worked with an organization determined to stop the human trafficking, and Aaden and I helped get much needed medical aid to war ravaged parts of Zimbabwe, Sudan, and the Congo.

Although we worked closely together, we were both so busy we barely had time to say "hello," let alone have a decent conversation. I think that was for the best since it would have been next to impossible to focus on the job I came to do had Aaden and I had a moment alone.

At the end of two weeks, we all meet back at the house to get our things before we head for Mrs. Maybelle's in Atlanta. She is expecting us to stay with her for a full week and help out. She insists we stay in her guesthouse so she can keep an eye on us like the true mother hen she is.

While we wait for the twins to return, I seek out Aaden. I find him in the kitchen with a bottle of what looks like a beer. I know it's Coy inside, but I can't tell what kind from where I am. He's talking to Ruin. The two of them are sharing a laugh.

Great…

"I wanted to—never mind," I say quickly as I start to leave.

"Wait, Pry. What is it?" Aaden asks.

Reading the tension in the room, the former Kaster gets up and excuses herself. I don't say a word until Ruin has gone completely.

"You wanted to talk to me," he says.

"Um…yeah. I did."

"What is it? Is something wrong? Are you okay?" he asks.

"No, I'm fine," I reply. He looks back at me suspiciously.

"Okay, I'm not one hundred percent but I'm getting there, look!" I reply as I hold my palms out towards the window and suck the life from the plant across the street.

"Pry, that's great!"

"Yeah, and watch this," I brag.

I look out the window again, and using my palm, I raise the level of fear in the human across the street from us. Without warning the human is sweating, short of breath, and fidgeting.

"Okay, I'm gonna stop because, well, it's kind of mean to do that to someone, but my powers are back at full force," I tell him.

"Yes!" he replies as he lifts me up and gives me a big hug. I laugh as we embrace.

While the hug started out innocent, when I pull away, we remain close. And a moment that was once pure is now thick with longing. We look into each other's eyes and exchange a heated gaze. My whole body tingles with excitement. We both take a step back, fearing the yearning will consume and overwhelm us.

"So…by any chance did you get your Rah back?"

"Yeah, Diana gave it back to me," he replies.

"Oh…"

"You know that there's no danger from being around you like before. Since The Center is gone…"

"Yeah, I get it. Having your Rah back is a good thing, right?" I ask.

"Yeah, it's very good," he replies with a suggestive smile.

"Listen…thank you for helping me get past this—"

"Pry, stop."

"I just want to thank—"

"Hey, stop. Don't thank me. When you were locked away in The Center, if felt like I was too," he says sincerely as he takes my hand.

"Okay, so remember that talk we were gonna have?" I start carefully.

"Yeah, the one about us?"

"Is there an 'us?'" I ask.

"I hope so, but it depends on you and what you want," he says carefully.

"Aaden, you know what I want. This. You and me."

"Yeah, but before you make that decision, I have something to tell you."

"Okay, what is it?" I wonder.

"I kissed Diana."

"Back when you two were together you mean?"

"No, recently. In the forest."

WTF??!?!?!?!?!?!?!?

"Oh," is all I can manage to say.

"We didn't plan it. It just happened," he adds.

"Okay…"

"Pry, you're the one I want."

"Yet you're kissing demons in the forest…" I reply, perplexed.

"There's no excuse for what I did. But you have to know that there was so much happening and I really thought I might lose you. And Diana was—"

"I really don't want to know why Ruin felt she needed your lips pressed against hers," I assure him.

"She was going through a lot."

Is he serious right now? RUIN has been through a lot? RUIN? And what the hell have I been going through—a cruise down the Riviera? Is he fucking kidding me?

"Pryor!" he says.

"Yes?"

"Talk to me. Are you upset? Look, I know it was wrong and that it hurt you. I'm sorry. I wasn't trying to—"

"Hey, don't worry about it," I interject.

"What?"

"Look, it's just a kiss and anyway you guys have history. No big deal. Kiss away," I reply with a smile.

"Pry, don't do this."

"Do what?" I ask, pretending to be clueless.

"Don't act like the kiss doesn't bother you when it clearly does."

"Why should it bother me? We weren't together. All I have is a hammer. She had a whole year with you filled with adventures and wild nights. She had your Rah and apparently your kiss. I just have a hammer."

"Pryor, I'm sorry about the kiss. I really am. But I want us to get past it."

"Past what?" I reply, shrugging my shoulders.

"Carrot, don't do this. If the kiss bothers you then let's talk about it," he offers.

"Look, you saved my life in many ways and on many occasions. I don't have a right to be mad because the guy who I'm NOT with, kissed another girl. Look, I'm good. Really. It's not even…Aaden you and I are just friends. Really good friends," I reply with a warm smile.

"And that's how you want to keep it, us being 'really good friends?'" he asks.

"Yeah! It's easier that way. And you know what, you can go on kissing whomever the hell you want to in the forest because I don't care."

"Okay, fine," he barks.

"Fine," I counter coldly.

We stand there and look at each other; neither of us speaks. The tension in the air is hostile and thick. Swoop does a handstand and lands right in front of us.

"Um...hello? What's going on with you two?" she says.

"Absolutely nothing," I vow, glaring at him.

Aaden is about to say something but thinks better of it and addresses Swoop instead.

"Bird, how was it?" he asks.

"Haiti is so beautiful. I only wish they could find a way to stop the infighting and come together," she replies as she embraces me.

"What was it like to build homes?" I ask.

"It sucked. It was hot and I couldn't wear my heels. I was forced to wear these things called 'flats,'" she jokes.

"So you didn't have a good time?" Silver says.

"No, I had a great time. The working on the house was sucky but when it was done and we handed the humans the key to their new home...it was incredible. Silver, you should have seen the looks on their faces. They cried because for some of them this was their first and only home. Given everything that happened to them, I can't believe they are so full of hope. It inspires me."

"Oh really?" I ask.

"Yes. So now I'm gonna help them build more homes when I have time. But even better, when I go there again, I'm bringing all the girls in the village heels. It's the right thing to do," she explains.

"I'm glad you had fun. What about Key? How is she?" Silver asks.

"Honestly, not good. She enjoyed helping but her mind was on other things," Swoop informs us.

"What do you mean?" I ask.

"I think she's breaking up with Bex."

"Bird, are you sure?" Silver asks.

"Yeah...she's hinted at it. In fact, she wants to head to another charity and stay out of New York for a while. She just came back so she could talk to Bex," Swoop explains.

"Oh no. He loves her so much," I reply.

"They've been headed down this road for a while; I mean, since you know..." Swoop replies.

"Since what?" I ask.

"Since he told Key and everyone else he had feelings for you," Swoop says before she can stop herself.

"Bex said what?" I ask, looking over at Aaden.

"Damn, I'm sorry; I thought you were caught up on everything," Swoop replies.

"Me too," I say, unable to take my eyes off Aaden.

"Okay, awkward moment. Leaving now," Swoop says as she summersaults out of the room.

"Why didn't you tell me about what Bex said?"

"There were a million things you missed. I couldn't get to everything so I told you the important stuff," he says.

"You didn't think that Bex saying he has feelings for me is important?"

"Are you really coming at me this hard over Bex?" he asks.

"I'm asking you a question."

"No, you're accusing me."

"I am not."

"The hell you aren't. You think I didn't tell you what Bex said on purpose?"

"Well, is that the case?"

"Hiding what Bex feels about you would have been pointless because everyone knows he wants you; everyone but you," he snaps.

"I don't want to be the reason they split up."

"You don't have any control over that," he reminds me.

"Bex is going through a lot right now. The Paras are on him about leaving us and he's dealing with the aftermath of everything. We can't let Key break up with him," I reply.

"There's nothing that can stop what's gonna happen with Key and Bex. And really, I don't care what Bex thinks about you. What I care about is how you feel about him."

"What?"

"Don't make me repeat myself," he counters.

I fold my arms across my chest and shake my head stubbornly.

"Pryor, do you have feelings for Bex?" he demands.

"You should have told me what Bex said. It affects this team. You will not withhold vital information from me again. Is that clear?" I order. He shakes his head in frustration.

"Are you really gonna go into 'official' mode with me right now?" he demands.

"Aaden, you are not to withhold anything from me that can affect this team. Am. I. Clear?"

"Crystal," he snaps as he storms off.

***

Swoop was right about Key. She intends to stay away for a while. Or so she explained in the letter she placed under each of our doors. In it she apologizes for putting the mission at risk and says she needs some time away to straighten things out in her head. She leaves us the address of the charity she's going to help and asks that we not contact her unless it's a team related emergency.

I thought Swoop would be upset, but she actually agrees with her sister going away. I think it's because she wants her twin to be as far away from the drug scene as possible. Key swears that she's not leaving the team but that she just needs time away. I get it. Yet I don't like her being by herself. In the end, she promises to let East fly in on his Port and look in on her. She says a temporary good-bye and heads outside to speak to Bex, who has no idea she isn't staying.

We overhear the two of them; their voices carry in the air and come through the open window. This is really going to suck. And yes, we should leave them alone, but it's just hard to believe that these two angels are breaking up. They've been together so long; you have to see it to fully believe it. So we all stand in the living room and watch the impossible happen.

"Where's the rest of your stuff?" Bex asks Key.

She holds up a small and sensible-sized carry-on.

"This is it," she says.

"Seriously, Key, where are the other forty bags you're taking with us to Mrs. Maybelle's?" he says.

"I'm not going to Mrs. Maybelle's with you guys," she replies with a sad smile.

"I don't get it," Bex says.

"Can we sit for a sec, please?"

"Sure, whatever you need," he replies.

The two of them sit on the steps of the house. He takes her hand in his and looks lovingly into her eyes.

"I know what I said about having feelings for Pryor hurt you. I don't know how to make it up to you, but I will. I promise, I'll make it better. I can move out of the house so that I only see her for missions and I could—"

"Bex, Pryor is not the problem," she replies.

"It's me. I rushed into being physical too soon after your ordeal. Damn, I'm sorry if I was being a jerk."

"No, you weren't. There's nothing wrong with you wanting to make out with your girlfriend. I'm the one who can't give you that right now," she says.

"I don't need to have sex," he lies. She tilts her head to the side in disbelief.

"Okay, I do need to have sex—but I can wait. Seriously, I am willing to wait for as long as it takes. Key, I love you. Sex is not the best thing about us; it's just one part of us. Please don't worry about it," he vows.

"That's very sweet, Bex, but that's not the problem," she replies.

"Then what is it?"

"Me. I'm the problem," she admits.

"I don't understand."

"I've been letting everyone down," she says.

"Key, it wasn't your fault. You can't—"

"Bex baby, please let me talk and no matter how much you want to interrupt, don't. I need to get this out. Okay?"

"Okay."

"I've let a lot of people in my life down these past few months. And yes, you were to blame for not being up-front with me about having feelings for Pryor, but in the end, my actions were my own. There is no one else to blame for me getting involved with drugs but me. I made horrible decisions. I hurt the angels who love me and I almost lost my sister in the process."

She inhales deeply and pushes herself to go on. She takes both of Bex's hands inside hers and looks deeply into his warm eyes.

"Bex, when we first met, I hated you on sight. It was our first day of training and you were pushy and stubborn. You kept yelling at me and pushing me to do better with my fight technique. You were relentless in battle and yet you had this big heart. You tried to hide that part of you away, but I found it; that night I hurt my leg after a training exercise went wrong, I saw you standing outside the Healers' room, looking in. You stood there all night to make sure I was healing. When I woke up you were the first angel I saw. I knew you would be.

"I saw things changing between us when Pryor came back. I fought it so hard. I almost killed you, trying to ensure that you stayed with me. And while you did drive me nuts, what I did to you was wrong. What I made the team go through was wrong. This whole time I was so worried about losing you that I didn't realize I had lost myself. When I think back to the way I have behaved and the things I allowed to happen…

"I was afraid to let you go because I love you. But love, *real* love, doesn't confine, it liberates. And I do love you, Bex. That's why I'm letting you go. I want you to be happy. I want you to…"

Her voice cracks as she speaks. Bex is about to say something but she gently places a finger over his lips. The tears well up in her eyes. She composes herself and tries to stop her voice from shaking.

"I don't know how I'm going to live without you but I know it's time I learned. And when the pain of your absence coils around me, threatens to drain the life from me, I'll fight it off by remembering that I was loved. For three years, four months and eleven days, I was loved."

"Key, no! I don't want to lose you" he pleads.

"Bex, we were protecting an empty shell. You and I weren't destined to make it. Let's not dishonor what we had by pretending now."

"But I love you; I still love you."

"I know. But I don't love who I've become trying to hold on to you. I need to find out what it's like to be alone. And you need to go find out what's between you and Pryor."

"There is nothing between us!" he vows.

"Bex, every battle we face could be our last. Please don't waste anymore time pretending she means nothing to you. You want her. You need her. And there's a good chance she wants and needs you too," she says as she stands up and gathers herself.

"Key, please don't do this. We can figure it out. I don't want to lose you. Please, Key, don't walk out on us," he insists.

"You walked out on us months ago. I know you didn't walk out to be cruel. I know you tried to stay in love with me. But the fact is your heart is somewhere else. Please, follow it." She gets up and starts gathering her things to go.

"You can't do this. You can't just end us. Key, please…" he says desperately."Wait, we need to talk about this. Where are you going?" he asks.

"My parents used to help out a small orphanage in Mexico. They took me and Swoop there many times. I haven't been back in a while and I think it's time I returned. It's the only time I really feel close to my parents."

"So you're just taking off by yourself?" he asks.

"Yeah, I'm gonna lose myself in charity. I think it's the only way I can really…find myself," she says as she heads down the steps and onto the sidewalk.

"Key, wait!" he demands. She sighs and turns back to face him. He goes down the steps and looks into her face.

"Bex, walking down this block knowing that it's really over between us is going to kill me. Yet, I'm gonna do it. I'm gonna walk away. But if you call me, if you even so much as whisper my name, I will turn back. So if you think some little part of you, no matter how small, wants to be with Pryor, please do the humane thing and remain silent as I walk away. Because I can't take being in love alone anymore; it hurts. It hurts."

She slowly turns and heads down the block. Bex reaches into his pocket and takes out a small black velvet box. He opens it and reveals the contents—it's a small glass case with a liquid-like substance inside. It's his Rah: the angel equivalent of a wedding ring. Bex was going to ask Key to marry him tonight.

Bex looks like he wants to go after her, yet he stands still. The Rah inside his palm gleams in the light of the fading sun. He watches, pained, as his former girlfriend gets further away. Judging by her shoulders, she's sobbing and beside herself. But to her credit she never once turns around…

***

The flight to Mrs. Maybelle's is a silent one. Bex hasn't said a word and judging by his demeanor, he's in no mood for conversation. Silver is pissed at me for not replying to his Bex question. But it's hard to give him an answer when I don't have one.

Meanwhile, Swoop and Randy try to cheer up East, who is still getting over Marisol. Ruin keeps sneaking glances at Silver when she thinks he's not looking. There's something on her mind, I can tell. Yet she has made no attempt to talk to Silver or anyone else. I watch her closely and not just because it's my job.

Once we arrive at Mrs. Maybelle's place, one of the kids takes us to the guesthouse about five minutes from the main property. It's a charming two level home with antique furniture and bright accent colors—a fusion of rustic meets romance.

Once we each pick a room and settle in, Mrs. Maybelle puts us to work. We help her build a playground in the backyard, make home repairs, and paint the entire house.

Mrs. Maybelle can get people to do this work, but I think she likes having us around. The little boy Kevin follows Bex around helplessly like a little puppy. By the end, Kevin looks like a mini version of Bex and has gotten everything down from Bex's "serious" glare to his feet apart "ready to fight" stance. Kevin becomes Bex's shadow. It is beyond adorable. Yet behind his smile, we can see Bex is hurting.

On our third night here, I find Bex out on the front porch of the guesthouse. He's checking his phone. I'm guessing it's to see if Key called. He's been checking it every twenty minutes, we all notice. Even Ruin feels kind of bad for him after a while.

"Hey, um…Mrs. Maybelle said there's a box of nails that might work better. It's out in the woodshed," I tell him.

"I'll go get it in a minute," he says with his eyes glued to the screen.

"Any luck?" I dare ask.

"No. She's probably just…busy. She'll call," he says, mostly to convince himself.

"Yeah, you're probably right," I lie.

I start to head back to the main house, but something keeps nagging at me. Should I confront him about his feelings for me?

"Hey Bex," I call out.

"Yeah?"

"Nothing," I reply.

How can I even bring up the subject of how he feels about me when he's still so hurt from his breakup with Key? If Bex does feel something for me, I doubt it will ever see the light of day…

CHAPTER TWENTY-EIGHT
HOLD BACK THE DARKNESS

On our last day, Mrs. Maybelle says she has one final job for us. So the team and I head out back to see what she needs help with. We're shocked when we walk out and find a crowd of angels, Quo, and humans gathered along the sprawling yard. There's a banner that floats in midair with letters that sparkle like fireworks and change every few seconds. The letters spell out the same words in every language: Thank You.

"Mrs. Maybelle, we're honored, but really you didn't have to do this," I reply.

"No she didn't, but bless you for doing it anyway!" Swoop says as she quickly kisses Mrs. Maybelle on the cheek and heads towards the nearest Quo hottie.

"You welcome, sugar!" she shouts back as she signals for the band to start playing.

Mrs. Maybelle orders us to have fun and not to even think about work or another mission. We promise to try and have a good time given the amount of work and expense she put into this party. I order the team to blow off steam and enjoy themselves. They all take off in different directions and mingle with the crowd.

Randy and I look throughout the vast lush grounds and I explain all the activities going on. I point out to him the Keeper that Mrs. Maybelle has hired. A Keeper is an angel whose job it is to secure animals long thought dead by humanity. Omnis pulls those animals out of circulation in order to make space for new ones. But if you have the money, you can hire a Keeper and he or she will come to your house with the animals of your choosing.

"That's so freaking cool," Randy says.

"Yeah, and it looks like Mrs. Maybelle has hired a Keeper with dinosaurs," I reply.

Randy turns slowly and sees three "medium" sized dinosaurs with elongated necks and tails. There are dozens of kids around the animals. He's torn between fear and fascination.

"Don't worry, Randy. They're all herbivores; they only eat plant life," I assure him.

"I know what I want for my birthday!" Randy says, overjoyed. He then takes a closer look at what the kids are doing.

"Wait, are they face painting them?" he asks, baffled.

"Yeah, what else would you do with dinosaurs?" I ask.

"Um…ride them," he says.

"Why would you ride dinosaurs when you have unicorns?" I reply, signaling to the half dozen stunning creatures across the yard from us.

"Unicorn rides? Man, I wish I knew you when you were a kid. I'd come to all your parties. I'd beg your parents to adopt me. In fact, I still might," he jokes.

Although I am used to lavish parties in the Angel world, I must admit this one is better than any other I've been to. From the music, to the extensive food buffet, to the impeccable aerial decorations and entertainment, Mrs. Maybelle has done an amazing job.

She even arranged to have a Zipper; a Zipper is a Ferris wheel that's pretty much like the ones the humans have except for two things: one, it is not bound by gravity, and two, it has no visible attachments.

So when the kids step onto the spot on the ground marked "Zip," they are suddenly lifted off the floor and hurled into midair with no visible means of support. Both angel and Quo kids love Zippers because they move in intricate patterns at top speed.

The kids on the Zipper shout gleefully as they wave their little arms and legs wildly in the air. The Zipper was my little brother, Sam's favorite ride.

He'd get on that thing for hours and refuse to go home. It always took a really big bribe to get him to get off the ride; that or a stern look from my mom.

I feel a sharp prick of longing for Sam. It starts in my soul and spreads throughout my body. I can't articulate the sadness that comes even months after his passing. There hasn't been a word invented to describe the loss I feel knowing he's no longer here with me. It's like waking up and finding that you have lost your arm. I love Sam so much; I keep thinking one day I will open my eyes and it won't hurt anymore, but that's just never going to happen.

Randy stands next to me and studies my face. He sees the sadness that replaces my smile as I look over at the kids on the Zipper. He takes my hand and kindly reminds me that I promised Mrs. Maybelle to have a good time.

"You're right, sorry. It sneaks up on me sometimes," I admit.

"I know, Carrot, but it's okay to miss him. Sam was lucky he had you as a sister. And he knew that. He loved you," Randy says as he leans into me.

"Thanks…hey, look over there," I tell him.

Randy follows my gaze and finds pretty, bright smoke appearing in spots throughout the yard. Randy asks what the smoke is and I tell him to just watch. Suddenly the smoke forms into a waiter holding a tray of treats.

"What the hell?" Randy says.

"They are called Shadow Servants," I reply, laughing.

Even after all that's happened, Randy is still fascinated with the little aspects of the Angel world. I find that endearing. When a Shadow Servant appears before us, Randy helps himself to the snacks on her tray with a big smile. When the Shadow Servant disappears in a puff of smoke, Randy shakes his head in awe.

"That's just so cool," he says.

"Come on, Randy, I'll introduce you to the Keeper," I said.

"Um…I think someone wants to talk to you," Randy replies as he looks out across the yard at the Noru leaning on a tree studying me intently.

Aaden's eyes have laser focus—on me. It's as if the hundreds of people around us don't exist at all. I'm the only being he sees at the moment. The intensity of his heated gaze makes me forget what I was saying. It makes me forget how to flap my wings and how to blink my eyes. I have Aaden Case's undivided attention.

"Have you guys talked at all since you've been back?" Randy asks.

"Um...yeah, when he was helping me get better and stuff," I reply, unable to take my eyes from Aaden's.

"That's not what I mean. Have you guys actually discussed being together?" Randy pushes.

"We've been...busy," I reply lamely.

"What the hell is it with you two? The only time you guys want to unite is when there's some evil force forbidding it. Enough already. Everyone knows you want each other. Just go for it," Randy says.

"I know. I just..."

"Just what?" Randy pushes.

"There's so much that could go wrong with us," I admit softly.

"If only you were a big, strong powerful angel and had a best friend who would be there for you no matter what the outcome is with Silver," Randy says sarcastically.

I look over at him and smile back. I know he's right. It's time that Aaden and I talked for real. We've been hiding behind missions, ex girlfriends, duty, and charity. But the time has come. If Aaden and I are to be together, it's now or never...

***

I look at him and without saying a word I head down the path that heads to Mrs. Maybelle's elaborate garden just past the guesthouse. It's my favorite place to go when I visit Mrs. Maybelle.

It has a small stone bridge with a koi pond filled with colorful fish. There's a cascading waterfall that flows into the pond. The sound echoes in the still night and sings a peaceful lullaby to the garden and all its inhabitants. There are a million stars above me and the scent of night-blooming jasmine lingers in the air. The night is perfect. So perfect in fact, I almost feel bad for intruding on its unequivocal beauty.

"Hi," he says simply.

I turn and find him standing behind me. His grey wings flap gracefully in the night air. He followed me just like I hoped he would.

"Hey," I reply as a thousand butterflies take flight in the pit of my stomach.

"You missed it. Randy convinced the Keeper to let him ride one of the dinosaurs. He was on there for about three seconds before he was catapulted into the air."

"Is he okay?" I ask.

"He's fine. He landed in Mrs. Maybelle's prized rose bushes, so she put him to work."

"Doing what?"

"Thanks to Randy they are one dinosaur short, so the kids now have a new face to paint," he says, smiling.

"Seriously?"

"A group of five-year-old Quo girls got their hands on him. He's sporting sparkling lip gloss, red blush, and a long curly blonde wig to match."

Aaden and I share a laugh at my wonderful best friend's expense. It feels good to laugh and be silly with Aaden. We so rarely get to do that now. But years before, all we did was joke around and find ways to make each other laugh. I miss that. I miss him.

"Look, before when I said I didn't care about you and Ruin…I did care…a lot," I admit.

"I'm so glad," he replies.

"You're glad that I was pissed about the kiss?"

"Yeah, because it means that you care what I do and who I do it with."

"Really?"

"Pry, kissing Ruin was a mistake on every level. I've been telling her that there's nothing between us and then I go and kiss her. It was an asshole move—one that I don't plan on repeating. Can we get past it?"

"I went through the hardest time in my life a few days ago and I don't want to argue with anyone, especially you. I thought about all the times you and I wasted and I swore if I got the chance to see you again…yes, I can let the kiss go but I need to know that kiss was a onetime thing."

"It was," he replies.

"Fine, but it's not just that. Why didn't you tell me about Bex?"

He sighs and signals for me to follow him. We walk over to the bridge and stand in the middle, looking down at the gleaming water below. Aaden is quiet for a while. I don't push him. Whatever he's about to say is hard for him, judging by the dark expression on his face.

"When you were gone…it felt like The Center had taken me too. I felt like I was there in hell with you. And the only way I could function and stay focused was to compartmentalize. I had to put what Bex said in a box and push it to the back of my mind. But then when everything got back to normal, Bex's words came back to me and…Pryor, I vowed I would never again let something stop me from being with you. That's why I didn't tell you. I feared you would go to him. And I don't know how to deal with that."

"Aaden, you can't keep things from me."

"I know. It was an asshole move and I'm sorry. But I need to know—do you have feelings for Bex?"

"That's a complicated question," I reply.

"Bullshit!" he snaps.

"Look, all this time Key and Bex have been together. They were the perfect couple: Romeo and freaking Juliet. Who's gonna go to the trouble of falling for Romeo when he already has his Juliet?"

"Maybe you never thought about Bex in that way because he was taken, but now he's not. So, now is the time to think about it. Now answer the damn question. Do you have feelings for Bex?"

"Why are you yelling at me?"

"BECAUSE I CAN'T TAKE IT ANYMORE!"

Shocked by his frank and frustrated outburst, I remain silent. He hangs his head in utter despair. Without looking up, he gathers the fabric of my shirt underneath his large hands. He then pulls me towards him, sighs, and bows his head. When he speaks again, his voice is vastly different. He's not enraged. He's exhausted and vulnerable.

"I want you, Pry. I want you so much. If you choose Bex…" His voice trails off.

A lump forms in my throat. I stroke his hair tenderly and whisper into his ear.

"I don't know about Bex. Maybe there's a little something there, like you said you have with Ruin. But at the end of the day, you are the angel I want. Aaden Case, how could you not see how much I love you?"

He finally looks up at me, puzzled and uncertain. I stand on the tips of my toes and place my arms around his neck.

"I've never stopped wanting you. Ever. You're my only constant," I say as I part his lips with mine. He kisses me back with hunger. Then he embraces me and lifts me off the ground. I squeal with joy, like a kid. Being in his arms feels as natural as flying. It's where I belong. It's where I have always belonged.

"Can you do something for me?" I ask, still in his embrace.

"Yes, I will do it," he replies.

"You don't even know what it is," I remind him.

"I don't care. I will do whatever you ask."

"Okay, remember how you were my first kiss?" I ask playfully.

"Wait, was that you?" he teases.

"Ha, ha. Seriously, Aaden. I'm ready for another…first."

I wait for him to say "no" yet again. The conversation he had with The Face really affected him. I'm afraid he'll fight me on us making love. He won't cave in until I'm sixteen or even seventeen.

Damn that old lady! I thought detention was the worst punishment she could inflict on me. Man was I wrong…

"Okay, let's go," he says, holding his hand out.

"What, really?"

"Really."

I grin like a major dork and take his hand. I'm going to make love to Aaden.

***

(PLEASE BE ADVISED THERE IS MATURE CONTENT BELOW. YOUNGER READERS CAN SKIP THIS CHAPTER WITHOUT MISSING ANY PLOT POINTS.)

It's a few minutes later and Aaden stands across the room, shirtless and tormented. The moonlight beams down on him, highlighting his broad shoulders, powerful biceps, and remarkable abs. His desire to come to me is evident in his fiery stare, yet he remains on the other side of the room.

I watch as a war rages inside him. The demon in him wants me; needs me. The longer he stays away, the more he desires to be near me. Yet the angel he is can't help but worry that I might not be ready for this. The angel in him worries he may take me down a path I'm not equipped to walk. He deathly fears that stripping away my innocence will leave me bare and unprotected; the second strongest angel in the world is at an impasse.

I walk over to him slowly and stand close so that the moonlight bathes us both. Aaden hangs his head in deep contemplation. The unrest inside him is growing, but so is the longing to touch me. I place my hand under his chin and gently raise his head so that we have eye contact. I have never seen him so tormented. His body is still and certain, but his eyes betray him.

"Talk to me," I whisper.

"I want this…badly. But I don't want you to regret it in the morning. I can handle anything, but not that," he replies urgently.

"You think you're taking something away from me. And maybe if I was with the wrong guy, that's exactly what would be happening. But Aaden, I'm exactly where I should be, where I've always wanted to be—with you. You aren't taking something from me, you're giving me something."

"What can I possibly give you?" he asks.

"Don't you know? Aaden, one smile from you gives me the strength of a million Paras. The care in your voice when you say my name restores me. Your touch is a superpower. It somehow heals me of all doubt, fear, and worry. We loved each other before we even knew what it really meant. But for so long we loved from afar. I don't want to do that anymore," I assure him.

He looks up at me longingly but doesn't speak. I place both hands on either side of his perfect face and confess something to him I have never said out loud to another soul, not even Randy.

"I've always thought of you as a light in my life. Even when you were far from me, I could feel you illuminating just beyond my reach. I've been lucky because I was surrounded by beings that loved and cared about me. I was bathed in light. But that was before Malakaro.

"You're afraid that 'Carrot' is a little girl and she's not ready to be with you. Well, guess what? I'm not 'Carrot.' My name is Pryor. I'm a strong young woman. I've lost my little brother, can't be with my parents, and I am keenly aware of the fact that every time I leave the house, there's a good chance I might not make it back.

"All I want right now is to feel something other than this overwhelming darkness. I want you to make love to me. I want you to push back the darkness, if just for one night. But I'm not going to stand here and try to convince you; that's not how a woman handles herself. So when you're ready—when you feel grown enough, come see me." I don't wait for him to reply. I just head for the door.

Without warning, he picks me up and carries me over to the edge of the bed. His movements are commanding and distinctly masculine. I look into his face once again. When he looks back at me, his eyes confirm what I already know: the war inside Aaden is over.

He kneels in front of me so that we are at eye level. He looks into my face and addresses me. The bass in his voice is thick with longing, yet steady and controlled.

"I'm going to remove all your clothes; nothing will stand between my lips and your flesh," he informs me.

His take-charge tone and certainty grips me. I can't speak; I just look into his intense gaze and nod slightly.

"This moment is about you. If you are hesitant in any way, now is the time to tell me. I've been making love to you every day in my head my entire life; once we start I won't be able to stop. When it comes to you…I'm just not that strong," he admits as he studies me.

I stand up and give him a head start by taking off my shirt, revealing my sky blue cotton bra. Before I would have worried that I wasn't dressed right. I would have given my soul for a quick Victoria Secret shopping spree where I would purchase something sexy, silky, and enhancing. Like I said, that was before.

Now I stand in front him certain that I don't need the fancy embellishments. I don't need to add polish, shine, or shimmer to my body because I'm enough. I know that because after he takes an article of clothing off me, he stops and marvels at what's been revealed.

When he finally has me completely naked, he steps back in awe. He looks at me like an art student who's uncovered a lost work of art, a masterpiece no one else has viewed, let alone touched.

He stands and summons up a vial of Tam. It appears just beside my head. Tam is liquid birth control. Although Aaden's ability to summon is impaired due to The Center, he seems to have no issue summoning small objects.

Thank Omnis.

I drink the Tam quickly and the vial disappears. Aaden gives me an ardent stare that causes me to shiver with anticipation.

I've always thought of Aaden as the boy I grew up with; the boy I was in love with. But the way he places his large hands against the small of my back tells me he's a grown man; a man who's going to officially launch me into womanhood. A change I've never been more ready to make.

He pulls me towards him and claims my mouth with sweeping strokes of his masterful tongue. He explores the seam between my lips with growing hunger. The more I give in to his velvet tongue, the more it demands of me. His mouth slides, sips, and sucks on my lower lip, eliciting a moan from the deepest depths of my soul.

I place the palm of my hands on his rock hard chest and feel the heat from his skin. I brush the tip of his nipples with my finger, causing him to swear. No longer satisfied with just my lips, he adjusts my head so that he now has access to the nape of my neck. He leaves a delicious trail of kisses from my earlobe down to my collarbone.

Aaden was serious when he said he would make this all about me. Everything he does is dedicated to one thing: ensuring my pleasure. The growing frenzy in me makes it hard to remain standing, but I don't want to move and disconnect from him—ever. So I remain standing but once he grazes the sides of my breasts with his fingers, standing becomes far more difficult. And once he goes from fondling my breasts to suckling them, my thighs liquefy.

"Please…" I beg him, not even sure what it is I need from him.

While *I* may not know what I need, Aaden does. He lifts me up, lays me flat on my back, and quickly takes off the rest of his clothes. I take all of him in with my eyes. From his flawless face to the stiff eagerness between his legs, this angel is perfect and I need him in me. Now.

He knows I'm on the brink and that I'm ready take him in because my legs part and impatiently invite him in. Yet he doesn't enter; not yet.

Instead he gets on top and uses his silky lips to bend my body to his will. I moan and writhe as lust and desire spread from the tips of my wings to the tips of my toes. He doesn't just suck on one or two spots; he plants fervent, in-depth kisses throughout my body: my wrists, the crux of my elbow, the back of my knees, across my stomach, and between my shoulder blades. Places I never thought needed attention; places that now can't live without his touch.

He is possessive and firm when he grabs hold of my legs and parts them. Yet when his lips make contact with my inner thigh, he's gentle. I try to steady myself as my desire grows, but once he starts using his tongue, I can no longer keep still. The ecstasy is almost too much to take in. It's a pleasure overload and I am losing all sense of time and space.

Despite my passion filled cries and moans, he's not ready to release me of his erotic hold. Instead, he yanks me further down on the bed so that he has full access to me. He gently parts the soft folds of my cleft with the tip of his tongue. He doesn't poke or pry crudely. Instead his mouth explores the lining of my center with grace, focus, and diligence.

When his tongue brushes the very peak of my center, I involuntarily arch my back and bite my lower lip until my teeth break the skin. I mumble incoherently as waves of ecstasy engulf me. I think I've hit the height of desire, but then he uses a combination of his lips, tongue, and fingers.

"Oh my Omnis," I cry out as I shake with longing while an ocean forms between my thighs.

I want him to stop because the pleasure is going to rip me in two. Yet he feels so good inside me, I think I will die if he so much as *tries* to pull away from me.

He does it again. Lips. Tongue. Fingers.

"Aaden baby…shit!"

He does it again. Lips. Tongue. Fingers.

I know it's happening and I can't stop it. The inner Arc, the human orgasm, that is coming my way is bigger than anything I could ever have conceived of. I grab hold of the metal railing of the bed frame beneath me and bend it as if it were made of soft clay. It's no use. The orgasm headed for me will take control of every part of me and won't be able—

"YES!!!!!" I scream as wave after wave of ecstasy ripples through me.

It takes control of my entire body and it seeps out of me using my powers as a vessel. A surge of power springs from my palm, ready to kill anything in sight. In the throws of passion, I can't control my power to drain life. All I can do is aim for something not human.

Thinking quickly, I aim my hand out the window and on to the garden outside. As the orgasm works its way though me, the surge in my power grows. It shatters the glass window and pulls all the green from the garden, draining it of all color.

I squeeze my legs tightly as the final current of desire runs through me; outside the window there now stands a black and white garden.

He climbs on top of me, concerned that I may have hurt myself. He's taken aback when I flip us so that I am now the one in control. He's about to talk but I stop him.

"Shhhhh…I got this."

I straddle him and place my knees on either side of him. I sweep my lips across his pecs and take his nipples in my mouth. He sighs and holds on to the back of my thighs. I taste his lips and dip my tongue in and out of his mouth. He makes a low animalistic growl as I playfully tease and tickle his hardened nipples. I feel him beneath me, he's hard *everywhere*.

I place my hand between his thighs and make contact with his middle by lightly grazing it. He takes in a sharp breath and looks back at me pleadingly. I use my hand to stroke his center again.

Again. Again. Again.

"Pry…" he groans as his eyes turn "full demon" black.

He's not the only one who's aching. My body is impatient and eager to have him inside me like he was before, but this time deeper; much deeper. Neither of us can stand being apart any longer. Our bodies need to merge. Right now. I wrap my hand around his core and insert him in me.

HDRRJRBSKSDKRFNLRLNGONOUROFWEKMFPWKPWM;W MFPWEMFW;INUYRJNW434983M4NFKOS85L3LGOKNOERNOR NGOEWKNKWENLK099K4MELKEMDLMDLNLNLNLRNLWNGL WKNVLKELFIJGPP1!!!!NIONOI!!!NON1ON1NJ11

"PRY!" I hear him shouting.

"How did…?" I ask from the floor, not sure how I got there.

He rushes to my side and gently places me back on the bed.

"You placed me inside you and the initial power was too much. I should have told you it would be. It's my fault. I'm sorry," he says, taking my face in his hand.

"You were speaking every human language all at once. It's the side effect of being so powerful and not having any control when you make love. Your mind can't take it," he explains.

"Has this ever happened to you?"

"Yes, in the beginning. I had to learn to focus."

"Teach me."

"What? You still want to…"

"Aaden, I'm not leaving this room until we have made love in every way possible," I declare.

"Pryor, no. I think we should stop here," he says, sounding official.

Without warning, I kneel down before him. I take him into my mouth. I don't know how it is that my body knows exactly what to do but it does. Together, my lips and tongue seek, slide, swirl, sip, sweep, skim, suck, squeeze, and slurp.

"Ah…" He groans as he leans forward and rests his head on my shoulder, unable to manage the surge of ecstasy running though him.

I want to be just as thorough at pleasing him as he was at pleasing me. So I add my fingers to the mix of tongue and lips. They explore him meticulously; they go over, under, and in between. They trail, taunt, tease, twirl, tickle, and tend.

Adding my fingers sends Aaden into overdrive; he growls, lifts his head off my shoulder, and sinks his teeth into my flesh. The pain travels down my body and ignites a spark between my legs.

Aaden is shaking helplessly and begging for me to stop. Finally, I slowly begin to release him from me but just when he's almost free of my lips, I greedily drink him back in.

"AHHHH…BABY YOU'RE GONNA MAKING ME SET YOU ON FIRE—FUCK!"

A massive swirl of blue flames spring up from each of Aaden's palms. He cries out as he hurls them on to the ceiling. The sea of sapphire flames rages just above our heads.

"Get over here," he orders. He grabs me by my arms and flings me over to the bed.

This time he gets on top of me and interlocks his hands with mine. Just being that close to him sends chills of lust down my spine.

I want him. I want him. I want him.

"Focus," he scolds. I nod and he leans in and whispers in my ear.

"I love you. And no matter what happens, do not let go of my hand. Do you hear me?" he demands.

"Yes."

"Keep your eyes open. I want to see your beautiful eyes the entire time," he says.

I nod in agreement. He showers me with long sensual kisses as I say his name with a sigh under my breath. In no time my center is pulsating and seeking again. He inserts himself into me. Slowly.

My first impulse is to flee in panic. It's too much. It's like looking into a thousand suns all at once. The most beautiful suns ever created. You can't look away, yet the sheer power of it hurts. He sees the fear in my eyes and calls out to me.

"Damn it, Pryor, stay with me!"

I fight the urge to run and submit to the ecstasy and agony of my first time. But the fear of being overwhelmed resurfaces. Concerned, Aaden makes me sit up so that now we are both upright and facing each other.

"Watch my wings. And flap them in time with mine," he instructs.

"I want to...it just...it feels so...the euphoria inside me...you feel so good. I can't think."

"Don't think. Just flap your wings in tune with mine."

I force myself to try again and do as Aaden says. It starts working. The panic is dying down. Our wings are flapping in tune with each other.

"Good, that's good, baby," he encourages.

"What now?" I ask, now that I can finally think again.

"When I'm inside you, know that I'm only there to do one thing: love you."

I look into his eyes. He's sincere and unwavering in his statement.

"That's it, Pry; for the rest of my life I only have one job: love you."

So when he places himself inside me again, I don't run or panic. I don't black out and wake up on the floor. Instead I let him do his job. I let him love me. He plows into me with force, yet he's not brutal. Instead his strokes are rhythmic, powerful, slow, concentrated, and all consuming. I raise my hips up off the bed to meet his sensual, seductive thrusts.

His rhythm is the only thing I am aware of right now. I don't know where I am. Or even what my name is. All I know is that this angel is making love to me like I'm more important than his very soul.

My eyes roll to the back of my head and I shudder as I say his name. This time when we have the second orgasm it's not loud and bigger than life. It's a slow, sensual, deep-rooted orgasm; the kind shared by soul mates.

The Outer Arc orgasm doesn't happen inside our bodies but outside. It appears in the room in the form of a shimmering orb. And as my lover and I are entangled inside each other, the Arc in the room grows. And like any two angels who truly connect, we trade characteristics and powers. My wings turn grey like Aaden's and he gets my purple eyes.

The orb splits into two. It goes inside me and tells me what Aaden was thinking while making love to me.

"Thank you, Omnis. Thank you…"

The other half of the orb makes its way inside Aaden and tells him what I was thinking.

"Home; he is my home."

The orb then pulls itself out of us and lingers in the room. By the time we are done making love, it expands past us and goes up into the ceiling where the flames are. It forms a makeshift coat of protection, guarding us from the flames.

Aaden wraps his arms around me from behind. He whispers my name over and over again; like it's the sweetest word he's ever spoken. He nuzzles my ear and the nape of my neck. Then kisses my forehead and tells me he loves me. And just like that, darkness lifts from my world.

EPILOGUE

I wake up in Aaden's arms and find him studying me. He had gotten up in the middle of the night and fetched a thick blanket to cover us. While I appreciated being warm and cozy underneath the covers, I would have been okay waking up to find him still naked.

"Why are you looking at me like that?" I ask suspiciously.

"I want to make sure you're okay. Your first time can be...traumatic," he admits.

"Was yours?"

"Um...yeah...it was."

"What was it like?" I ask carefully.

"It was a rush. I had a lot of nervous energy," he says ruefully.

"So...who was it with?"

"Ah...I can't say."

"Why? I mean it's not like it's someone we know, right?"

He clears his throat and turns away.

"Oh, so it's someone we know. Who?" I push.

"Pry, it was a long time ago. I was crazy young and stupid. But yes, she is someone we all know, who isn't on the team."

"What happened?"

"Pryor, I am not going to run down the details of a misguided one-night stand from a million years ago. That is improper, young lady," he says, doing his best "Face" imitation. We share a laugh. He then gently grazes my lips with his thumb and speaks with a concerned tone.

"Seriously, are you okay with...last night?" he asks.

"If you're asking if my soul died because we had sex, the answer is no. If you're asking if I have regrets, then the answer is yes."

"You regret what happened last night?" he asks, wounded.

"Yes. I regret that the night ended."

"You're...amazing," he says, relieved.

"You mean the sex was amazing," I reply.

"No—well yeah, it was. But it's not just that. I don't know how to explain it without sounding like I'm crazy," he says as he kisses the palm of my hand.

"I happen to like crazy, so let's hear it," I reply while I run my fingers through his hair.

"Have you ever been to the Ukraine?" he asks.

"No, why?"

"There's a series of underground caves there called 'Blue Dove.' It's called that because the aqua blue entryway resembles birds' wings. There's a river that passes through the cave and when the light hits it at the right angle, it looks like a sea of stars coursing through it. When I stand in the middle of it, I swear it's like Omnis lowered the light and placed it at my feet.

"Blue Dove is the only place I ever truly felt hopeful. The impossible beauty of it makes all things seem...possible. But once I leave Blue Dove, the hope I feel fades—quickly. Eventually I stopped going there because I knew I could never retain the awe and wonder I found in the caves.

"Then this morning, as the sun was coming up, I looked over at you and there it was—that same feeling I found in the cave. Only now, I don't have to go looking for it anymore because I have it right here, with you. You're my living version of Blue Dove. And I get to have you in my life every day. I mean, if that's what you want," he says.

"It's what I've *always* wanted," I reply.

We kiss tenderly at first but then it quickly starts to escalate. I leap out of bed and playfully signal for him not to follow me.

"No, Aaden! We have to go. Mrs. Maybelle wants the team to have breakfast with the kids." I remind him as I start to gather my clothes.

He playfully tackles me and drags me back to bed. I'm laughing so I can't form words.

"I'm only gonna keep you for just five more minutes," he lies.

"Get dressed, Noru!" I reply, trying to sound official, but the laughter in my voice betrays me.

"Okay, okay. Wow, we're together for a few hours and you're already trying to control me?" he jokes.

Suddenly, I stand still and watch as he gathers his clothes. He looks at me and sees that I'm no longer smiling.

"Pry, what's wrong?" he asks, alarmed.

I rush into his arms and cling tightly to him.

"Hey, hey, what is it?" he asks again.

"Thank you. Thank you for protecting the team while I was gone. And thank you for not giving up on me. And for being there when I needed you most. The whole year you were gone I missed you *so* much. And now we're here…I'm not scared anymore. I'm not scared," I reply.

He tightens his hold on me and presses me against his chest. He whispers in my ear that he loves me. It's a long time before I finally break away from his embrace.

"We really should get going," I tell him.

"Okay, but how do we explain the scorched ceiling and the faded garden to Mrs. Maybelle?" he says.

"Aliens?" I suggest.

"I'm gonna jump in the shower while you figure out a better lie," he says as he heads for the bathroom.

I call out after him; he turns to face me, smiling.

"What is it?"

"I wanted to make sure this was all real," I admit.

He walks back towards me and takes my face in his hand.

"Hey, this isn't a dream. This is long overdue. We are finally together and nothing's going to change that."

We kiss one last time and I head back to my room to get ready. Before going in, I check to see if the other members of the team are awake. Everyone's door is closed except Bex's and Ruin's.

I look out the window to see if they are out there but I can't see them.

I head downstairs to look for them. I hear two voices coming from the kitchen. I peek behind the door; Bex and Ruin are standing on opposite sides of the counter. He watches her as she drinks more of the mixture that Mrs. Maybelle made for her.

"What's in that drink?" Bex asks.

"Why do you care?" Ruin counters.

"Because something's going on with you," Bex replies.

"What are you talking about?"

"Something has been off about your whole situation from day one. I mean, really, why are you hanging around knowing Silver has other interests…"

"I couldn't care less about the redhead."

"I think that's far from the truth," Bex counters.

"And I think you have a lot of time on your hands since Key left you and you need a hobby. Maybe stamp collecting or how about couponing?" she quips.

"You would not let us scan you with the device Harris gave us. Why? And why did the Queen of Furies spare you on the island? Was it because she saw good in you or something else?"

"I'm done with your pointless questions. I know you want me gone. Your leader tells me to go and I will. But until then, stay out of my business and out of my way," she snaps as she drinks the rest of the mixture.

"Okay, fair enough. But I have one last question," Bex says.

"What is it, Para?"

"Which one of us is going to tell Silver he's gonna be a father?"

END OF BOOK III

Dear reader:

I know how difficult cliffhangers can be and I will try very hard to finish the book 4 as soon as I can. However I can tell you that the baby is in fact Aaden's and it's not a mistake. I also want to remind you that this is only the 3rd book in the series so keep the faith. Thank you for your continued support and patience.

Yours,
Lola

PS: Stop by and like us on Fb and sign our mailing list to get updates:)

http://eepurl.com/W-scP

YOU CAN ALSO READ MY FIRST SERIES, CALLED "THE GUARDIANS" AND FIND OUT WHAT DRAMA, SCANDAL AND ADVENTURE TOOK PLACE BEFORE THE NORU.

READ THE FIRST CHAPTER OF THE "GUARDIAN" SERIES WRITTEN BELOW, AND THEN DOWNLOAD BOOK ONE IN THE SERIES FREE!

****

Free Preview

CHAPTER ONE
THE BOY

Okay, it's official: I'm a coward. No one is in class today but me—and the new twin foreign exchange students from Japan. The boy's name is Rio. He's tall, lanky, and on the cutting edge of fashion. His hair is flaming red and falls into a shaggy bob cut that usually covers his face. His lips are plum red and he has eyebrows most girls would die for.

Rio looks like a Harajuku poster boy. This I learned from Wikipedia; it is a fashion trend in Japan where the kids dress in bold colors, patterns and off-the-beaten-path clothing. I find him sexy in a dark, mysterious way.

His twin sister, Miku, is more bohemian. No matter the weather, she can be found in dresses that are usually soft, flowery, and flowing. She has almond-shaped gray eyes like her brother. Her hair is jet black, bone straight and falls down to her waist. Her bangs frame her soft face beautifully. She wears a single honey blonde braid on the right side. But where Rio stands at 6'0, his sister is nearly a foot shorter.

We've said hello to each other in passing, but I've never struck up a conversation. I wonder what it would be like if I had that kind of charm. Would I take over governments? Start wars? Or maybe, just try to get a date for senior prom?

It didn't surprise me that the twins are here. They never miss a day of school. Since they arrived, I've been fascinated by the way they are with each other. They could be laughing quietly and joking around, but if a student enters the room looking worried or upset, it changes the mood of the twins. Suddenly they are concerned as well. Of course this is all me— having way too much time on my hands to analyze other people's behavior.

Still, I imagine their lives are somehow filled with adventure. I wish mine were. I'd like my life to be as exciting as Joan of Arc's or Queen

Elizabeth's. Their existence changed the world. I daydream about being that kind of girl. But those women were brave and defiant. Me, on the other hand, I can't even cut one lousy class.

The reason for such a low turnout in my last class period is the weather. New York City rarely has temperatures above 30 degrees in January. But here we are just two weeks in to the new year, and it's a blissful 70 degrees outside. So everyone said a silent *"Thank you"* to global warming and ditched class.

My friend Sara was trying to coax me to join her, but at the last minute, I chickened out. I never go against the rules. Not because I don't have a desire to, but because I am afraid of the repercussions. What if I cut class and got caught? They'd call my mom and I'd be grounded. Not that I ever really go anywhere but still....

It isn't just the weather that has made people skip Mr. White's history class, it's Mr. White himself. He rarely makes eye contact with the class, or even asks questions to see if we are following along with the lesson. It's as if he's talking to himself. He's a one-man show, and we inconvenience the hell out of him by being there.

I raise my hand and get permission to go to the bathroom. I head down the hallway and encounter the Armani- Dior-McCartney parade. Fashionistas come towards me armed with posh handbags, perfect teeth and utter disapproval.

I am the only kid at Livingston Academy that doesn't have old money. Actually, I don't have new money either. My Grandfather was a janitor here for twenty years before he died. As a favor, the dean arranged it so I could get a partial scholarship. It's still out of our price range but my Mom won't hear of public school.

Standing there, I thought I'd get my stuff and make a break for it, but no, I walked right past my locker and into the girls bathroom. Like I said: big coward.

I look at myself in the mirror and sigh. I am so uninteresting. My face is too round, my eyes are too far apart and my cheekbones lack the height needed to elevate me to exotic. The only things that stand out about me are my eyes: they're as purple as the stupid dinosaur. And, well, that's just weird.

What's even weirder is that they go various shades of purple depending on my mood. If I'm angry, they become such a deep shade of purple they appear black. When I'm sad, they lighten up and take on an electric, neon glow. I hate my eyes. They come from my father. He had encountered my mother on her way home from school—and raped her. She went to the police, but they never caught him. She tried to put that night behind her, but then I came along.

My mom, Marla, calls me the one good thing in her life. Funny, I never saw it that way. She had a scholarship to Columbia University and was going to be pre-law, but she had to postpone school to have me. Then my grandparents died in a car accident and she had no one to help support her.

So, she put off school and got a series of dead-end jobs to make ends meet. Law school became a distant fantasy. She poured all her dreams into me. She wants me to be what she would have been had she not had me: a brilliant attorney slash striking social butterfly.

But it takes a full night of cramming to squeeze out a C+ or B- on my exams. That is not brilliance. And as far as being striking goes, as I said, the only remarkable thing about me are my eyes. I *always* get asked about wearing contacts. I get so fed up with that question.

So here I am, Emerson Hope Baxter, a fifteen-year-old, purple-eyed freak living in New York City. I look at myself in the mirror once again. I smooth out a wayward strand of ink colored hair and tighten my ponytail. I take one last look at myself. I'm 5'4" without a curve in sight. I sigh, again.

I wash my hands and head out the door. The urge to ditch doesn't last long. Besides, even if I had ditched class, where would I go? Everyone who cut class today had something fun and exciting to do. Their life had urgency and meaning. My life, on the other hand, is routine and ordinary.

So, no ditching, but I'm doing the next best thing; I head to the nurses office, my safe haven. The nurse's name is Cora. She lets me crash on one of the cots when life at Livingston Academy has gotten to be too much. I run to the safety of the Lysol-scented office until I get enough nerve to face the world again.

As I head down the hallway I hear a moan coming from the janitor's closet. I walk up and press my ear to the door. I turn the knob half expecting it to be locked, but it isn't. The person moans even louder.

"Hello?"

"Help!" a male's voice says weakly in the dark.

I gently drag him out of the closet and prop him up against the wall. I know I have seen him before. I can't remember his name, but he works in the main office. He's about fifty or so, balding with dark rimmed glasses and kind eyes.

"They're coming for him. Must stop them...hurts so much," he says in barely a whisper.

His face is pale and his lips are pressed together so tightly they form a thin white line. I put my hand on his shoulder to calm him. That's when I first see the blood. It has seeped through his white shirt and tie and continues to spread its way across his abdomen. By the time I find the origin of the blood, it's seeped down to the floor. I put my hand on the hole in his stomach but that does little to slow the bleeding.

"Help! Somebody help!" I cry out. The hallway answers back with staunch silence.

"Help me!" I call out again. Nothing.

He's trying to say something. I lean in closer.

"Find him. Tell him to run."

"Find who?"

He hands me a crumpled blue 5x7 index card. The kind all the students have to fill out detailing their address and other important information. It's covered in blood.

"Find him," the man insists again.

"Okay I will," I promise, hoping that would get him to stay calm.

I call out for help once again but this time I don't wait for the silence to mock me. I stuff the index card in my pocket and I run down the hallway as fast as I can. It doesn't seem fast enough. Should I have left him alone?

Can he hang on until I get back? How long does it take an ambulance to come? *Stop thinking, just go!* My heart is pounding so hard my chest hurts. I scan the hallways. Not a person in sight.

As I call out again, something hurls itself at me and throws me down to the ground with the force of a category five hurricane. I hit the floor. I would have thought I were dead save the acute pain traveling from my shoulders down to my ankle. I groan in agony as the thing that attacked me pins me down to the ground. I stare into the face of my attacker.

It's Rio from my history class. But before I can be sure, he covers me with something. Everything goes dark. I don't have time to pinpoint what it was because just then gunshots rang out.

I don't know who is shooting because my attacker won't let me up, so I fight him. I know in my head that it is a bad idea to stand up, what with a hail of bullets flying overhead, but panic steps in, and I just want to flee. I have to get up and run away. I punch him repeatedly. I kick and scream for him to let me go. It's hard to tell if he can hear me over the sound of the gunshots. If he does, it in no way affects him. He holds me down effortlessly with his body and what I think must have been some kind of dark blanket. But where did it come from?

I make one last desperate attempt to free myself; I push past the pain running down my side and hurl myself forward to get out from underneath the boy holding me captive. He doesn't even budge. How can he be so strong? He's only 120 pounds or so.

Suddenly, I hear the most beautiful song ringing out into the hallways. It sounds like the kind of melody you've heard at a funeral. Sad. Haunting. Sorrowful. Tears sprang instantly from my eyes. I'm heartbroken but I don't know why. It's as if the melody has etched the saddest possible memories into my heart. The pain is worse than any physical thing I could have experienced. I want to die. My captor looks into my eyes.

"Don't listen," he begs as he holds me closer to his chest.

The blanket he has spread over us has somehow gotten darker and heavier. The song sounds far away now. And although I no longer feel the desire to die, I am so saddened by what little melody I can make out; I continue to weep, loudly, into his chest. Somewhere in between the sobs I think I hear groaning, but I can't be sure.

The shots stop just as suddenly as they had started, and the hallway is silent again. The blanket is pulled off of me. I was right. It was Rio who held me down.

"What the hell is—." My voice dies in my throat. Lying about ten yards away from us are three bodies. And standing a few feet away from them is Miku, Rio's twin sister.

Horrified, I make my way over. Three men lie lifeless on the floor. I've never seen them before. They have on dark suits and ties. A trail of bloody tears has run down their faces. Each of them had torn their shirts open, exposing large blue and green bruises on their chests. I lean in closer and see several bloody self-inflicted gashes. It's as if they were trying to rip their hearts out.

"What did you do?" My voice is filled with so much anguish, I barely recognize it. Before Miku has a chance to reply, Rio comes towards us shouting, "We have to go! They're coming."

No sooner had he gotten the words out than a group of men comes barreling down the stairs wearing suits and carrying guns. They begin shooting.

"Emmy, let's go!" She doesn't wait for me to move. She grabs my hand and drags me down the hallway towards the exit. I fall in step with her for fear that if I don't she'll hurt me like she did the men on the floor. I knew it was her. She was the one singing. She had killed three people without putting a hand on them. And now I'm being dragged down the school hallway by a murderer and her brother. But I figure I'm better off with them than the "Wall Street" mafia back there, right?

The wonder twins and I dodge into the stairwell. Bullets whiz over our heads. The singer pulls the fire alarm. Kids quickly flood the stairwell. The PA system comes on. I can't hear what the principal is saying as the brother and sister team and I run at breakneck speed past the student body and out the door. Once outside, a red sports car comes towards us at top speed, jumps the curb and stops just short of hitting us. The door flings open. The driver, whose face I can't see, says, "Get in."

They try to get me inside the car but I fight them off, kicking and screaming. I'd rather die here than get in this stranger's car and end up bruised and broken in some dark alley.

"Get off me!" I shout back.

Had it not been New York City, the sight of a group of teenagers fighting would have been disturbing. But seeing as how the city is always full of strange characters and even stranger happenings, not one person even stopped. Although, there were a few who looked on as they walked by but dismissed it as juvenile horseplay.

Rio somehow gets both my arms behind my back and holds them there. I struggle, but it does no good. His grip is too tight.

"I got her. You clean up," Rio instructs his sister.

"I cleaned up last time," Miku replies.

"So you should be familiar with the process," he retorts. She stares back at him coldly.

Rio lets his guard down for a half a second. That's all I need. I shoot off down the street. They grabbed a hold of my shirt from behind. I scarcely manage to slip out of it. I thank myself for layering this morning because I didn't trust the weather to stay this warm throughout the day. I'm half way down the block. My muscles beg me to stop or even slow down, but I don't give in.

What's going on? The question bounces inside my pounding head with every labored breath I take. *Don't stop to analyze,* I reason with myself. *Just get some distance.*

I spot a cop car halfway down the block; seeing an end to their pain in sight, my muscles fully cooperate. I'm now running at top speed, mere yards away from help, when she appears before me, stopping me dead in my tracks.

She looks to be about my age, maybe a year or so older? She stands at a statuesque five feet nine inches. Her beauty defies logic. No one that stunning can be real. Even if she wasn't blocking me, I would have had no choice but to stop and marvel at the sheer radiance of her face. Her skin looks as if it had been carved out of the night sky: smooth, black, glowing. Her eyes are the color of gleaming pennies; her full lips spread across her face and form a spectacular smile.

Her hair reaches past her shoulder and down to her lower back in thick curls with streaks of copper matching her eyes. She wears black leather pants that hug every flawless curve and a matching fitted black leather vest. I gasp at the impossible perfection before me.

I want frantically to reach out and touch her for two reasons. First, to make sure she is real, and second, I long to put my hands on something so flawless. But I can't reach out and touch her. That's not to say that she isn't real. She's real, as is the silver handgun she's pointing at me.

I hear a car pull up, but I can't tear myself away from the girl in front of me. "Get in," she orders. She doesn't need the gun. I know from the chill going down my spine that she is dead serious, and disobeying isn't in my immediate best interest. I tear myself away from her face and see the same red car, its door open. I get into the car.

Once inside, the car zooms up Broadway going at nearly twice the speed limit. The twins are seated next to me. I want to ask where they are taking me, but I'm afraid the minute I open my mouth, I'll cry. I refuse to give my conquerors the satisfaction of seeing me weep. Instead, I look out the window at the crowds of New Yorkers passing by. As usual they are all in a hurry to get where they need to be or leave where they've just been.

They remind me of my mom. She's always racing home to make me dinner. But neither of us are good cooks, so we always end up ordering out. I wonder if I'll ever see her again. I had been in such a rush this morning, I didn't say good bye. I didn't even say goodbye to Ms. Charlotte, my cat. She waits for me on the windowsill at exactly 3:30 p.m. everyday. I don't know how she knows it's time, but I swear she does. She'll be waiting today....

I try to swallow but can't. A big lump forms in my throat. Tears stream down my face. Then I remember the emergency card the man in the closet gave me. I had told him that I would help find this boy and tell him to run.

It made no sense to me, but it had mattered to the man, and I should have done it. Oh well. I'm sure this boy is safer than me, wherever he is.

I surreptitiously remove the crumpled, blood-stained paper from my pocket. I can't make out the home number or address of the boy the closet man had failed to reach. But there, printed clearly underneath light splotches of blood, it reads:

"Emerson H. Baxter."

****

I was wrong about the alley. We pull into a quiet, charming, tree-lined street somewhere on the Upper East Side. Everything about the neighborhood says "old money lives here," from the rows of five story brick townhouses to the pristine community garden. When we get to the townhouse at the end of the block, the car pulls into the driveway. The twins get out of the car and hold the door open for me. I know I should try to run, but I'm sure my limbs won't comply. I slowly get out of the car.

I see the driver for the first time. He's black and slightly taller than Rio, but his muscular body makes him a hundred times more intimating. He's wearing a black hoodie and a platinum twisted chain. I can't make out his eyes under his Gucci shades. The twins motion to me to go into the house. Sensing I'm about to object, Rio sighs impatiently, and Miku takes my hand and walks me through the frosted glass door.

The house is breathtaking. From the high-dimension ceiling to the smooth wheat-colored finished floor, there isn't one square inch that's not appealing to the eye. The house has a historic feel, but the décor is modern with sleek, clean lines. The browns and reds that highlight the décor make the space warm and cozy. The paintings are mostly Monet. Some I recognized but two I have never seen before. The bay window looks out onto the Park.

Rio and the driver come in behind us and close the door. I'm feeling lightheaded and find it hard to focus. Miku looks at me, smiles brightly and says, "I'll get you a soda," as if this were any other day and I'm a good friend who happened to come by. Rio goes into another room and comes back with a small trash can and places it at my feet. "Don't bother," he says to Miku. Just then a wave of nausea hits me. I double over and vomit. I miss the can completely.

Miku goes away and comes back with a wet towel. She bends down and pats my face. "I want to go home. You can't keep me here. Please," I beg her. She walks me over to the plush sofa and sits me down.

She turns to Rio. "How is she?"

"Tired. Shocked." I hate being talked about like I'm not in the room.

"Why are you asking him? I'm right here."

She pays me no mind. "She should sleep," she says to the driver.

Is she kidding me? I've just been in a shoot out. I've seen a man bleeding to death and I'm being kidnapped. How does she think I could possibly sleep?

"Tell me what's going on. Who are you? Why did you force me into your car and who was shooting at us?" The more questions I ask the more hysterical I become.

"I want to go home," I shout at the top of my lungs. The driver comes up to me and takes his shades off to reveal soft, warm, hazel eyes. He places a hand on my shoulders. He looks into my eyes and speaks with a soft velvet voice oozing charm. "You would like to go to sleep," he says simply. After he said that, nothing mattered more than the desire to close my eyelids. I've fought off sleep before, but this isn't like that. There's no fight. I want nothing more than to give into darkness. The last thing I see before I drift off is the girl who held me at gun point coming towards me.

****

"She's got to be a part of this whole thing. Why else would Lucy send half a dozen Runners after her?"

"She looked genuinely surprised when they came. This girl has no idea what's going on."

"That doesn't make sense. The council would never expose a human to that kind of danger."

"I'm telling you she knows nothing."

"It doesn't matter if Emerson knows something or not. If Lucy thinks she's involved, she's dead."

As I listen to the conversation taking place in the living room, I keep my eyes closed. They had carried me into one of the bedrooms when I fell asleep. This is all a dream. This is what I get for falling asleep watching the SyFy Channel. But even as I'm saying it to myself, I know it's a lie. This is real. And this Lucy person sent a bunch of guys to kill me. What did they call them—"Runners"? What have I done to this Lucy to make her want me dead? I'm gonna lay still and keep my eyes closed. This nightmare has to end.

"Is she awake?" I think Miku is speaking. Rio answers.

"She is, but she's trying to wish this whole thing away."

"We don't have time for this." I recognize the voice of the girl who pointed the gun at me.

She sounds irritated and on edge. I open my eyes and scan the room looking for a phone. There isn't one. I snort at the absurdity of my situation. What would I say to the cops if there had been a phone? *"Hi, my name is Emerson Baxter and I'm being kidnapped and held hostage inside, what looks to be, the centerfold of* Architectural Digest.*"*

Someone knocks on the door of the room. Miku's voice calls out to me sweetly behind the door, "Emmy, it's time to get up." She opens the door and comes over with a tray of food. She sits beside me. On the tray is a small bowl of broth with pieces of a few white squares and a handful of green onions. "It's miso soup. It's good. My mom used to make it. Oh, and a turkey sandwich. I got Jay to make it for you. He's a culinary genius, but he's a little stingy with his talent."

"Who's Jay?" I question.

"The driver."

"He should have his license revoked."

"He did." She laughs and hands me the tray.

"I'm not hungry."

"Rio says you are."

"How does he know what I feel?"

"It's a long story. First food then Q&A, okay?"

I was ready to argue, but the aroma of the soup hit my nose and my stomach growled. I take one spoonful of the soup intending to stop there, but it is so good I end up drinking the whole thing.

Miku studies me. "Now, try the sandwich."

"No, I'm fine. Really." She looks pleadingly at me.

I'm such a pushover. I take a bite of the sandwich. It's the best thing I have ever put in my mouth. It has some kind of spread that gives the turkey a kick. There's also a light sweetness to it but I can't figure out from what. I look at Miku in awe.

"I know. It's amazing huh? You should try his parmesan potato bread. It's his specialty. But he really has to like you to make it."

I gobbled it up in four quick bites.

I am making a pig of myself, but Miku doesn't seem to mind. She hands me a can of soda. I drink it down and wipe my mouth with the napkin she had thoughtfully placed beside the tray. I thank her. She smiles and motions for me to follow her. I take a deep breath and walk after her out of the bedroom, into the living room.

I must have been asleep for hours, judging by the dark sky. The living room is lit softly by track lights. Someone has cleaned the spot where I'd thrown up; the sour smell is gone. The house now smells of green tea and jasmine. There's no one in sight.

"Everyone's waiting outside," Miku informs me as she leads the way. We walk up a few flights and through a black gated door onto the roof. Standing there beside Rio is the driver, Jay, and the gun girl.

It seems impossible but she is somehow even more striking than she was when I first saw her. She walks up to me. Her voice is official and impatient. "I'm Ameana. And this is Jayden." She motions towards the driver. He says, "It's cool, call me Jay."

Ameana continues without the slightest concern as to whether I respond or not. "You have something in your possession that is vital to me and many others. We need you to hand it over."

"I don't know what you're talking about," I stammer. She looks at the others, then back at me. "You have no idea what I want from you?" she asks again. I try to keep my voice from trembling.

"N-n-no," I say weakly. She turns to Rio. He replies, "She's telling the truth. The Runners haven't told her anything. She has no idea what's going on."

I don't know where the anger came from. All I know is that I had had enough of this sci-fi bull. I direct my comment to Ameana. "Look, warrior princess, I don't know what you are talking about, okay? I was just trying to help some guy I found in the hallway and then all hell broke loose! If you plan on killing me before this Lucy person, then fine, do it. If not, I have to get home."

"How do you know Lucy? Has she come to see you?" Ameana turns to Rio.

He answers her unspoken question. "She has one. I would know if she didn't."

"One what?" I ask.

"How do you know about Lucy?" Ameana demands again.

Hoping that if I give her some answers she'll give me some, I reply, "I overheard you guys talking. So, who is she? Why is she out to kill me?" I look into their faces and see something in them I didn't see when bullets rang out over our heads—fear.

"Is she some kind of super bad girl? I mean how many guns can a girl carry?" All my attempts to lighten the mood fail. "Please, tell me what's going on. I may be able to help. But you guys have to talk to me," I plead. They confer silently with each other.

Before anyone can speak, a boy pops out of thin air. Seriously. He came out of nowhere. Startled, I jump back, lose my balance and fall head first down the side of the five story building. I don't even have time to register that I should scream. I try to prepare myself for the pain. My head will hit the ground first, so maybe death will come swiftly. *Please, please come swiftly.*

There is no pain. I feel no pain. Yes! Somehow I must have been knocked unconscious so quickly, the pain never had time to register. I'm dead. I'm dead. I'm dead.

Then I hear Rio's voice. "Emmy, open your eyes" I do. I am lying safely on the floor of the roof. I look up at the faces staring back at me; Rio, Jayden, Ameana, Miku and the new pop-up guy. He looks like a J Crew model. He's wearing a designer military-style jacket, a royal blue stretch pullover that brings out his eyes, and white cargo pants.

Well, if I am dreaming, at least I'm dreaming about pretty people. Everyone on this roof is hot. Well, aside from regular looking old me. Pop-up guy says to me, "I'm Reason. But you can call me Reese." He extends his hand. I go to shake it when I see something big and dark like a shadow hovering above. I look up at Reese and gasp. Protruding out of his shoulders blades, are wings! Honest to goodness wings! Huge, disturbing, flapping-in–the-wind wings!

He sees the freaked out look on my face and then it registers with him. "Oh, sorry, I always forget." Suddenly the wings disappear.

"Am I dead?" I choke. I look over at Miku.

She answers coyly, "No, but we are." In the hallway shootout earlier I had thought *this is as confused as I can get.* I was so wrong.

Reese kneels down on one knee and takes my hand. "I'm sorry to startle you. It's rude and very 'un-angel-like.' I get on Jay for *gliding* rudely, and here I am doing the exact same thing." He helps me up.

I whisper something about it being okay. But I don't think he buys it.

Ameana stares out into the dark night. The worry in her voice is obvious. "I thought he'd be back tonight...."

"You know Marcus; he won't come back until he's found out something. In the meantime, check on Emmy for me," Miku says.

Ameana looks at me as if she is scanning me, as if she can see inside my body. "She'll live," she says dismissively—wait, can she?

Miku takes my hand. "Good, let's all go back downstairs and talk. I'm guessing you have questions." *Um, one or two.*

We all take a seat in the spotless kitchen. It has everything a cook could want, from the top of the line sub-zero refrigerator to the stainless steel eight-burner stove. It looks like no one has ever used it. If they did use it, they were obsessed about cleanliness. To stop myself from hurling all my questions out at them, I occupy myself by counting the tiny flicks of gold embedded in the black marble countertop.

"We don't have time to play twenty questions. We only have time for one. So make it good," Ameana instructed.

"What? I can only ask one question? Are you serious?" She looks at me and glares. "Fine" I paused. There is so much I don't know. I have no idea where to even start. I think for a moment and ask the most important question.

"Did the man in the closet get help? Is he okay?" Miku grins as if she's just she won the lotto. Rio shares her joy, as does Reese and Jayden. They all look at me strangely. Like I revealed something important but didn't realize it.

"That's what you want to know?" Ameana says incredulously.

"Well, there are lots more, but you said I could only ask one," I say bitterly.

"He's been taken to the hospital. He's critical but stable. There's a good chance he'll make it."

"Thank you," I say curtly, matching her tone.

She gets up to leave the room. As she is almost out the door she says, "Fill her in. Tell her what she needs to know." *And nothing more,* I think, reading between the lines. Then she walks out.

I can't hold it anymore. "Are you angels? Who's Lucy? Why did she send those guys after me?"

Miku gets up and pours me a glass of water. "Here, you'll need this."

I take it from her and drink it. I'm not thirsty, but I have a feeling she won't take no for an answer. She sits back down and Jay prepares to addresses me. But before he can get started, Rio tells him to hold on. Then out of nowhere he says loudly, "Emmy's cold, bring her a sweater, please."

How did he know I was cold? I didn't make any gestures to indicate being cold, but he's right. I've been getting goose bumps for 10 minutes. I just didn't want to stop them now that they're finally talking.

Rio points to something next to me. I follow his gaze. I don't see anything. He points up and there right above my head, hanging in the air is a rust colored wool sweater. It's just hanging there in thin air. Miku nudges me to take it, and so I do.

Then she shouts towards the entry way, "Thanks Mina."

"Wait, how did she—"

"She can move objects and people. Cool, huh?" Miku explains.

If I ever did drugs, I would stop today. But since I've never done them, I can't explain what has just taken place in the past few hours.

"Miku, please! What's going on?" I beg.

Jay comes to my rescue. His voice is steady, but he seems very far away.

"In the beginning there was the creator; the highest measure of good. Over time, this entity has been given many different names. But its original name was Omnis, which is Latin for *All*. Omnis created nature and with it, a law that no one element can exist without an opposing element. This is known as the law of opposites. This concept encompasses all things, except for Omnis himself.

"Omnis then created humanity. Everything had been perfect. So perfect, in fact, that humanity began to doubt the need for Omnis, and, over time, their connection to him all but disappeared.

"Omnis concluded that, like nature, humanity needed the law of opposites to keep it balanced. If humanity never felt despair, it could not seek out the hope he provided. If they never experienced sickness, they would not marvel at the grace of good health.

"And after seeing how wasteful humans were with the life he had given them, he knew that the only way for them to appreciate their own existence was to make it ephemeral. But because he loved humanity far more than anything he had ever created, it was difficult for him to be objective.

"So he created a council of impartial judges that would look at the complicated design of humanity and do what was necessary to keep it in balance. Omnis created three council members: Death, Time and Fate. Although the council honors and respects him, it operates independent of Omnis, to assure that balance is maintained.

"In addition to the council, Omnis decided he needed the opposite energy of himself. He is grace, forgiveness and goodness, so he wanted a force filled with rage, bitterness and evil. This force of evil would serve as an incentive for humanity to strive to be good and follow in the path that led to Omnis' welcoming arms, or they would suffer at the hands of evil.

"He called on his favorite and most cherished angel, Atourum, and told him what he needed done. The angel readily offered to serve, but Omnis cautioned that in order to become the personification of evil, there had to be hate in one's heart. Not just for humans but for Omnis himself. But Atourum could never imagine hating his creator.

"Omnis explained, 'The only way for them to believe in me, Atourum, is for them to believe in you. Go, be merciless. Be savage and cruel. All the world will say your name with fear and contempt. Then, and only then, will they seek out salvation from me.' Atourum bowed to his master and vowed to do as told.

"In order to become evil, Omnis sent Atourum to Earth several times for him to witness firsthand the flaws of man. Each trip to Earth made Atourum more and more susceptible to human influence and less connected to Omnis. The more affected Atourum was by humanity's shortcomings, the harder it was to get back into heaven. Eventually Atourum gave in to the savage ways of man and committed murder. This caused Omnis to ban him from heaven forever.

"Atourum said to Omnis 'I am now your opposing force, just as you wanted. Humanity will recognize your light by measuring it against my darkness. You take souls and put them in your mansion in the light. But humans will not appreciate this gift until you create an opposing space to the light. The only way to measure the beauty of your house is to measure it against the horror of mine.' And so it was Atourum was granted Ren, meaning 'house of fire.'

"They also came to an arrangement: Omnis would take all children and Atourum would take all the adults who had committed unspeakable acts. But they could not agree on who would get the souls that died as teenagers, souls that had yet to choose either the path of darkness or the path of light.

"They left it up to the council. The council decided to put souls that died between the ages of 13 and 19 on a bridge. The bridge is halfway between the light and the House of Fire. The souls would linger there until they choose the path to which they felt more connected. They would not know which is which. They would only follow the path that felt right to them.

"Neither side was allowed to guide the souls; they had to find their own way. It was called 'The Walk.' Each soul lingers for as long as it is undecided and then once it accepted either the light or the dark, it would go in that direction.

"Omnis and Atourum were each allowed to choose six souls from the bridge to be Watchers. A Watcher's job is to keep an eye on the bridge and ensure that neither side intervenes in 'The Walk.'

"Omnis chose six of the purist souls. He called them "The Guardians." Atourum chose six of the darkest souls on the bridge and named them "Akon" meaning "chaos."

"There were only two rules both sides had to abide by: neither side could tell a soul which way to go, and neither Omnis nor Atourum could know the location of the bridge.

"Centuries passed, the bridge would fill up, and the souls would take 'The Walk' and go on into the light or the darkness. Each time the bridge was empty, The Guardians and Akons would go to the light or to Ren and be promoted.

"On the first cycle of the bridge, the soul chosen to be first Guardian was a soul named Julian. He watched vigilantly and made sure that nothing interfered with 'The Walk.' All the souls were left to choose their own path.

"One day he took notice of a soul on the bridge that seemed to be having more trouble than the rest. It seems this soul wanted to follow the light but was drawn to the darkness. Julian watched it waver back and forth. It couldn't decide which path to follow.

"Julian talked to the soul. Her name was Femi. She lived in a small village in Nigeria. Her whole family was killed when her village was raided. She was subsequently beaten to death for standing up to the men who did it.

"She told him that she was drawn to the darkness because of what it offered her: power, strength, and control. Since her life on Earth had lacked those things, she ached to have them. The other side offered her peace, happiness and hope, but she had seen those things on Earth and they were easily taken away.

"When Julian was on the bridge just as a soul, it never appealed to him to follow any direction but the light. But as he talked to Femi, he began to understand her and sympathize with her dilemma.

"She was hopeful and filled with peace, but when violence came this last time it had stripped her of those things. 'Why run to happiness if it can get taken away?' she asked. Julian understood for the first time that 'The Walk' was easier for some than others; there were souls that could not feel the inferno of hell or the glory of heaven. That would have made it too easy for them. They'd have to decide what they wanted most: peace or power. That was the only question that stood between heaven and hell.

"Julian couldn't stop watching Femi go back and forth on the bridge. He thought about her constantly. He spoke to the other Guardians. They encouraged him to keep a distance and not interfere. They were certain she would follow whatever path she was destined to take.

"Souls had come and gone on the bridge, but Femi was still undecided. *She's so confused.* Julian reasoned. *She's not evil, she's just broken.* So one day, unable to watch her suffer indecision anymore, Julian pointed the way to the light.

"Not long after, Atourum summoned the council and asked Omnis to attend. Once all of them had gathered, Atourum told everyone that, according to the Akons, Julian had broken the rules. Atourum was livid and demanded revenge.

"'She was my soul. She would have gone to me,' Atourum spat.

"'You don't know that. She has goodness in her,' Julian responded.

"Omnis told Julian to approach. He addressed his servant warmly but firmly. 'You have disobeyed me. I know your heart is true and you have goodness and purity in you, but you have yet to learn obedience. I will send you back to Earth as many times as it takes for you to learn to follow my directions.' Then Julian was cast out of the sky.

"The council asked Atourum what he would like as retribution for the rule that had been broken. Atourum said: 'I ask to know the location of the bridge.' The council flatly refused. They knew that once Atourum found the bridge, there would be an invasion. All the souls would go towards darkness by fear or by force. That would more than triple the size of Atourum's followers, enabling them to destroy all of humanity.

"Furious, Atourum reminded the council that they were supposed to be objective. He accused them of siding with Omnis. The council went behind closed doors to talk the matter over. When they reached a decision, all parties were once again gathered.

"Death, Time, and Fate all spoke in unison. 'We, the council appointed by Omnis, have come to a conclusion on the matter of the bridge and the broken rule. While we will not give Atourum the location of the bridge, we will create a triplex that holds a map to the bridge. The triplex will then be placed somewhere on Earth every six hundred and sixty-six years. You, Atourum, will be given a chance to seek out the triplex.

"'If the map is found before midnight of that year, you will be permitted on to the bridge to do with the souls whatever you wish. If Atourum does enter the bridge, all balance will be lost and the Earth will be plunged into chaos and fire. Therefore we are also granting the Guardians a chance to seek out the map and destroy it.

"We will hide it somewhere on Earth. Each side can go about seeking the map any way they choose. However, the same basic rules still apply: Guardians can not kill human beings. If this is done, they will be thrown down to the flames. Only the first Guardian can take a life; and although

Akons can kill a human, they can not take a soul unless that soul is willing. Each side will be given a name with which to start their search.

"Only humans that are integral to the search can be informed of the mission. If humanity as a whole should find out about the search, the council will intervene and both sides will be punished. Humanity must remain, with a few exceptions, unaware of what is happening. We can not and will not tolerate exposure, as humans are frail and panic when faced with uncertainty.'

"And so, every six hundred and sixty-six years, Guardians and Akons come down to Earth to find the Triplex."

Panic rises inside me as I say out loud what Jay won't. "This is the sixth hundred and sixty-sixth year."

"I'm sorry, Emerson, but we're going to need that in the form of a question," Reese jokes in his best announcer voice.

I ignore him and go on. "That means you guys have to find an object that could be anywhere on Earth? If you don't find it, we will all die a fiery death?"

"That's about right," Jay chimes in.

My stomach feels queasy again. Maybe eating was a bad idea. Okay, note to self: news of the end of the world is best taken on an empty stomach. I'm fighting back bile. My hands are clammy and won't stop shaking.

"It doesn't have to be fire. It can come in many ways, like a flood, earthquake, or tsunami. Most people think hell on earth would just be fire, but really, it's a combination of things," Miku says casually as if we were discussing where the best lunch specials can be found. We all stare back at her.

"What? It's true."

Rio looks at her dubiously. "You're a creepy little angel."

"So, what's the name on the paper?"

Everyone looks at me as if to say "don't be stupid," but I had to ask. I need to hear it out loud. The look of sympathy on Miku's face confirms my deepest fear.

"My name is the clue."

"You, Ms. Baxter, have just gotten to the final round! Now, will you choose door number one or door number two?" Reese is getting on my nerves.

Apparently I'm not the only one. I feel a soft breeze beside me. I look over and Jay is still seated beside me. But I know he moved because Reese's mouth has literally been taped shut. Jay leans back in his chair to admire his handy work. I look at him bewildered.

"How did you…?"

"Skills baby girl," he smirks. Even as I'm hearing news of impending doom, I can't get over how amazing he looks. And when he called me "baby girl," I felt a warm feeling wash over me. Wow, he is so hot. *Focus, Emmy. Focus.*

Not one to be out done, Reese rips the tape off his mouth and "pops" up behind Jay. He holds him in a headlock.

"Where you gonna go now, speedy? Come on. I'd like to see you glide out of this," Reese says triumphantly.

They wrestle back and forth, each trying to pin the other one down. Every time Jay gets the drop on Reese, Reese disappears. And whenever Reese manages to get the upper hand, Jay moves at an impossible speed.

Rio announces that he has dibs on Jay. Reese, offended, pops up behind Rio and pulls the chair out from under him. Miku howls with laughter. Apparently the end of the world is a light-hearted subject.

"Excuse me!" I snap, not bothering to hide my irritation. "Are you guys kidding me? Was this all a joke? I thought this was serious. You guys just brought me here as some stupid elaborate game?"

"No, it's real Emmy." Miku puts her hand on my shoulder. I shake it off.

"If this is real then why aren't you guys taking it seriously?"

"We're just tryin' to be easy," Jay says.

"How can you 'be easy'? We're talking about the end of humanity. Forever!" I am seething.

"Emmy, calm down," Rio says gently.

"Don't you get it? I can't help you guys. I have no idea where your map is. Your council made a big mistake." I look at all of them with a mixture of hysteria and disbelief.

Miku chimes in, "You're the clue the council gave us. They're never wrong."

When I speak my voice is unsteady. "They're wrong about this; I'm just some girl. I watch bad TV and spend way too much time reading about things that can't possibly happen to me."

I stand up and look into their all-too-calm faces. I'm so frustrated, I could scream. "If I'm your clue then we're all dead. Do you understand?"

"Well, we're already dead, so...," Reese joked.

"Fine, you just sit there and keep making jokes. It's obvious you don't care." I storm out of the kitchen. They all follow, with Reese heading me off.

"Stop popping out in front of me!" I shout.

"It's called blinking," Reese states matter-of-factly.

"Whatever. Knock it off." I can feel rage welling up.

Jay comes from behind me and blocks my way.

"Move! I'll fight you, angel or no angel." The sheer thought of being confronted with violence by a girl who's half his size and only a fraction of his strength, amuses him to no end. I ball my fist and speak through clenched teeth. "Move!"

He can barely keep from laughing. He holds his hands up as if to surrender.

"Alright, baby girl, it's all you. I'll just glide back to my spot, *killer*. It's cool."

He moves so fast that by the time his words hit the air, he is already out of my way. He looks like light reflected on a car window going 120 miles an hour. Now only Reese remains.

"Before you storm out, at least give us a chance to apologize," he says as he silently appeals to Miku to intervene.

"We were just blowing off steam and we're sorry," Miku offers from behind me.

"No, you're not. It's not your life that's coming to an end. It's not your mother whose—"

I freeze. *My mom.* She's probably got half of New York looking for me.

"It's okay. We called her. We told her you were studying with us and you fell asleep. She knows you'll be home late," Rio says in an effort to calm me down.

"Who did you tell her you were?"

"Classmates of yours."

I'm weak with relief. I crash onto the sofa and sob. They let me. They don't approach or try to comfort me. I'm grateful for that. I need the space to fall apart.

My mind wanders from my mom and on to my neighbor, Donna. She has a four-year-old son, Benjamin. I take him to the park on weekends. He loves the swings, and he's sure if he keeps trying he can go high enough to touch a cloud. The thought of his little body pulverized by some evil force makes me sob even harder.

And just when I think it's not possible to shed any more tears, a fresh salty stream runs down my face. Sorrow and desolation engulf me. I stop trying to hold myself together and let the weight of my grief pull me into the fetal position. My body steadily rocks, sob by sob.

They don't speak or impose on me in any way. They allow me all the time I need. Maybe patience is another power that angels are granted. And even though I'm ensconced in misery, I'm certain that if they were not with me, I would be worse.

Finally I stop crying. I don't feel better, I've simply run out of tears. So I just lie there and take in the silence. My head is throbbing. I'm light-headed and empty. I should eat something but the thought of chewing is exhausting.

"I have some questions," I say to no one in particular. My throat is raw and strained. I speak so softly I think they don't hear me.

Rio asks, "What do you want to know?"

"What's a tri thingy?"

"A Triplex. It's a cover coat that protects the object inside it by taking the shape of its surroundings. It's what our wings are coated with. That's why you can't see them even though they're out all the time; it blends into whatever surroundings we're in. If it's snowing, the Triplex will take the form of falling snow," Rio explains.

"Can't people feel your wings when they're standing beside them?"

Reese responds, "Not with the Triplex. It takes no space. It has no definite form. You can only find it if you expect it to be there. I can always see Miku's wings because I know that they are there."

"Why did I see yours before then?" I inquire.

"Because you thought you were dead. You were expecting angels; so you saw one. I'm not sure you realize it but you screamed the whole way down… and even after you were safely back on the roof." He's trying hard not to make fun of me. "I think I lost all hearing in my left ear." Apparently he can't help himself, nor can I really blame him.

I must have looked like a nut. I didn't even realize I had screamed. "Sorry about that," I mumble.

"What? I can't hear," Rio shouts back.

I throw a pillow at him and he blocks it with his wings. It didn't get anywhere near him.

"So the map of the bridge is in the Triplex, making it virtually impossible to find," I surmise.

"Virtually," Jay chimes in. "But since your name is our clue, we think that the council met you and decided to leave the Triplex with you."

"I think I would remember running into Death, Time and Fate, don't you?"

Miku replies "Actually, no, you wouldn't. The council would have used someone you know to put the Triplex somewhere in your life where you wouldn't discard it, either because of necessity or sentiment."

"Nothing jumps out at me. Sorry."

"Don't worry. It will," she says encouragingly.

"We're already two days into the New Year. Why did it take so long for you guys to come to me?" I ask.

"There are 53 Emerson's in New York City alone," Reese retorts.

"So, how do you know that I'm the one?"

"You're the only one being shot at today."

"Oh." Point taken.

"It's more than that. I'd felt dark waves heading toward you and thought that it would be a good idea for us to keep a closer eye on you," Rio adds from across the room.

"You knew they'd attack me?" I am amazed. "Can you tell the future?"

"Why, you play lotto?" Rio jokes.

"Seriously. How do you do it?"

"All Watchers, Guardians and Akons have at least one power. It comes from their last moments on earth. Let's say you were crushed by a car on your last night on Earth—"

"Ooh, that's a good one," Miku says, completely taken by the image of carnage in her head.

"—Anyway." Rio rolls his eyes and continues. "Let's say after being crushed to death, you get chosen to be a Guardian. Your power would be the ability to manipulate metal because at your time of death, that is what your spirit asked of Omnis. Everyone's powers have to do with the way they died."

"So, you can't see the future," I state, half-deflated by this additional downer to death.

"No, but I can feel the emotions and desires of people miles away from me. Their emotions give way to their actions. I knew you were feeling nausea even before it registered in your body. "

"That's why you brought over the trash can," I say, amazed.

"Yeah I could tell by your color wave you were feeling unsettled and overwhelmed. I knew you'd get sick but I didn't know the exact moment or where to place the trash," Rio clarifies.

"You see people's feeling as colors?"

"Yep, he's our very own mood ring," Jay teases.

Rio ignores him and continues. "They appear in colored waves. Humans usually emanate the same three colors; orange, gray and blue. That usually means worry, insecurity and fear. It can change throughout the day. If they meet a loved one or find out there's a baby on the way, the change is powerful. They radiate a soft white glow."

"So you know what the guy down the street is feeling right now?"

"I know what Manhattan is feeling. That's how I was able to find you in the hall. Your color wave is almost always…" He was going to say something but then thought better of it.

"Let's just say your color changed to onyx. That means the person fears for their life."

"Can you change what people are feeling?" I have to know.

"No, but along with Jay's ability to 'glide,' he has suggestive powers. So if you radiate deep sadness and you're near me, I'll get Jay to suggest something to lift your spirits."

"That's sweet," I can't help but say.

Rio smiles, "Can't you tell by now what a nice guy I am?"

Miku scoffs, "Yeah, tell her what you and Jay do when you see a cute girl radiating purple."

"What does purple mean?" I ask.

"It means she's … thinking private thoughts," Miku says coyly.

"You know when a girl's turned on?"

"And then he has Jay go up to her and 'suggest' she gives him a kiss," Miku volunteers.

"Jay!" I scold.

"On the cheek," he says, unable to face me.

"What kind of angel are you?" I accuse.

"What kind of angel would you like?" End of the world or not, that boy's a flirt.

"He has to use his powers. How else would he get a girl with me around?" Rio taunts.

Jay shouts back, "You're crazy. My game is foolproof."

I quickly interject before they decide to fight it out. "Do all of you have a protective shield?"

Rio says "No, only me."

"So, what were you doing when you died that you asked for a shield?"

Right away I know that I shouldn't have asked that question. The mood of the room instantly changed. They all stiffen up. Reese looks up at the ceiling as if it were suddenly the most interesting thing in the room.

Jay looks down at the floor. Miku avoids her brother's eyes. Rio's jaw tightens. And for the first time since we've been talking, he looks pained. Miku says, "Excuse me," gets up and goes to the kitchen.

"I'm sorry. It's none of my business how you died. I'm sorry Rio. Don't be mad," I say trying to fix this major error.

He smiles but it doesn't reach his eyes. He's just being polite. I've offended him.

He gets up and says, "I'm gonna go look out for Marcus." He moves quickly and heads up to the roof.

I made an angel sad. What kind of monster am I? "Why don't I take you home? Tomorrow we'll be at your school just in case the Runners come back." Reese gets up and holds out his hand. I take it and stand up.

I want to know what "Runners" are, how they'd all died, and who Lucy is and why she's after me, but I don't want to risk saying anything else to upset them. Jay senses my dilemma.

"Don't worry," he says. "We'll fill you in on the rest tomorrow."

"Okay, thanks. And can you tell Rio I'm sorry, again. Please?"

"He already knows, remember?"

"Oh yeah, right," I say, now feeling even more inadequate.

Just then Ameana comes out of her room and addresses the guys. "It's too late for her to go home by the usual means. Reese, Blink her a block from her house."

"No problem," he says, taking my hand.

Panic spreads through my body. What is she talking about? I can't just pop in and out of places like Reese. What if I get home and half a leg gets left behind? No way. Not gonna happen.

"It's okay, Emmy. Blinking is much safer than driving. Or at least it is when Jay's behind the wheel," Reese jokes.

"I'm right here. You wanna go? Let's do this!" Jay counters.

Ameana is not amused. I look down and remember that the sweater I have on doesn't belong to me. "Just let me put this back in the room."

"It's Miku's. She's cool if you take it home," Jay offers.

"No, it's not mine. And it looks like it costs a lot of money. My mom will wonder where I got it," I explain.

I head back into the bedroom where I had slept. It's decorated in lace and satin. Teddy bears from different countries are displayed throughout the room. It's not really my style, but it's pretty.

Miku enters the room. I don't even give her a chance to say anything. I give her a big hug. "I'm sorry if I said anything that hurt you. I was just—"

"Stop. It's okay. And why are you returning the sweater? Don't you like it?"

"I do but—"

"But nothing."

"I'll keep it here. And get it whenever I come back, okay?"

I can tell that she is about to argue her point, so I rush on ahead.

"Miku, there are six Guardians, right?"

"Right. The first Guardian is in charge of the other five."

"Is Ameana the first Guardian?" I ask.

"She acts like she is, but Marcus is the first Guardian. He's our leader. Just like Julian was. The second-in-charge is Ameana, then me and Rio, and then the two knuckleheads out there."

"You guys don't seem worried about finding this Triplex thing. That must mean you're close, right?" I ask, trying to downplay my fear.

"We've been trying to track down Julian. He's the best link into how the council thinks. He can give us a better idea of what we need to look for. Marcus went to check out a few places he could be. We'll find him soon. Try not to worry."

"Why did the council leave him to roam the Earth when he knows where the bridge is?"

"Julian was sent back by Omnis, so the council could do nothing about that, but they stripped him of some of his memory. He doesn't remember where the bridge is, but he does recall the council."

"He remembers them?"

"Yeah, but he thinks they're aliens who abducted him," Miku quips.

"So, all the alien stuff is true?" I have to ask.

"Well, Julian's aliens are true, I can't say for the rest of them."

Reese shouts to us from the living room, "C'mon ladies. Some of us have to recharge!"

I look at Miku blankly, "We find a spot that is absolutely quiet and perfectly still. It recharges us. Like what sleeping does for you," she explains.

"Oh, like meditating?"

"Without the annoying sound of the ocean and the smelly mats," she smiles.

"Okay. Five more seconds and I'm coming in. You two better be ready!" Reese barks.

So much for the patience of angels, I think.

Someone calls out from the living room. This time, it's Jay. "He's back!"

"Good, I bet he has a lead on Julian. C'mon." She drags me back into the living room.

Standing there among a room full of gorgeous angels is the most perfect creature I have ever seen. If beauty were measured by water, all of them would be a full glass, while I would be the proverbial half-empty. But Marcus' beauty spans two oceans; *seriously*, he's flawless.

He stands at 6'1. His hair is chestnut with natural auburn highlights. His eyes are blue green with flecks of gold. His lashes, jealous of the attention the eyes are getting, stretch out like a proud peacock. His nose, lips and cheeks are the original blueprint of beauty. His shoulders are broad and strong. His arms and legs are well defined but not bulky.

He's wearing dark Diesel jeans, a charcoal gray cashmere sweater, and an open black leather jacket. The simplicity of his outfit in no way detracts from his stellar beauty. The only time I've ever encountered something close to the beauty of Marcus was when I first met Ameana. And even that encounter would be a distant second.

I refuse to blink and miss a moment of him. The water builds up in my eyes. It stings. It burns. No, I won't blink. It's like having a thirst so deep water cannot quench it. The more I drink him in, the more of him I want.

Tears gather in my eyes, waiting, begging for me to blink. I won't. So the tears run down my face. My vision gets blurry. No, I won't blink. My eyes feel like they're being pricked by hundreds of small pins. It stings badly. But I remain steadfast. The second round of tears falls from my eyes. I won't blink. I will not move from the vision before me.

My stomach quickens. My whole body is warm with the exception of my hands, which are ice cold and trembling. I don't know a lot about the heart, but I'm certain it's not supposed to beat this fast. I want to look anywhere besides his face, but the thought of looking away from him makes me dizzy with despair.

Suddenly I'm very aware of how I'm dressed: faded jeans and a Winnie-the-Pooh "Piglet" T-shirt with the cartoon pig trying to catch a runaway balloon and saying "Oh, d-d-dear." *Great, Emmy, that's real sexy.*

And if my hair looks the way it usually does after I've slept, right now I resemble a mad scientist. I want to go back into the room and fix it, but it's too late. He's already seen me. I mean, it's already time to go.

Miku, whose existence I have all but forgotten, pokes me lightly. I blink. A third round of tears make their way down my face. It's embarrassing but I'm powerless. Not for the first time today. *Get a hold of yourself.*

He had been studying a small red leather-bound book. Miku introduces us. "Marcus, this is Emerson Baxter. She's gonna help us save the world." He looks up at me, says a quick "hey" and goes back to the book. His dismissal stings worse than my eyes.

"Tomorrow we need to go over your life and find out about everyone you know, everyone who knows you. They know that you're not a boy like they originally thought. We're going to keep you in school because you're safer in a crowd of humans," he contends.

"They attacked me in a crowd today," I say.

He continues to flip through the book and responds without looking up. "They weren't trying to kill you, they just wanted to get you before we did. If Lucy wanted to kill you, she would have sent Akons. But since we got to you first, she's gonna have to get past us now. The only way she can do that is to send out all six Akons."

"So, this Lucy person isn't out to kill me?"

"She is, but only after she's tortured you and gotten enough information out of you to locate the Triplex. Then she'll have the Akons finish you off or do it herself, if she has time."

"Oh," is all I can say.

He is speaking about my death so casually; Miku and the others exchange a look. I guess I'm not the only one who thinks he's being rude.

"The council forbids Akons from attacking in public. So you should be okay if you stay in public places. You are never to be left alone unless we are standing watch. Do you understand?" he asks, once again never looking up at me.

Why isn't he looking at me? I know I'm not "angel-good-looking," but I'm not a dog. What's his problem?

"Where do we pick up Julian?" Miku asks.

"We don't. Lucy got to him first. There's a good chance he's dead."

"Wait, you told me that the council couldn't kill Julian but this Lucy woman can? Who is she?" I ask Miku.

"Don't worry, Emmy. We're not gonna let her get to you," she says.

"Who is she?" I demand.

"Atourum," Marcus says plainly.

I can't breathe. The air is too thick that I've forgotten how. I lean against the wall for support.

"The devil is a woman?"

"You tellin' me!" Jay jokes in an attempt to lighten the mood.

"For this cycle, yes," Miku says.

Jay looks into my ashen face and what he sees there causes him to worry. He comes up to me. "I can calm you down, if you want."

My voice cracks, "No. Just take me home. Please."

Marcus speaks with the authority of a general. It sounds strange coming from a boy barely eighteen. "Jay and Rio will watch over you tonight. Reese, when you're done taking her home, get back here and help Miku search a few Runner hangouts. See if anyone knows anything." Reese nods in agreement.

Marcus turns his attention to Ameana and says, "Mina, can we talk?" There's something in the way he says her name. It bothers me. Then it bothered me that it bothers me.

She leads the way and he follows her into her room. Why can't they talk in front of the rest of us? Wasn't all business talk done on the roof or in the living room? Why did he want to be alone with her? He said her name with such care....

I try hard not to look at Rio. I don't need an angel mood ring to tell me what I'm feeling. I don't want to know. I just want to get as far away as possible.

I tell myself it's because I'm being hunted by the source of all evil. I tell myself it's because the fate of the world rests on information I don't have.

But when Reese lifts me up into his arms and Blinks me out of the house, the thing that I'm upset about isn't Lucy or the end of the world. There's only one thing that upsets me: *He said her name with such care....*

TO READ THE REST OF
"GUARDIANS: THE GIRL" FOR FREE, VISIT:

http://www.amazon.com/dp/B006VRXR42

Made in the USA
Columbia, SC
23 December 2023